THE E-FINANCE REPORT

THE E-FINANCE REPORT

Ezra Zask, Editor
Advisor Software, Inc.
and
Princeton University

McGraw-Hill

New York   Chicago   San Francisco   Lisbon
London   Madrid   Mexico City   Milan
New Delhi   San Juan   Seoul   Singapore
Sydney   Toronto

332.10285
Z38ν

Library of Congress Cataloging-in-Publication Data

Zask, Ezra.
    The E-finance report / by Ezra Zask.
        p. cm.
    Includes bibliographical references.
    ISBN 0-07-136427-7
    1. Financial services industry—Computer networks.   2. Internet banking.   3. Electronic commerce.
4. Internet.   I. Title: Efinance report.   II. Title.

  HG151.8 .Z37   2001
  332.1'0285'4678—dc21

                              2001030148

McGraw-Hill

A Division of *The McGraw·Hill Companies*

1 2 3 4 5 6 7 8 9 10 AGM/AGM 0 9 8 7 6 5 4 3 2 1

ISBN 0-07-136427-7

This book was set in Times New Roman by Patricia Wallenburg.

Printed and bound by Quebecor World/Martinsburg.

This publication is designed to provide accurate and authoritative information in regard to the subject matter covered. It is sold with the understanding that neither the author nor the publisher is engaged in rendering legal, accounting, futures/securities trading, or other professional service. If legal advice or other expert assistance is required, the services of a competent professional person should be sought.

> —*From a Declaration of Principles jointly adopted*
> *by a Committee of the American Bar Association*
> *and a Committee of Publishers*

McGraw-Hill books are available at special quantity discounts to use as premiums and sales promotions, or for use in corporate training programs. For more information, please write to the Director of Special Sales, Professional Publishing, McGraw-Hill, Two Penn Plaza, New York, NY 10121-2298. Or contact your local bookstore.

 This book is printed on recycled, acid-free paper containing a minimum of 50% recycled, de-inked fiber.

CONTENTS

Chapter 3

www.Online_Trading.com   27
George R. Monahan, Vice President and Director, Industry Studies
Securities Industry Association

Chapter 4

The Internet Revolution in the Brokerage Services Industry:
An Unfinished Play in Three Acts   43
Carlos Otalvaro-Coronado, Chairman
WallStreet Electronica
WallStreet. E
Noah Otalvaro, President
Net International Inc.
Francisco Otalvaro, President
WallStreet Electronica
WallStreet. E

Chapter 5

The Internet Brokerage Industry   51
Ezra Zask, Executive Vice President
Advisor Software, Inc.
and Visiting Lecturer
Bendheim Center for Finance,
Princeton University

Chapter 6

Online Fixed-Income Trading   79
Robert Knox, Senior Vice President
Zions First National Bank

Chapter 7

The Democratization of the Foreign Exchange Market   97
Richard Olsen, Chairman
Olsen and Associates

Chapter 8

The Future of Venture Capital   105
David Starr, Co-Founder of Vcapital, and currently
Client Partner at Culture Worx

Chapter 9

Retail Internet Banking   115
Octavio Marenzi, Managing Director
Celent Communications
Isabella Cagnazzo Fonseca, Analyst
Celent Communications

Chapter 10

Online Banking   133
D.R. Grimes, CEO and Vice-Chairman
NetBank

Chapter 11

Internet-Based Bill Payment and Presentment   149
Gerhard Kschwendt, Senior Consultant
Dove Consulting

Chapter 12

Online Credit and Banking   179

Scott Gregory, Director
PriceWaterhouse Coopers Consulting

Chapter 13

Financial Information   189

Jeremy Pink, Vice President, News and Programming
CNBC Europe

Chapter 14

Financial Services Portals: The Winners in a New Era   197

Amy Butte, Financial Services Analyst and Managing Director
Bear Stearns
Christine Haggerty, Managing Director
Bear Stearns

Chapter 15

Online Asset Management   213
Kevin D. Freeman, Co-Founder and Chairman
Separate Account Solutions, Inc.
Erik H. Davidson, Co-Founder and President
Separate Account Solutions, Inc.

Chapter 16

How to Build and Monitor E-Commerce Insurance   231
Burke A. Christensen, Vice President, Operation and General Counsel
Quotesmith.com, Inc.

Chapter 17

The Insurance Industry E-Volves   237
Thomas Holzheu, Ph.D., Senior Economist
Swiss Re, Economic Research and Consulting
Thomas Trauth, Ph.D., Senior Economist
Swiss Re, Economic Research and Consulting
Ulrike Birkmaier, Senior Economist
Swiss Re, Economic Research and Consulting

Appendix A

Leading Financial Services Websites   249

Appendix B

Contributors

Jeffrey P. Anderson   Principal, Bond & Pecaro, Inc.   (Chapter 2)

Ulrike Birkmaier   Senior Economist, Swiss Re, Economic Research and Consulting (Chapter 17)

Amy Butte   Financial Services Analyst and Managing Director, Bear Stearns (Chapter 14)

Burke A. Christensen   Vice President, Operations and General Counsel, Quotesmith.com, Inc.   (Chapter 16)

Erik H. Davidson   Co-Founder and President, Separate Account Solutions, Inc.   (Chapter 15)

Isabella Cagnazzo Fonseca   Analyst, Celent Communications   (Chapter 9)

Kevin D. Freeman   Co-Founder and Chairman, Separate Account Solutions, Inc.   (Chapter 15)

Scott Gregory   Director, PriceWaterhouse Coopers Consulting   (Chapter 12)

D. R. Grimes   CEO and Vice-Chairman, NetBank   (Chapter 10)

Christine Haggerty   Managing Director, Bear Stearns   (Chapter 14)

Thomas Holzheu, Ph.D.   Senior Economist, Swiss Re, Economic Research and Consulting   (Chapter 17)

Robert Knox   Senior Vice President, Zions First National Bank   (Chapter 6)

Gerhard Kschwendt   Senior Consultant, Dove Consulting   (Chapter 11)

Octavio Marenzi   Managing Director, Celent Communications   (Chapter 9)

George R. Monahan   Vice President and Director, Industry Studies, Securities Industry Association   (Chapter 3)

Richard Olsen   Chairman, Olsen and Associates   (Chapter 7)

Franciso Otalvaro   President, WallStreet Electronica, WallStreet.E (Chapter 4)

Noah Otalvaro   President, Net International, Inc.   (Chapter 4)

Carlos Otalvaro-Coronado   Chairman, WallStreet Electronica, WallStreet.E (Chapter 4)

Jeremy Pink   Vice President, News and Programming, CNBC Europe (Chapter 13)

Humberto Sanchez   Research Associate, Bond & Pecaro   (Chapter 2)

David Starr   Co-Founder of Vcapital, and Currently Client Partner at Culture Worx   (Chapter 8)

Thomas Trauth, Ph.D.   Senior Economist, Swiss Re, Economic Research and Consulting   (Chapter 17)

Ezra Zask   Executive Vice President, Advisor Software, Inc., and Visiting Lecturer, Princeton University   (Chapter 1, Chapter 5)

THE E-FINANCE REPORT

The Changing Landscape of E-Finance

Ezra Zask, Executive Vice President
Advisor Software, Inc.
and
Visiting Lecturer
Bendheim Center for Finance
Princeton University

BACKGROUND

The financial services industry has been dramatically altered by the financial, technological, and competitive forces let loose by the Internet revolution that started in the mid-1990s. It is not surprising that the financial services industry, with its reliance on the storage, transmission, and analysis of information, is arguably more advanced in its use of the Internet than any other industry. For this reason, the financial services industry is ideal for studying the impact of the Internet on business in general.

E-Finance is the use of the Internet to deliver financial services to consumers, businesses, and financial institutions. In the course of the migration of financial services to the Internet, many of the traditional services—brokerage, banking, insurance, asset management, investment banking—have undergone a profound transformation. The Internet has opened a myriad of new opportunities and technologies for the delivery of financial services, forever changing the industry and its participants.

While the changes caused by the Internet have been dramatic, one of the central themes that emerges from the readings in this book is that the worlds of online and offline (more commonly referred to as "clicks and bricks") are converging as traditional companies adopt Internet strategies and dotcom companies establish a physical presence through branches and financial intermediaries. If the trend continues, the

Internet will soon be just one of the various technology or medium choices available to all participants in the financial services sector. Especially, it may become an alternative channel of distribution for "real" corporations that have the brand, infrastructure, resources, expertise, and customers that many dotcoms lack.

Competitive Dynamics

The E-Finance revolution can be broadly divided into two phases. The first, spanning the years 1995–1999, was dominated by Internet start-up companies, best exemplified by E*Trade and Ameritrade (brokerage), Quotesmith (insurance), E*Bank and Wingspan (banking), and Wit (investment banking). With ample venture capital backing and funds raised through initial public offerings (IPOs), these firms were able to gain early advantage in market after market.

However, as the permanence of the Internet became clear to all, traditional firms responded by developing their own Internet strategies. With a speed unanticipated by most observers, firms such as Merrill Lynch (brokerage), Citibank (banking), AIG and Prudential (insurance), and Fidelity (asset management) rolled out impressive and competitive Internet offerings. In fact, the advantage in many cases has shifted to the established firms, whose greater wealth, existing client base, branch network, brand names, and marketing experience are proving formidable in defining the Internet. Thus, the most often heard question of 1999, whether the large financial institutions would be able to withstand the onslaught of the dotcoms, has given way in 2000 to the question of which of the dotcoms will survive the challenge from the financial giants.

Some of this change in perception stems from a growing sense of reality that has replaced some of the more far-fetched speculation of the past few years. Internet companies are increasingly being held up to the same scrutiny and standards of performance as traditional "bricks and mortar" companies. Thus, we hear less and less talk about how Internet companies and the "new economy" follow different economic and financial laws than traditional firms.

This is especially true for the driving business model of the early phase of the Internet economy: "Build the brand first. Make money later!" On the basis of this model, billions of dollars have been allocated to Internet start-ups to be spent largely on marketing to develop brand name. However, the renewed emphasis on profits rather than revenues has led to a drought from these financing sources, throwing Internet companies back on traditional expense control and financing strategies. The metrics favored by early Internet firms (i.e., eyeballs, unique visitors, etc.) are increasingly being replaced by "old economy" measures of profitability, cashflow, and return on equity as indications of success. The result has been a drop in the valuation and stock market prices of pure Internet companies, a drop in some cases that approaches 90 percent and threatens many with merger or even bankruptcy. (See Appendix: The ENC Marketplace in Chapter 5 on p. 74.)

The Battle for Customers

The Internet has revolutionized the nature of marketing and customer relationships. Winning customers is cheaper online, where targeting customers is easier and less expensive than building branches and bricks-and-mortar plants. However, retaining customers and getting them to pay for services is a challenge for all online firms. Recent evidence points to the overall decline in the use of the Internet for shopping in general, along with revised downward projections for advertisement revenues. Furthermore, studies indicate that as much of 70 percent of the available Internet advertising, a major source of income for Internet firms, goes to the 10 most widely viewed sites, with 90 percent going to the top 50.

Online service providers have increasingly differentiated customers based on their wealth and the amount of capital they have to invest. The marketing strategy has been refined to encompass two tactics. First, firms target all customers with financial services once reserved for the affluent served by private banks, including information, analysis, and basic funds management tools. However, as customers move up the wealth pyramid, they receive fee-based services, including pay-for-advice services and contact with personal advisers.

Internet marketing is different from traditional marketing. In *Digital Capitalism*, for example, the authors point to a number of unique features of marketing on the Web.[1]

- All Web users communicate in all directions, so that marketers can no longer tightly control customer perceptions.
- Internet customers have greater power since buyers, as much as sellers, determine pricing.
- Rather than tout products, firms build relationship capital by using comprehensive communication strategies.
- A company's brand (and the trust that accompanies that brand) serves as the relationship capital for the Internet.

This last point is crucial. One of the problems confronting online ventures (and a large plus for established companies) is that customers have been reluctant to deal with a company that does not have a recognized name. Established firms not only have established brand names, but also have greater resources to maintain and expand their brand. A $100 million branding campaign is much more manageable for a large, established firm than for a newly established dotcom.

THE BROKERAGE INDUSTRY

While online banking and online brokerage began around the same time, the brokerage industry was the first to fully utilize the power of the Internet, forever

---

[1] Don Tapscott, David Ticoll, and Alex Lowy, *Digital Capitalism*, Harvard Business School Press, Boston, 2000.

changing the relationship between investors and the financial markets. Online brokerage firms (now numbering over 200) claim well over 10 million accounts, representing nearly 20 percent of the brokerage market. With over 50 percent of U.S. households now owning stocks, online brokerage has much more room to grow. The online trading industry was aided by the existence of a long-standing discount brokerage industry. It is no coincidence that the largest discount broker, Charles Schwab, has also become the largest online broker, as discount customers found the Internet to be another channel for broker-free execution of trades.

Prior to the Internet revolution, brokerage firms, brokers, and financial planners served as gatekeepers between the trading and investing public and the financial markets. They monopolized information, research and analysis, distribution and execution of trades in the various stock markets, as well as the IPO markets. The online brokers (using the facilities of the electronic communication networks, or ECNs) were able to circumvent this barrier and provide investors and traders with direct, broker-free access to the stock markets.

The result has been a fragmentation of the traditional brokerage functions and a free-for-all among traditional and online brokers, banks, insurance companies, online portals, and asset-management companies all vying for the pieces. While brokerage firms have had to face greatly increased competition under the new regime, they have also been able to enter into new areas—such as banking and insurance—as some of the lines blur between financial institutions.

While there are more than 200 online brokers, the industry is actually quite concentrated, with the top 10 online brokerage firms controlling over 96 percent of customer accounts and 98 percent of the assets held by these customers (see Table 1-1).

As competition between online and traditional brokers has increased, transaction charges have steadily declined to the point where many doubt the viability of a business model based on revenues coming largely from transaction fees. As a result, the emphasis has shifted to capturing online customer assets, especially the assets of the more affluent clients, to fee-based advisory services, and to cross-selling services such as online banking and insurance. This has driven some online brokerage firms to resemble financial portals in their diverse product offerings. It has also reintroduced the broker and financial planner into the equation in a prominent role. Unlike early predictions of the demise of the financial intermediary, it turns out that investors, especially the more affluent investors, prefer financial planners and are willing to pay for access to them.

According to one analysis, U.S. millionaires represent 7.1 million households, 20 percent of whom will use the Internet to manage their finances. The online trading battle has recently moved upscale as brokers compete for the affluent investor with online services. J.P. Morgan (with www.MorganOnline.com) and Goldman Sachs (with www.GS.com), for example, have combined traditional wealth management services with an online site to appeal to the affluent client

TABLE 1-1

Total Online Brokerage Customer Accounts and Assets (Feb. 29, 2000)

Online Broker	Online Customer Accounts (millions)	Online Customer Assets (billions)
Schwab Online	3.7	$418
Fidelity Online	4.2	328
TD Waterhouse	1.7	118
E-Trade	2.4	62
Ameritrade	1.0	39
DLJdirect	0.4	27
Datek	0.5	15
Fleet Online	0.34	13
National Discount Brokers	0.2	12
Scottrade Online	0.2	6
Others	0.6	21
Total	**15.24**	**$1059**

Source: Salomon Smith Barney and The Industry Standard.

base. Credit Suisse is following a similar course in Europe, appealing to the "new affluents" with www.credit-suisse.net.

NONEQUITY FINANCIAL MARKETS

The U.S. and foreign equity markets were the logical starting points for online information and transactions. Other financial markets quickly followed suit, although with a mixed record of results and very different business plans. In the major nonequity markets—currencies, bonds, and derivatives—the institutional players tend to control a large part of the volume. Thus, these markets have tended to follow the business model typical of business-to-business (B2B) markets: A dotcom start-up creates a marketplace through good alliances and management and establishes a strong position. The major players (banks, brokers, and investment banks) realize their power of volume trading and create their own marketplace. As volume and liquidity pick up, spreads narrow, making competition on price and liquidity more difficult and placing the smaller firms under pressure.

Another difference in many of these markets, as contrasted with most equity markets, is the use of an electronic share-matching system by professional participants in the market. The currency market, for example, has long used this type of system in lieu of a centralized exchange. The ECNs that have captured 30 percent of the NASDAQ's trading activity also use the share-matching approach, potentially bypassing the exchanges by crossing deals on their own books. The largest

ECN, Instinet, even has a plan to extend its share-matching system to individual investors rather than just the brokers.

The foreign exchange market, the world's largest, with a daily turnover exceeding $1.5 trillion, has only begun to use the Internet, as described in Chapter 7. In recent months, a number of large commercial and investment banks have teamed up to establish currency sites. For example, FXall.com was set up by Goldman Sachs, Morgan Stanley Dean Witter, J.P. Morgan, Credit Suisse First Boston, Bank of America, UBS Warburg, and HSBC to transact currencies between the partners and other wholesale firms. It is anticipated that this site will provide access to research and currency rate pages from all the banks with which they have preexisting relationships. Similarly, Deutsche Bank, Chase Manhattan, and Citigroup teamed up with Reuters to develop an online foreign exchange (FX) service. To date, Currenex, which gives corporate customers access to bank currency desks, and MatchbookFX, which matches FX trades on its own platform, are leaders among dotcom companies for FX services.

The fixed-income universe has also produced joint ventures, including that between Schwab and ValuBond, to offer municipal bond trading and corporate and convertible bonds, and that between J.P. Morgan, Goldman Sachs, and Merrill Lynch, which created BondBook, to trade corporate, junk, and municipal bonds. TradeWeb, a site that allows dealers and institutional customers to trade Treasury bonds online, has been successful in entering a number of fixed-income markets. Even the U.S. government has entered the area with www.TreasuryDirect.com, a site that allows individuals to purchase U.S. Treasury bonds. MuniAuction.com, which started in November 1999 with $57 million general obligation bonds for the City of Pittsburgh, the first bond offering without an underwriter, now does online trading of more than $206 billion in primary and secondary bond markets for 201 issuers. Plans are on the table to develop Websites to trade mortgage-backed securities and other fixed-income derivative products.

The Europeans have also joined the fray with EuroCredit MTS, a new electronic trading system for nongovernment bonds, and BondClick, an online fixed-income trading site developed by ABN AMRO, BNP Paribas, Caboto Sim, Deutsche Bank, Dresdner Bank, and J.P. Morgan. BrokerTec Global, owned by the 12 largest bond dealers, provides an order-matching system for the U.S. Treasury and European sovereign market. With the expanding capabilities of the online fixed-income market, it is possible to contemplate a time when the local Moscow government could raise money from the Internet by issuing bonds directly to investors in the United States and Europe.

The derivatives and futures markets have also been active online, with a deluge of proposals and early efforts to place every traded market on the Web. The United Kingdom's LIFFE, for example, launched Connect electronic platform, a B2B system that it also sells to other exchanges around the world. LIFFE has developed futures to enable users to hedge their risks on nonfinancial B2B exchanges in a merging of financial and nonfinancial disciplines such as risk management, which is becoming a part of everyday business. Other futures exchanges, including the Chicago Board of Trade, have developed Internet-based systems and strategies, often over the protests of their own members. A growing impetus for exchanges to develop online capabilities is the fear the ECNs will encroach on their turf as they have in the underlying equity markets.

As the Internet becomes more sophisticated, so do the markets and instruments that can be traded on the Web. A short list of the Internet-based derivatives sites includes SwapsWire (interest rate derivatives); creditex Inc. (credit derivatives), OnExchange (financial and commodity derivatives); Internet Commodity Exchange (commodities), IntercontinentalExchange (over-the-counter energy, metals, and other commodity-based products founded by leading banks and Royal Dutch/Shell Group), and Altra Energy Technologies (bulk commodities).

Risk management has made its way onto the Internet with offerings from RiskGrades, a spin-off of J.P. Morgan's RiskMetrics. The site offers risk analysis of thousands of traded instruments and portfolios for individual investors. ERisks.com provides enterprisewide risk management along with management consulting, while NetRisk also provides enterprisewide risk management on the Web.

The massive corporate finance market has also come under the Internet's sway. CFOWeb.com, Integral Development Corporation's capital markets trading portal, offers research and portfolio and risk management to 2500 members. A number of major international banks have committed to provide liquidity for the system. In a similar vein, Commerzbank will develop a portal to link financial departments of corporations with financial departments banks, controlling payments and treasury and financial risks online in a secure way and offering access to information and reports about financial markets.

ONLINE INVESTMENT BANKING

Brokerage firms and banks have increasingly diversified into investment banking in search of fee income to offset the uncertainty of trading commissions. Online brokers are also seeking an entry point into investment banking for the same reason. One of the key advantages of the full-service brokers has always been their access to IPOs. To the extent that online brokers are able to compete in this area, they will be able to more easily convert high-net-worth clients from Wall Street firms.

The announcement by Schwab, Ameritrade, and TD Waterhouse that they (along with three venture capital firms) will establish an online investment bank to offer IPO shares to high-net-worth individuals points to the importance of this trend. (It may also show the need for these firms to pool their resources to compete with the established Wall Street firms.)

The SEC's approval of online marketing (under some rather rigid guidelines) will provide a further impetus to online investment banking. The SEC's recent ruling that restricts analysts from gaining information on IPOs before the general public may also provide a great impetus for online dissemination of IPO information and, eventually, transactions.

The stakes are extremely high for all participants. The Wall Street firms have staked out a lucrative franchise in the IPO arena, with fees firmly fixed at 7 percent of the offering. This virtual monopoly has been based on key attributes these banks bring to the party: name recognition and legitimacy, research and distribution capabilities, and market-making abilities. In all these areas, the online firms have some level of capability and may be able to offer a long-term challenge to the traditional investment banks.

While online underwriting now accounts for only 2 percent of the total IPO activity (distributed among DLJ Direct, 0.9 percent; Wit Capital, 0.8 percent; E*Offering, 0.2 percent; FBR.com, 0.2 percent; and W. R. Hambrecht, 0.2 percent), the growth of this sector will, as elsewhere, place downward pressure on the margins of the big three underwriters: Goldman Sachs, Merrill Lynch, and Morgan Stanley Dean Witter.

In other areas of investment banking—mergers and acquisitions (M&A) and private equity financing—the Internet has proved to be an inhospitable place to date. Merrill and CSFB joined CapitalKey Advisors to provide investment banking services (especially M&A and private equity financing) to small business. CapitalKey has established a database of institutional investors who may be interested in smaller businesses and has developed an investor-targeting technology. OffRoad Capital, an Internet company that matches seekers and providers of capital, has also instituted a service that provides a "basket" of private equity shares for the small institutional investor with $100,000 minimum. Vcapital provides a similar service, as described in Chapter 8.

In an example of the consolidation that has affected the Internet as well as the rest of the financial services industry, WitSoundview, which originally started as Wit Capital, an online effort to provide IPOs to the retail marketplace, has announced its intention of entering every area of capital markets including M&A, IPOs, and venture capital.

The potential power of the Internet for disintermediating investment bankers and brokers is shown by an innovative program by which Ford Motors Corporation's treasury has been using the Internet to raise funds through its securitized asset pools, commercial paper, and corporate bonds.

NEW SYSTEMS AND TECHNOLOGY

In the medium term, two technological trends on the horizon—broadband and wireless—are likely to quicken the pace of change in the future. While still in their relative infancy, they have the potential to revolutionize financial services and usher in a new era of investment, banking, and money management. Not surprisingly, all the major participants in the financial services industry are developing the technology and products to exploit the new technologies. The technology enablers—a rapidly expanding group led by AFS, Vantra, digiTRADE, Kingland, Reality, SunGard-EMS, S1, and Taho, will grow, according to Celent Communication, by 50 percent a year–which provide Internet platforms for financial businesses.

Longer term, the technology will focus on the decision-making mechanisms that enable the Internet to more effectively meet the needs of investors. Customized financial services will meet client needs based on the information available on the Internet and such powerful techniques as neural networks that monitor spending and viewing habits over time (10, 20, or 30 years).

FINANCIAL INFORMATION AND RESEARCH

Financial information was a natural early denizen of the Internet and includes sites such as CBS's www.marketwatch.com, the mostly widely used financial information site, and the early research site www.fool.com, managed by Motley Fool.

One of the interesting questions in this area is the extent to which non-Internet information services such as Bloomberg and Reuters will fare in the Internet environment. Table 1-2 compares these services with Internet-based financial information services.

E-INVESTMENT SERVICES

E-investment has come to the forefront as the latest growth area, following the rapid growth of e-brokerage (and ECNs) and e-advice. Online investment services can broadly be divided into four types: 401(k) investment services, managed account and wrap account services, stock and mutual fund "basket" trading, and professional financial planning services.

401(k) and Long-Term Investment Services

There has been a growth of service providers with online products for the 401(k) markets, for the retirement market in general, and for longer-term financial asset savers. Providing information on 401(k) plans is a natural for the Internet. Forrester Research, for example, estimates that online advice will reach 4 million 401(k) participants by 2002, with distribution through brokers and through employers. With $11 trillion accumulated in U.S. retirement accounts, and $1.5 trillion in 401(k) accounts, the market is certainly interesting. With the amount of money involved, it is no surprise that the space has become highly competitive with advice providers such as mPower, FinancialEngines.com, Advisor Software Inc.'s VirtualAdvisor.com, and Morningstar ClearFuture competing with the large, established brand players such as Fidelity and Merrill Lynch (see Table 1-3).

TABLE 1-2

Financial Information Services

High-End, Fully Loaded Terminals	Internet-Based Applications for the Professional Investor	Services on the Web
$800 to $1600 per user per month	$100 to $500 per user per month	Free
Bloomberg: Detailed information on all types of securities; global markets data; customizable analytical tools; analytics and fixed-income securities information	**S&P ComStock:** Real-time quotes; charting; company information; detailed trading information; technical analysis	**Yahoo Finance:** Delayed quotes; basic charting; basic company information; Zack's earnings data; news wires; portfolio tracking
Bridge: Detailed real-time market data and securities information; customizable analytical tools; rich charting features; news search	**Thomson's ILX W3:** Real-time or delayed market information; charting; options information; company and equity information	**ThomsonInvest.net:** Real-time quotes; financial educational center; bond guides; equity research; basic charting; alerts; portfolio tracking
Reuters: Global market data; real-time news, data, and television feeds; historical securities information; customizable analytical tools	**Reuters Plus:** U.S. market information; real-time price and volume data; alerts; fundamental analysis and historical data	**ClearStation:** Focus on technical analysis—stock trends based on price and volume data; portfolio tracking; recommendation lists

Typically, these online programs create an asset allocation plan tailored to the user's financial objectives and risk tolerance using forecasted rates of return for each asset class. They project return rates for different asset categories using historical data and the historical correlation between asset classes. The rates of return are then used to develop model asset allocation portfolios. These are measured against the investors' financial objectives, risk tolerance, cash inflows, and needs to calculate the probability that the investor's portfolio will meet those objectives or the projected shortfall, all taking inflation and interest rate into account.

Managed Accounts

A more recent type of e-investment service is managed accounts and wrap accounts, traditionally the preserve of investment banks and mutual fund companies. For example, RunMoney.com, myMoneyPro.com, WrapManager.com, and PrivateAccounts.com are setting up Internet separate accounts, without a broker or investment adviser acting as intermediary and with minimum accounts as low as $50,000. Managed and wrap accounts are similar to mutual funds, but they are not pooled investments, and the investor actually owns each security in the portfolio. A broker or investment adviser now sets up the account, and then the

TABLE 1 - 3

A Sampling of E-Investment Services

Mpower.com	Oldest and most widely used online advice provider, with access to more than 16 million retirement plan participants, uses historical returns and inflation to build around 20 asset allocation plans for a range of levels of risk tolerance. Employs 30 analysts and uses quantitative and qualitative techniques, including returns-based-style analysis and interviews with money managers.
FinancialEngines.com	Builds models at mutual fund rather than asset class level (although asset class determines 85 percent of outcomes). Using Monte Carlo analysis of economic variables, historical correlation between assets and inflation, it generates range of possible outcomes to calculate how large the user's nest egg will be in retirement and the likelihood (in %) that the use will meet the investment goal.
Morningstar ClearFuture.com	Goals-based (rather than user tolerance for volatility) analysis derives three portfolios (based on 65% large cap, 3% small cap, 15% international equities) and varies stock-bond mix for different risk levels.
DirectAdvice.com	Retail product with fixed allocation (20% U.S. large cap growth, 20% U.S. large cap value, 10% U.S. growth and 10% U.S. value; 15% large cap foreign growth; 10% large-cap foreign value; 10% foreign small cap; 5% emerging market stock). Uses 37 core "recommended," largely index, equity funds that users can pick.
Quicken 401k (TeamVest)	"Bootstrap distribution methodology" developed by Frank Sortino to project asset class returns at the mutual fund level, and use Monte Carlo analysis to forecast how 21 different preset model portfolios would be likely to perform in the future, with equity levels ranging from 0% to 100% in 5% increments. Risk is represented as the chance of falling short of retirement goals and in terms of user's ability to withstand short-term volatility.
Standard & Poor's 401(k) Advisor	Markowitz-type mean-variance estimate of the efficient frontier. Review funds' performance and suggest 6 to 8 standard portfolios (put together by analyst and reviewed by investment policy committee). When user answers questionnaire, software matches recommended allocation to fit his or her risk-reward profile. Avoiding Monte Carlo, it does return-based style analysis to derive asset classes using historical returns and economic conditions.
Fidelity Investments PortfolioPlanner	PortrfolioPlanner generates one of four target allocations based on responses using Monte Carlo simulation to generate a range of probability and best and worst outcomes over an investment horizon.
Vanguard Group	Matches 401(k) participants with one of seven model portfolios derived from data from 1960 using only S&P 500 and Lehman Brothers Government Corporate Index because the most important factor is the equity risk premium.
401kExchange.com	Provides information, due diligence, and ratings service for the 401(k) qualified plan industry and an online exchange between plan buyers and 401(k) service providers.
VirtualAdvisor.com	Provides a risk questionnaire–based approach to asset allocation. Based on a comprehensive financial and risk profile, a recommended asset allocation based on stock and mutual fund data is generated and compared with existing portfolios. The program includes an account aggregation feature to bring together diverse security holdings.

money manager makes the stock picks. Fees are as low as 1.25 percent, compared with 2.25 percent of assets with traditional separate accounts. Assets in managed accounts have tripled since 1996, to $425 billion, according to the Money Management Institute, compared with $7 trillion invested in mutual funds.

Customized Portfolios

Foliofn, founded by Steve Wallman, former commissioner with the SEC, offers "folios," or portfolios of stocks, for a flat annual fee of $295. Investors choose from preselected folios of stocks that represent different industry groups or risk parameters. Or investors can put in their own financial goals and constraints, which are run through stock-selection screens to produce customized portfolios. Merrill Lynch and other firms have started to develop their own equivalent products. The Merrill Lynch product, HLDRS.com, provides a similar service to Foliofn. Recently, E*Trade, the second largest online brokerage company, purchased Electronic Investing (known as eInvesting) and will offer a similar service in the near future. Other companies in this space include SmartLeaf Advisor, BUYandHOLD.com, NetStock Investor, and NetFolio. Unx.com provides basket portfolios for investment professionals.

Financial Planning Services

Providing the hundreds of thousands of financial planners with information, analysis, and investment services on the Internet has become a highly competitive area with product offerings from brokers, asset managers, banks, insurance companies, and newly formed online firms such as InvestorForce.com, which provides a comprehensive range of services to the professional planning community, and FinancialPlanAuditors.com, which offers analytics for running historical back tests of financial plans.

ONLINE BANKING

Online banking has yet to gain the momentum that its financial services cousin, stock trading, has made on the Net. In fact, a study released in the summer of 2000 by Cybercitizen Finance, a division of online market researcher Cyber Dialogue, found that approximately one-third of U.S. online bank customers discontinued their accounts during the previous 12 months. While 3.2 million people opened online bank accounts during the period, another 3.1 million stopped using theirs altogether, according to the report, a net growth of only 3.5 percent.

Despite the early lead by online banks, it is the traditional banks that have been able to leverage their client relationships and brand leadership to capture online customers. As indicated in Figure 1-1, brick-and-mortar banks have the overwhelming majority of online banking customers, with no online bank show-

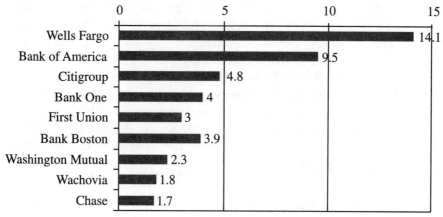

Source: Gomez Advisors Inc.

FIGURE 1-1

Market share of Internet banking.

ing up among the top nine. Traditional banks benefit from the customers' desire for security, privacy, and secrecy, all attributes of familiar, established banks.

The three largest online banks—NetBank, WingspanBank.com, and CompuBank—have less than 3 percent of all 6 million online accounts, compared with 14 percent for Wells Fargo and 9.5 percent for Bank of America. One major problem for online banks is the inability of customers to get ready cash and limited bill-paying options, pointing to an obvious strategy of developing branch networks or joining with an established bank.

However, fending off newcomers will be expensive as service pricing becomes more transparent, fees are reduced, and banks become disintermediated from some services as competition from brokerages, asset managers, online portals, and specialized sites increases. To meet this competitive pressure, banks are being forced to continually add a greater range of services and products to their sites, including nonproprietary products. The financial supermarket that has been the aspiration of many banks may come to the Internet more quickly than to the nonelectronic world.

Electronic Bill Payment and Presentment

Electronic bill payment and presentment (EBPP) presents a tremendous opportunity for banks online. These applications continue to be one of the fastest growing and "stickiest" on the Web. Surveys show that consumers will use bill-paying services as the centerpiece of their online financial activity. While banks are the logical providers of these services, they face tremendous competition from outside vendors, forcing them to develop joint ventures to thwart competitors. For example,

Chase, First Union, and Wells Fargo developed Spectrum, a hub that enables financial institutions to route electronic bills and payments through a single connection. This technology enables consumers to pay any vendor either by paper check or electronically over the Internet.

Unusually for the Web, the market leader is CheckFree, a dotcom company, with a monthly volume of roughly 16 million EBPP transactions, an estimated 75 percent to 80 percent of the business-to-consumer EBPP market. Other sites here include PayMyBills for bill management, Bottomline (EPAY) and Fundtech (FNDT) for e-payments, and MisceCyberCash for processing online payments and credit card payments.

Credit and Mortgage Services Online

The Internet has been a crucible for loans and mortgage companies, with dozens of sites competing with traditional lenders. Since small mortgage banks and brokers handle the majority of today's lending, it is no surprise that this area is also fragmented on the Internet, with Mortgage.com, LoanCity, and E-Loan ahead in the mortgage-lending area. Other notable Internet service providers in the credit and bill payment area include NextCard (NXCD) for consumer credit, and ELoan (EELN) and NetEarnings for consumer loans.

INSURANCE

The insurance industry is proliferating on the Web, with dozens of dotcoms including InsWeb and QuickenInsurance. The nearly trillion-dollar U.S. insurance industry provides clear opportunities for increased efficiency and cost savings on the Web. However, the complexity of the industry is also reflected in the complexity and diversity of strategies adopted by companies on the Internet. For example, while the ING Group will sell life insurance to consumers via a new online subsidiary, John Hancock Financial Services is marketing its long-term insurance product on www.quickeninsurance.com, term insurance on www.ansercenter.com (a portal for employers), and its variable annuity product on www.johnhancock.com.

A key force within the online insurance industry is the aggregator site, perhaps best represented by InsWeb, in which insurance agencies provide leads for carriers or agents. For insurers, this business model allows for a greater reach over the Internet, lowering their acquisition costs.

FINANCIAL PORTALS AND ACCOUNT AGGREGATION

One of the Internet trends that may fundamentally change the nature of financial services is the proliferation of financial portals and account aggregation services. These services are potentially important because they promise to provide some-

thing close to one-stop shopping for financial consumers, encouraging brand iden-
tification, stickiness, and cross-selling opportunities.

Financial portals bring together a range of financial services in one location. For
example, Yahoo!Finance.com provides a soup-to-nuts range of financial services,
including brokerage (Datek), mortgage (e-loan), online insurance (InsWeb Corp.),
taxes (H&R Block), an online financial network with original product, and morning
calls with analysts. Microsoft MoneyCentral (www.moneycentral.msn.com) offers
investment advice and services, bill paying, portfolio management tools, commen-
tary, and many other financial services in its financial portal.

Online account aggregation services allow investors to consolidate account
information from a variety of sites and financial firms in one location using a technology known as screen scraping. The technology enables an Internet site to bring
together banking, credit card, investment, and other account information in one
place, accessible at a secure site with one password. The service is being provided
by a number of independent firms and technology service providers, including
Yodlee.com, Vertical One Corporation (a subsidiary of S1Corporation),
MyAccounts, and ByAllAccounts.

Using these services and their own technology, a large number of banks, brokerage houses, mutual fund companies, insurance companies, and others are now
offering or soon will be offering account aggregation. The reason is obvious.
Consumers are likely to leave their assets at sites that they use to gain a comprehensive look at their financial situation. Furthermore, these sites tend to be sticky
since changing vendors will most likely be time-consuming. The opportunities for
cross-selling are also large since account aggregation sites will bring together
financial information regarding banking, brokerage, insurance, and other financial
areas.

The appeal of this Internet space in indicated by the offering of General
Electric Corporation's Financial Network (www.gefn.com), which provides insurance, banking, bill payment and presentment, financial information, and advice.
GE hopes to transport its brand recognition and reliability into the financial portal universe.

Finally, it seems highly likely that financial portals and account aggregators
(which often go together as in the case of AOL, Quicken, and Yahoo) will find the
transition to providing investment advice, execution, and recommendations hard to
resist.

CHAPTER 2

Internet Financial Services Company Valuation

Jeffrey P. Anderson, Principal, and Humberto Sanchez, Research Associate
Bond & Pecaro, Inc.

INTRODUCTION

The stock market downturn beginning in March 2000 dramatically changed the valuation landscape for Internet companies. Prior to March, the abundance of capital in the private markets and an exceedingly strong stock market drove the values of Internet companies beyond traditional measures of valuation. The availability of capital continues to be restrictive early in 2001. Buyers and investors have begun to focus on profitability in addition to strong revenue growth. Despite the downturn, company valuations still exceed traditional benchmarks and remain volatile. There are many new financial metrics associated with the valuation of Internet companies. When examined more closely, most, if not all, have a basis in traditional valuation methods.

QUALITATIVE ISSUES

Given the nascent stage of the Internet industry, a qualitative analysis of the key economic and financial factors is critical. A qualitative analysis is particularly important in the case of early-stage companies where an entrepreneur may possess an underdeveloped technology, product, or service. Likewise, it is a crucial component of a traditional financial services company's e-commerce strategic analysis. The analysis provides general insight into the value proposition of a potential acquisition, subsidiary spin-off, or in-house product development effort. Selected key considerations may include those shown in Table 2-1.

TABLE 2-1

Key Considerations

Key Considerations		Financial Services Criteria
Market	Size	Overall size of market—number/value of brokerage transactions, number/value of loans/mortgages/insurance policies, number of banking accounts, value of assets under management, number/value of e-commerce financial transactions
	Fragmentation	Number of players, segment by size and product/service
	Competition	Identification of competitors' (pure online, traditional, hybrid), strengths and weaknesses
	Stage	Life cycle of industry segment, companies, or products and services
Operating	Value proposition	Price, convenience, product and service selection, content, transaction transparency, aggregator
	Revenue model	Interest income, commissions, fixed fees, subscription fees, transaction based, advertising, referral fees
	Management/ employees	Experience, compensation package, incentive clauses, retention rates, culture
	Technology	Proprietary and nonproprietary considerations, patents, intellectual property, ability to scale
	Sales/marketing	Advertising and marketing intensity, clickstream analysis capability, customer service quality
	Partners	Key operating partners—product and service offerings, distribution channels
	Customer base	Size, type, retention/attrition rates

VALUATION METHODS

The three primary valuation methodologies consist of the cost, market, and income approaches. A valuation using the cost approach measures the worth of a business through the summation of the costs necessary to replicate the concern. The investment or cost approach rests upon the familiar principle of substitution, which recognizes that the value of a property is commonly limited by the cost of reproducing or replacing it.

In applying the cost approach, an analyst must examine the factors that would make the subject more or less useful, and, hence, more or less valuable, than a substitute or replacement item. To the extent that suitable replacements exist, the market value of an item is presumably limited by the prices of such substitutes. Since Internet financial service companies often retain proprietary technology, it is important to consider whether replacement technologies are superior, and thus whether an obsolescence discount is warranted. Similarly, Internet companies are primarily composed of intangible assets. Therefore careful consideration should be given to assets such as intellectual content, proprietary technology, management, distribution and licensing agreements, brand, and customer base.

In the case of an Internet financial services entity, a meaningful cost analysis must quantify the various investments, both tangible and intangible, required to replicate the technology, brand, and resources in place at the company. These investment expenses may include costs for equipment, technology, and advertising and promotion, as well as legal, accounting, and consulting fees, among others.

The market approach can take many forms. The comparable sales approach analyzes the sales transactions of businesses similar in structure, market position, and size to determine the value of an enterprise. A valuation multiple, which is simply a ratio or measure, can be developed to compare relative values of businesses.

Finally, the income approach measures the expected economic benefits, expressed in cash, that an asset brings to its holder. The fair-market value of a business is expressed by discounting these future benefits. The discounted cashflow method used to value Internet businesses incorporates variables such as projected operating metrics, revenues, expense projections, operating margins, and various discount rates. The variables used in the analysis reflect historical market and company growth trends, as well as the anticipated performance of the business. The stream of annual cashflows is adjusted to present value using a discount rate appropriate for the technology and Internet industry.

Additionally, a projection is made for a terminal value. The terminal value represents the hypothetical value of the business at the end of the projection period. After appropriate adjustments for taxes, the net terminal value is then discounted to present value.

Traditional methods have been challenged to keep pace with the public and private market valuations of Internet businesses. For example, the discounted cashflow approach relies upon projections of revenues and operating profits. Many Internet companies have short histories, modest revenues, and large operating losses. Operating metrics and financial measures are volatile and difficult to predict. Owners of such companies have tended to focus upon growing market share and revenues as rapidly as possible, not managing operating cashflow. For most companies, operating losses are projected for many years.

VALUATION LIFE CYCLE

Based upon our analysis of Internet company transactions, operations, and values, it is clear that different valuation methods tend to be useful during different stages of an Internet company's life cycle. During the conceptual or seed stage of a company's life cycle, the cost approach may be most appropriate to value the business concept. By measuring the costs associated with procuring acceptable substitutes for a particular group of assets, it is possible to make inferences about what a rational buyer would be willing to pay. A meaningful analysis would quantify the various tangible and intangible assets required to replicate the resources in place at the business.[1]

As an Internet company moves into the early stage of its life cycle, where it begins to develop, produce, and market products or services, the market approach becomes more applicable. The market approach is based upon comparable sales transactions negotiated between willing buyers and sellers.

The availability of venture capital is an important component driving the value of early-stage technology companies. As such, the venture capital method[2] is one form of a market approach useful for valuing start-up and early-stage Internet companies. In the venture capital method, venture capitalists and company owners negotiate the inherent value of the business and the respective early-stage financing. The prefinancing valuation represents the value of the company prior to the cash investment. The postfinancing valuation is the indicated value of the business after the investment is made.

A comparable sales analysis is also useful during a company's early development. This market approach analyzes recent sales transactions of similar businesses. The purchase price paid for a business enterprise can be divided by an appropriate metric. Metrics for Internet companies could include trailing or projected annual revenues or could make use of measures such as unique visitors, page views, customers, or number of transactions at the time of the sale. These metrics may be an indicator of potential value. It would be ideal to have cashflow as a measure of comparison, but the majority of these pure Internet companies are unprofitable.

As a company develops a history and moves into a later stage, the market approach remains a powerful indicator of value. However, it is at this stage that the income approach also becomes more useful. Once a company becomes public and begins to mature, valuation is largely dictated by the income approach in the form of the discounted cashflow method, in conjunction with a comparable sales analysis.

Nonetheless, the income approach remains difficult to apply given the short history of the industry. As in any emerging industry, many firms have not developed a performance history. In addition, buyers and investors expect strong, sustained revenue growth and operating profits over the next 12- to 24-month time period.

Table 2-2 indicates the applicability of valuation methods during the various life cycles of Internet companies.

COST APPROACH

The cost approach has been the least applicable method for company valuation given the high valuations. However, in light of the public market pullback and the

---

[1] The cost approach may also be warranted when the owners or investors try to recover the cost of their investments.

[2] Robert M. Johnson, "Valuation Issues in Start-Ups & Early-Stage Companies: The Venture Capital Method," London Business School, December 1997, pp. 2–3.

TABLE 2-2

Valuation Methods and the Life Cycle of Companies

Stage of Development	Financing	Valuation Method
Start-up/business concept	Seed equity	Cost, market
Early stage	Venture capital—initial rounds	Cost, market (venture capital, comparable sales)
Later stage	Venture capital—later rounds	Market (venture capital, comparable sales), income
Pre-IPO	Venture capital, private equity	Income, market (comparable sales)
Public	Capital markets	Income, market (comparable sales)

closer examination of deals by venture capitalists, it is quite likely that many entities will not be able to continually fund operating losses. Owners and investors will seek to recover the cost of their investments.

MARKET APPROACH

The capital markets have been the primary drivers of Internet company values. Historically, mergers and acquisitions in the Internet sector were largely strategic and funded by an inflated stock currency. The pullback in the public and private sectors has forced buyers and investors to pay closer attention to valuation and the due diligence process.

Timing is critical to value in the acquisition process. The current state of the capital markets will affect valuations although company fundamentals may remain unchanged. Cumulative operating losses and the need for cash will also influence the value that sellers may be willing to accept. Finally, the number of parties interested in a target will also play a factor in the transaction price.

The market approach has been the most useful method to gauge Internet company values. It is particularly important to be careful in selecting comparables. The structure, market position, and size of the comparable companies analyzed should be similar to the target business entity. It is becoming exceedingly difficult to compare companies in the financial services sector as a result of the convergence of pure Web-enabled entities, traditional financial services companies, and hybrid businesses.

There have been a number of mergers and acquisitions within the last 18 months in the financial services sector. Recent transactions are shown in Table 2-3.

The purpose of mergers and acquisitions is to create value. However, buyers and investors purchase for different reasons. Some may purchase companies to diversify products and services; others may seek to increase scale and customer base, add key intellectual property and technology, or eliminate competitors.

TABLE 2-3

Selected Financial Services Acquisitions

Industry	Entity	Buyer	Date	Transaction Value (millions)	Product or Service
Online banking	Telebanc	E*Trade	06/1/1999	$1800.0	Online banking
	SoundView Technology Group	Wit Capital Group	11/1/1999	325.0	Investment banking services
	first-e	Terra Networks	03/6/2000	2280.0	Irish online banking service
	E*Offering	Wit Capital Group	05/15/2000	302.0	Online investment bank
	Entrium Direct Bankers	Bipop-Carriere SPA	06/26/2000	2000.0	German online bank
Financial portals	NetRoadShow	Broadcast.com	03/16/1999	50.0	IPO and financial services
	ClearStation	E*Trade	04/21/1999	46.2	Financial media Website
	IQC.com	Go2Net	05/14/1999	20.0	Financial information Website
	Market Guide	Multex.com	06/25/1999	159.0	Financial news and information for Websites
	Virtual Stock Exchange	Predict it!	07/8/1999	5.5	Financial investment portal
	Quote.com	Lycos	09/9/1999	78.3	Financial information portal
	MoneyLine.com	Accel Partners	07/9/1999	7.0	Real-time financial information Website
	Morningstar	SOFTBANK	07/9/1999	91.0	Online mutual fund rating firm
	Patagon.com	Banco Santander	03/9/2000	585.0	Latin American financial services portal
	Consumer Financial Networks	Gateway	05/25/2000	150.0	Financial services firm
	InvestNews	PT Multimedia	06/16/2000	37.5	Brazilian investment news
Online brokerage	E*Trade UK	E*Trade	01/13/2000	100.0	Online broker
	Deal Wise Ltd.	TD Waterhouse	05/4/2000	n/a	Online brokerage
	Online Trading Group	Omega Research	01/26/2000	300.0	Online broker
	Execute Direct.com	PSA, Inc.	9/20/2000	21.0	Internet day trading facilities
	Private Accounts.com	E*Trade	10/31/2000	4.3	Online access to money managers
	Share People Group	American Express	12/5/2000	44.0	British online brokerage
Online loans	eStudentLoan.com	Collegestudent.com	09/20/1999	n/a	Online student loans
	Rock Financial	Intuit Inc	10/7/1999	370.0	Online home mortgage business

Take for example, E*Trade. It continued its aggressive customer acquisition strategy with its purchase of Telebanc for $1.8 billion. With that acquisition, E*Trade obtained the nation's largest online bank, enabling it to take advantage of both company brand names. The merger allowed E*Trade to diversify its product lines by offering customers a full complement of online transactions, including FDIC-insured cash management accounts, ATM access, and online bill management.

Multex.com serves as another example. It purchased Market Guide for $159 million in June 1999. The acquisition allowed Multex.com to expand the quality and content of its financial services, as well as gain access to Market Guide's extensive online and offline distribution network and proprietary financial databases.

Public company valuation multiples provide insight into potential valuation. Table 2-4 presents a selection of brokerage companies and related valuation metrics.

Despite E*Trade's explosive growth in revenue both on a sequential quarterly and annual basis, the market correction has severely impacted its enterprise valuation multiple. The market has penalized pure online brokerage company valuations yet is willing to pay a higher multiple for an established brokerage firm such as TD Waterhouse, which effectively makes use of the technology benefits of the Internet and has a larger, more stable base of clients.

Financial portal company valuations can vary dramatically and be quite volatile as well. Table 2-5 shows a selection of valuation metrics for financial portals. Many financial service portals have fallen out of favor of late. It has become evident that firms in this sector need to expand revenue streams beyond subscription fee and advertising-driven models. Buyers and investors are rewarding those firms that can continue to grow revenues dramatically through incremental products and services and show strong progress toward profitability.

TABLE 2-4

Selected Companies and Valuations

Brokerage Company	Ticker	Enterprise Value*	1999 Revenues	2000 Revenues	Enterprise Value/1999 Revenue	Enterprise Value/2000 Revenue
E*Trade	EGRP	$1786.9	$895.1	$2373.2	2.0x	0.8x
Ameritrade	AMTD	1447.2	384.6	671.2	3.8	2.2
TD Waterhouse	TWE	4399.0	960.0	1540.8	4.6	2.9
Knight Trading Group	NITE	1179.1	800.7	1257.0	1.5	0.9
				Average	3.0x	1.7x
				Weighted Avg.	2.9	1.5
				Median	2.9	1.6

Source: Company financial statements, Hoovers Online.
*Enterprise value is based upon market capitalization as of December 29, 2000 plus debt, less current assets.

TABLE 2-5

Selected Financial Portals and Valuations

Financial Portal	Ticker	Enterprise Value*	1999 Revenues	2000 Revenues	Enterprise Value/1999 Revenue	Enterprise Value/2000 Revenue
MarketWatch.com	MKTW	$–4.7	$23.3	$54.2	–0.2x	–0.1x
TheStreet.com	TSCM	13.6	14.3	24.9	1.0	0.5
Multex	MLTX	350.5	35.6	86.0	9.8	4.1
Hoover's	HOOV	4.7	19.1	29.7	0.2	0.2
Edgar Online, Inc.	EDGR	6.7	0.4	1.5	16.8	4.5
				Average	5.5x	1.8x
				Weighted Avg.	4.0	1.9
				Median	1.0	0.5

Source: Company financial statements, Hoovers Online.
*Enterprise value is based upon market capitalization as of December 29, 2000, plus debt, less current assets.

It may be helpful to look at public company values as a potential benchmark when valuing a private company. However, it is important to recognize that large premiums have typically been ascribed to publicly held Internet companies compared with private transactions. The value accretion can be quite significant from a pre-IPO to post-IPO stage. Therefore, it is often appropriate to apply large discounts to public market values to account for control, marketability, and scale factors.

INCOME APPROACH

Although the financial markets have been the driving force in the value of Internet companies, the income approach, in the form of a discounted cashflow analysis, remains the primary method for company valuation. There is no question that this approach is extremely difficult to apply to companies that have few revenues, no cashflow, and an underdeveloped business model. However, it does provide insight into the ability of a company to sustain long-term value.

In a discounted cashflow approach, many of the key variables used to value traditional brick-and-mortar finance companies certainly apply to Internet company valuations. Important variables include the projection period or time horizon, key revenue metrics, sales and marketing expenses, operating expenses, and discount rates. However, the assumptions that are employed in financial models are quite different.

1. *Time horizon.* A shorter time frame is typically used in the analysis of an Internet entity. A projection period of 5 years may be appropriate, compared with a 10-year time horizon for a traditional financial services company. However, it is important to consider the long-term scenario. With rapid technology changes, it

is difficult to look beyond the short term, but an analysis should consider the implications on value when a company reaches a steady state or mature stage.

2. *Revenue drivers.* A key component to projecting revenues is the growth level of the underlying metrics that drive revenues—growth in unique viewers, customers, page views, registered users, transactions, accounts, and advertising. Is growth accelerating or trailing off from quarter to quarter and year to year? How can the company derive incremental revenues above and beyond the initial operating model?

3. *Sales/marketing expenses.* Excessive sales and marketing expenses were the downfall of many portal and Internet e-tailers during 2000. The steep customer acquisition costs compared with potential customer revenue streams were not showing improvement. An analysis may consider whether the sales and marketing costs to total operating expense percentage is comparable to that of similar companies. What are the customer acquisition costs, and what is the best way to measure them? Are they decreasing with an increase in the customer base? What are the incremental revenues that can be generated from making additional marketing expenditures?

4. *Operating cashflow margins.* Most pure Internet financial services companies are not generating operating profits. With the exception of the big hybrid players such as Charles Schwab and Ameritrade, many have large operating losses and a very high cash burn rate.

   However, the pure Internet companies that do survive have low-fixed-cost structures and will have the potential to generate cashflow margins greater than the 15 to 20 percent levels seen for traditional investment and financial services companies, once these entities reach a mature, steady state. Certain commodity products such as trading prices will continue to fall, and yet there will be opportunities to build margins through enhanced productivity and higher-margin product and service offerings.

5. *Discount rate.* Compared with the valuation of traditional financial services companies, a much higher discount rate is justified to account for the inherent risk of new financial services companies. A rate of 18 to 20 percent, or higher depending upon the stage of development, is quite typical.

6. *Sensitivity analysis.* An analysis of alternative scenarios takes on added importance with emerging companies or concepts. It is essential to examine every possible scenario. What is the impact of changes in technology and competitive markets? What happens when capital is not readily available? Is there a willingness to fund losses for a new business and for how long? What happens when the current business model fails?

There are a couple of key points to keep in mind when using a discounted cashflow analysis. A change in a variable can have a dramatic change in the valuation results of the model. As a result, careful selection of assumptions is essential. In addition, because of the fast-changing nature of the industry, it is helpful to perform several valuation scenarios and weight the valuation probabilities accordingly or employ real options analysis in the valuation of companies.[3]

The discounted cashflow model can be used to test the reasonableness of current values in the marketplace. For example, Multex.com's enterprise value as of December 29, 2000, is approximately $350 million. Given this enterprise value, what are the revenue, expense, and operating profit assumptions required for this current value to be realized using a discounted cashflow approach? Using a 10-year time horizon, historical income statements, and a discount rate of 20 percent, Multex.com will have to achieve the following results:

- *Revenue growth.* Achieve a compound revenue growth rate of 30 percent in years 1 to 5 of the projection period and a 15 percent revenue growth rate for the remainder of the time horizon
- *Operating profit margin.* Achieve an operating margin of 20 percent by year 3
- *Cashflow multiple.* Realize a terminal value at 13 times year 10 operating cashflow

The purpose of this example is not to project Multex.com's most likely financial performance but to illustrate a method to test current value against future expectations. The example shows that despite a deep connection in the public markets strong growth is still required for certain Internet companies to sustain current values.

CONCLUSION

The volatile nature of Internet company values will provide acquisition and investment opportunities for financial services businesses. Along with strategic and operating considerations, valuation has taken on added importance.

As in any emerging industry, Internet company valuation continues to be challenging. Market volatility, the availability of capital, high risk, and the rapid convergence of online and offline companies complicate analyses. Although some valuation methods may lend themselves better to certain situations, an analysis using as many methods as possible is recommended. Done properly, the methods will give insight into a reasonable range of values.

This is also a time to dig deeper into the fundamentals of companies. Buyers and investors want to see profitability. With a new company or division, operating cashflow may not be the first priority for operators and investors. Like different valuation methods, the importance of operating metrics changes as a company moves from gaining market share in the growth and expansion phase to revenue conversion and eventual profitability. Ultimately, value must be equated to cashflow.

---

[3] Internet financial executives and analysts have begun to utilize real options analysis in conjunction with the discounted cashflow approach to help quantify the value of emerging companies where the market for products and services is rapidly changing.

www.Online_Trading.com

George R. Monahan, Vice President & Director, Industry Studies
Securities Industry Association

No matter where you turn today, it's "this.com" or "that.com." The Internet, more specifically e-commerce, is becoming, if it is not already, ubiquitous. Screaming out at you everywhere is that omnipresent dotcom, whether you're watching the PGA Open on ESPN, catching Power Lunch on CNBC, listening to station W.COM in your Accura while commuting, or scanning mutual fund discounter ads in *The Wall Street Journal* (that is, if you still read hard copy instead of viewing the interactive. WSJ online or having its headlines e-mailed to you each morning).

The Internet's pace of adoption eclipses that of all other technologies that preceded it, notes the U.S. Department of Commerce. Radio was in existence 38 years before 50 million listeners tuned in. It took 13 years for TV to reach the same audience level. It even took 16 years after the first PC kit came out to reach 50 million mouse clickers. But once it was open to the general public, the Internet crossed that threshold in 4 years. And the number of users doubled to 100 million by the end of 1997. Traffic on the Internet itself is doubling every 100 days.

The explosion in Internet usage is hard to overstate. Today, the majority of computer users send more e-mail than they make long distance calls. Further, one-third of PC users send more e-mail than they make local calls!

After e-mail (and some prurient clicking), the fastest-growing consumer use of the Internet is online stock trading. From the first Internet stock trade 5 years

---

ago, via K. Aufhauser & Co., online trading is approaching half a million trades per day—and that's just counting equity and mutual fund trades.

GROWTH OF ONLINE TRADING

According to Forrester Research (www.forrester.com), there are about 4 million online brokerage accounts today (3.7 million at year-end 1998). But that's only half the number reported by Gomez Advisors (www.gomez.com), with 7.5 million at year-end 1998. It's also half the 7.3 million estimated by U.S. Bancorp Piper Jaffray (www.piperjaffray.com). Looking forward, Forrester projects 9.2 million online brokerage accounts by the year 2001, again about half of Gomez's projection of 18 million for the same year and less than the 14 million projected for just next year by Deutsche Bank (www.db.com). (See Figures 3-1 and 3-2.)

Part of the confusion comes from the way different services, and for that matter different online brokerage firms themselves, identify the number of online accounts. Some firms count anyone who has access to their account information online, whether or not they do, or even can, actually trade online. Some try to distinguish between active online accounts, those that have actually made an online trade during the year or quarter and, inactive or view-only accounts. Most also count telephone and direct PC (non-Internet) access. Merely having a password counts as an online account at some firms.

We tend to be conservative and think the lower estimates are more relevant to the securities industry—those that are trying to track active, online trading accounts. But no matter what the methodology or the source of the data, the

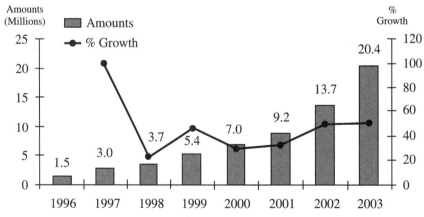

Source: Forrester Research, Inc.

FIGURE 3-1

Online investing accounts.

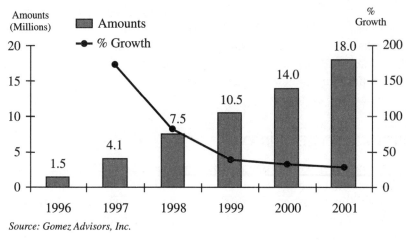

Source: Gomez Advisors, Inc.

FIGURE 3-2

Domestic Internet brokerage accounts.

growth trend is clearly the same. Following triple-digit growth rates after the online's initial introduction, the growth in the number of online accounts fell last year into the double digits, and projections are for roughly 50 percent growth rates for the next few years—still an impressive trend.

Part of the initial explosion in online accounts was simply enabling existing discount brokerage accounts to trade online. When Charles Schwab (www.schwab.com), the online industry leader by far, began offering online brokerage, the number of online accounts soared—without even adding one new customer. Simply allowing existing accounts to obtain a password to trade online skyrocketed the numbers. The explosion was also fueled by accounts from the "early-adopter" types who switched accounts from their non-online broker (or opened an additional account) to gain Internet access. Adding in the new, first-time accounts simply compounded this explosion.

This also happened with the other dual-account (traditional full service/discounter adding online) leaders: Waterhouse Securities (www.waterhouse.com); Fidelity Investments (www.fidelity.com); DLJ Direct (www.dljdirect.com), the online subsidiary of Donaldson, Lufkin & Jenrette (www.dlj.com); and Discover Brokerage (www.discoverbrokerage.com), the online subsidiary of Morgan Stanley Dean Witter (www.msdw.com).

Adding to the online account growth of the traditional firms offering online access was the growing account base of the predominantly online-only brokerages—E*Trade (www.etrade.com), Ameritrade (www.ameritrade.com), Datek Online (www.datek.com), etc. Put altogether, the online account figures inevitably zoomed.

In just 3 years' time, the number of brokerage firms offering online brokerage services increased to 100 from merely one firm (see Figure 3-3). Although many are new entrants—firms launched to take advantage of the opportunity afforded by the merger of new technology with personal finance—most are the online offspring of traditional financial services firms: full-service brokers, discounters, banks, and mutual fund companies.

BOTH EVOLUTION AND REVOLUTION

The online brokerage phenomenon has been as much an evolution of the discount brokerage business as a revolution in Internet-based e-commerce. Cerulli Associates (www.cerulli.com) estimates that more than half of the 7.5 million online accounts reported by Gomez Advisors and others at the beginning of this year are attributable to conversions from traditional brokerage accounts to online accounts. Cerulli notes that the largest discount brokers have already offered most of their client base the option of going online. It cites Charles Schwab, which alone has witnessed its online account share of its total account base to jump from 5 percent 5 years ago (including telephone and PC access) to 60 percent today.

Echoing this view is International Data Corp. (www.idc.com). It shows the number of online accounts growing from 6 million in 1998 to 25 million by 2002, with comparable growth in the number of investors and commission revenues.

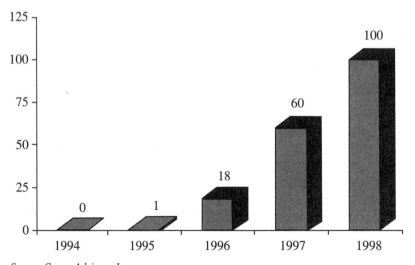

Source: Gomez Advisors, Inc.

FIGURE 3-3

Online brokers—1 to 100 in just 3 years.

Data Corp. attributes most of this growth to traditional investors looking for cost savings online. We feel that convenience was a large, but secondary, consideration.

Further, IDC predicts that 90 percent of today's discount brokerage customers will trade online by the year 2002.

Conversions are only half the picture, however, According to U.S. Bancorp Piper Jaffray (Piper), online brokerages today are no longer just converting discount brokerage customers and the early-adopter types from the client base of traditional brokerages. They are now signing up first-time, self-directed individual investors with an eventual eye toward building a customer base from the affluent bread-and-butter customers of full-service firms. They note that the bulk of the current new, first-time accounts are coming from the 401(k) mutual fund investor types who are discovering what they can do online. In fact, mutual fund companies are one of the main online brokerage groups that offer such 401(k) fund investor services.

Piper and other firms currently tracking the online brokerage industry predict that full-service firms will likely begin offering online investing, only or at least initially, to a select group of high-net-worth accounts structured like wrap fees driven by assets under management. A recent Gomez Advisor Alert discussed just why full-service firms are now embracing online trading within their wrap-fee revenue-type arrangements. Gomez notes that the cost of a trade has become commoditized and the price has fallen precipitously, leveling out at just under $16 per trade on average at the largest online firms (see Figure 3-4)—but people are still more than willing to pay fees for helpful investment advice. Since full-service firms dare not directly compete with a commoditized service against their broker work force, 20 percent of which bring in 80 percent of their retail revenue, they are wrapping up this ability inside the fee-based, asset-based products and services they already offer in order to not lose part of their core customer base who want online ability.

SELL-SIDE GENESIS

On the sell side, we've already seen online trading's epiphany from only one sell-side firm to at least 100 truly "online brokers" in just 3 years. Securities firms that have at least an Internet presence have blossomed from virtually nil to about half of the community today.

When SIA began exploring the possibilities of the Internet for our membership in the summer of 1993, the Internet as a communications medium for the public and business (nonacademic/government) was in its gestation period. With very few exceptions, the business and general public's Internet's use, let alone e-commerce, was embryonic at that time. Very few people even knew what www or AOL was. And it would still be another 2 years before an online stock trade occurred.

Then, in June 1995, SIA launched its own home page (www.sia.com) at its Technology Management Conference, when e-commerce was merely reaching its

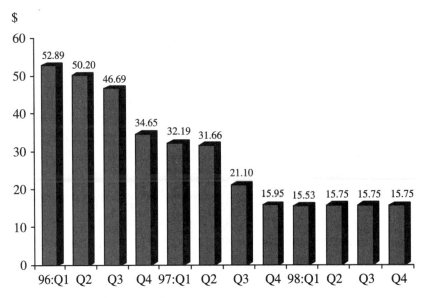

Source: Credit Suisse First Boston Corp.

FIGURE 3-4

Average commission by top 10 online trading firms.

infancy stage. At that point, only five securities firms within SIA, less than 1 percent of the membership, even had a Website, and online Internet stock trading was just coming off the drawing board. Today, just shy of 4 years later, fully half of SIA's nearly 800 members (http://www.sia.com/about_sia/html/members.html) have a Web presence with links to their sites spread all over the World Wide Web.

TODAY'S ONLINE INVESTOR

Who's online in today's investment field from the buy side? Both institutional and retail customers who have discovered, or more often than naught been sold on, the varied benefits of the Internet and online trading. For retail customers, the major advantages are low-cost trading and information access. For institutions, the prime advantage of the Internet lies in its use as a low-cost medium to access services the institutions previously had through proprietary networks or via traditional media, i.e., clearing services, research, etc. For this chapter, we'll look at retail on the buy side.

A recent Forrester survey of 50 brokerage and mutual fund companies revealed that 72 percent already had their core customer base online. However, many noted that, although online, these customers are not yet moving their transactions online, but they are expected to do so to within 5 years.

As we've already seen, a major segment of today's online investors were not new to the investing scene, but rather previous or current customers of traditional brokerage firms, particularly discount brokers. Therefore, the demographics of today's online investor does not differ dramatically from that of other retail investors. The household incomes of online investors versus all retail investors are markedly similar—71 and 74 percent, respectively, have household incomes under $100,000 (see Figure 3-5).

Looking at the ages of all retail brokerage customers versus the online investor, again we see not much difference (Figure 3-6). There's a bias towards younger investors being more active online, no different from every other activity relating to PC and Internet use. The only age group where there is a 10 percentage point difference is the under-29 age group—8 percent of all retail investors versus 20 percent of online investors—but this is also the least affluent age group, those with the smallest net worth, account balances, assets under management, etc.

The demographics according to gender are slightly more disparate (Figure 3-7). Here the demographics of both investing and computer use dovetail to show a male-dominated activity. Three-quarters of online investors are men—not a surprising statistic if you combine the fact that the majority of retail investors are male with the fact that the majority of PC and Internet users also are male.

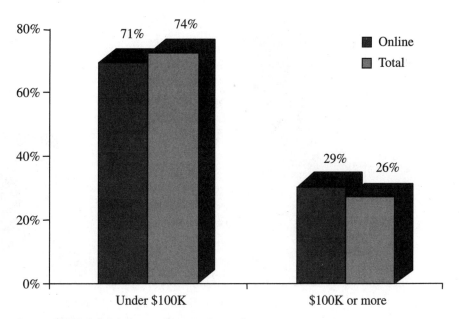

Sources: SIA/Yankelovich Partners; Forrester Research

FIGURE 3-5

Household income of retail investors.

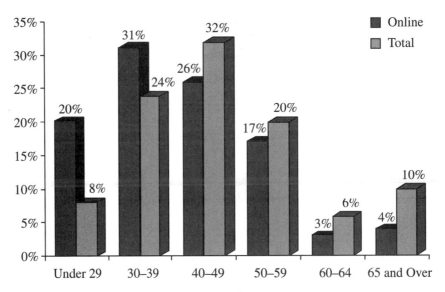

Sources: SIA/Yankelovich Partners; Forrester Research

FIGURE 3-6

Age of retail investors.

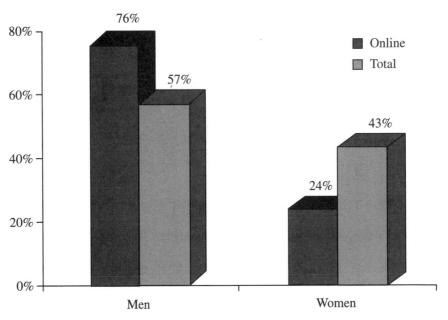

Sources: SIA/Yankelovich Partners; Forrester Research

FIGURE 3-7

Gender of retail investors.

WHERE BROKERAGE E-COMMERCE IS HEADED

In accordance with Forrester's more conservative, or more activity-focused, estimates, there will be 5.4 million active online accounts this year, and that number is projected to nearly quadruple to 20.4 million in 4 years. The accounts are owned by 3.1 million households, or nearly two accounts per household. These figures are projected to increase to 9.7 million households in 4 years, or just over two accounts per household by 2003.

But the distribution of these online accounts, households, and customer assets among different-type brokerage firms varies widely, as does the projected growth rates for different-type firms. Just over half, 55 percent, of online accounts today are held with deep discount, online trading firms such as E*Trade, Ameritrade, and Datek. The bulk of the rest, 43 percent, are held at what Forrester dubs "mid-tier" online firms that offer upscale investment services and advice with reasonable prices, i.e., Schwab, Fidelity, and Vanguard Brokerage Services (www.vanguard.com). Only 2 percent of these accounts are with full-service firms, most of which are only now beginning to offer online access, often with limited or no online trading capabilities, but with everything else—account information, quotes, research, broker e-mail access, market information, etc.

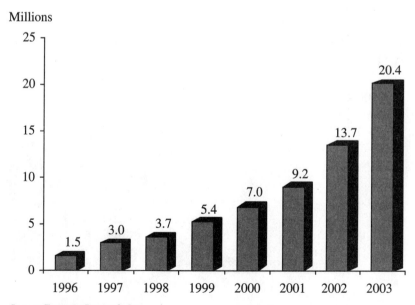

Source: Forrester Research, Inc.

FIGURE 3-8

Online investing accounts.

Looking forward 4 years to 2003, the full-service firms are expected to dras-
tically increase their share of these households and accounts, understandably coming from a virtual zero base. However, the major part of this growth is projected
to come mainly at the expense of today's deep-discount firms, which offer mostly
electronic interfaces with the client. Meanwhile, the mid-tier online firms, which
pretty much mirror many of the services of the full-service firms, are projected to
hold their own—increasing their market share of households and accounts but losing their share of customer assets.

The deep discounters are projected to drop from 45 percent of all online trading households today to 22 percent in 4 years. Similarly, their share of online
accounts is expected to fall from 55 to 26 percent. Consolidation is an inevitable
scenario here. Mid-tier online firms are expected to see their share of total online
accounts grow to 52 percent in 2003 from 43 percent today, while their share of
households will increase slightly to 56 percent from 52 percent this year.

The total assets in these online accounts will reach about $374 billion this
year, which translates into roughly $69,000 per account, or $121,000 per household (Figure 3-9). That's estimated to grow to about $3.1 trillion in 4 years, or to
$152,000 per account and $319,000 per household by 2003.

It's in this online customer assets area where the full-service firms, again
coming from a near-zero base, really gain market share at the expense of all other

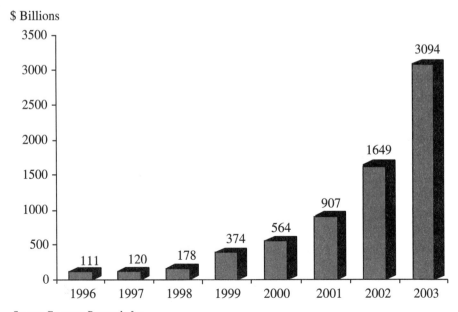

$ Billions

Source: Forrester Research, Inc.

FIGURE 3-9

Assets in online brokerage accounts.

firms but particularly the deep discounters. Because of their higher-net-worth customer base, the full-service firms have an 18 percent market share already in
online customer assets even though they have only 2 percent and 3 percent of
online accounts and households, respectively. In 4 years, when their respective
share of those two measures jumps to 22 percent and 23 percent, their share of
online assets is projected to zoom to 45 percent. Vice versa, the deep discounters'
current 25 percent share of online assets is projected to decline to a mere 8 percent, and the mid-tier firms' 1999 share of 57 percent will fall to 48 percent.

Driving Forrester's figures are the projected $310,000 of assets per online
account for full service firms versus $137,000 for mid-tier firms and a mere
$45,000 for deep discounters. Forrester notes that the deep discounters' growth
will slow because most active traders have already moved online and discounters
will struggle to convert mainstream, full-service-firm customers as these firms
offer their own online services. Also, pricing wars for customers have already driv-
en down the cost of trades to the bare bones, and now the war for customers is in
marketing. This is already costing some deep discounters more than any other
expense item and producing net losses—firms can only operate in the red for so
long. Again, this is a ripe environment for consolidation.

ONLINE'S RETAIL MARKET SHARE

The number of online equity trades per day has been growing at a phenomenal 35
percent rate in each of the past two quarters, according to Credit Suisse First
Boston (www.csfb.com). The number of trades reached 459,000 per day in this
year's first quarter. The top 10 online firms control 90 percent of online daily trading, and half of it is controlled by the top 3 firms.

CSFB estimated that at least two of the "online-only" firms show average
trades of 25 per account per year, five times the average trades per account at full-
service firms (Figure 3-10). CSFB and Piper both show the top six online firms
controlling 80 percent of this equity activity. Estimates show anywhere from 25 to
30 percent of the online customer base generating 75 to 80 percent of the daily trading for these firms. In other words, day traders are a large factor in this increase in
online trading as well as overall trading and higher-share-volume levels today.

As a result of this growth, online trading reached a 14 percent share of all
equity trades at the beginning of this year, again according to CSFB estimates.
Both CSFB and Piper translate this into a 27 percent share of *all* retail equity
trades in 1998 (Figure 3-11). Piper further estimates that by excluding mutual fund
trades, this rises to a 37 percent share of all retail pure equity trades by online
accounts last year. Of course, much of the recent growth is concentrated in trading
in Internet-related stocks.

CSFB showed that the 35 percent growth rate in online trades for the fourth
quarter of 1998 was fueled by an increase of 47 percent in stock volume of its own

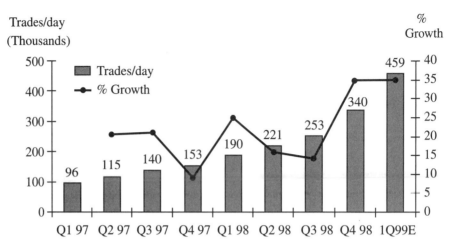

Source: *Credit Suisse First Boston Technology Group*

FIGURE 3-10

Online equity trades/day explode.

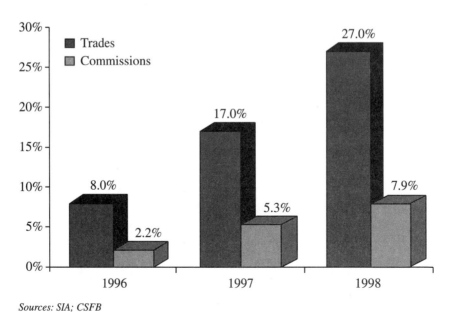

Sources: *SIA; CSFB*

FIGURE 3-11

Online firms' share of retail trades and commissions.

Internet-focused e-commerce group. Meanwhile, overall volume at the NYSE and NASDAQ was up only 2 percent and 14 percent, respectively, for the quarter. As CSFB noted, "The online trading industry is a case of Internet users (often working at Internet firms) using Internet brokerages to trade Internet stocks."

These are just estimates, as there is no industrywide reporting of what trades were retail versus institutional, and other data must also be estimated. Thus, not everyone agrees that the market share has reached this level, but everyone does agree that it has become meaningful and is certainly increasing. NASD president Frank Zarb recently estimated that online trading accounted for more than 10 percent of NASDAQ *volume* (not trades), and that share is rising.

CSFB also showed that commission revenues from online equity trades increased nearly fivefold in the 2 years from 1996 to 1998, rising from $268 million to $1.3 billion. As shown in Figure 3-11, this translates into a rise in the online share of all retail equity commissions from 2.2 percent in 1996 to 7.9 percent in 1998.

The commission growth was phenomenal, 81 percent in 1997 and 70 percent last year. However, as mentioned, the rapid growth will now diminish, as most of the easily converted accounts are already online, and it will take new entrants to keep the growth figures above the overall growth in commissions. CSFB estimates a 31 percent increase in online commissions this year to $1.7 billion and about 17 percent growth rates the next 2 years to $2.3 billion by the year 2001 (Figure 3-12).

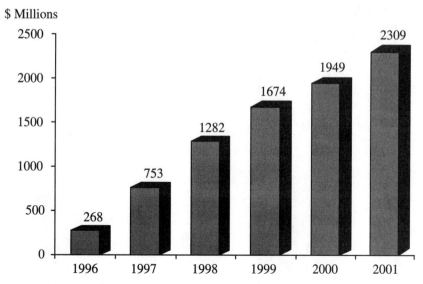

Source: Credit Suisse First Boston Corp.

FIGURE 3-12

Online trading commissions.

Again, this is not the only estimate: International Data Corp. also cites $1.3 billion for online commissions last year but projects $5.3 billion by the year 2002. Of course, IDC predicts a 90 percent conversion rate of all discount customers by then.

INTERNET IPOS

In March 1999, there were 13 Internet-related IPOs with proceeds of $1.2 billion (see Figure 3-13)—a record and the first month ever to exceed $1 billion in Internet IPOs. More impressive, March's total was nearly equal to the $1.5 billion in total Internet IPOs for all of last year.

Those 13 deals were nearly half of the 30 firm-commitment IPOs underwritten in March. This is a record percentage and provides impressive proof of how much Internet-related deals are dominating the IPO calendar so far this year, including 13 percent of January's IPOs (2 of 15) and 24 percent of February's (8 of 33). (See Figure 3-14.)

ONLINE TRADING BROKERS' PROFITABILITY

Data on the profitability of online trading for securities firms are minimal. First, most firms are not publicly owned, and thus they have no public financials avail-

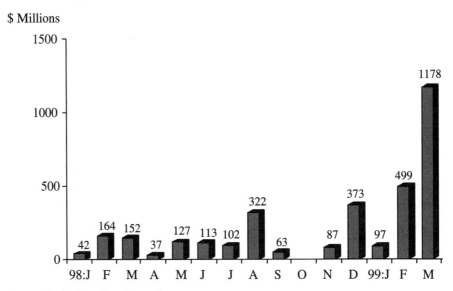

Source: Credit Suisse First Boston Corp.

FIGURE 3-13

Internet IPOs.

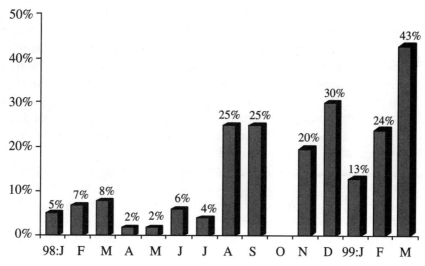

Source: Credit Suisse First Boston Corp.

FIGURE 3-14

Internet IPOs percent of total IPO deals.

able, i.e., 10Ks or 10Qs. For those public firms with both traditional and online brokerage, the results of online businesses or online subsidiaries are buried in the financials. DLJ Direct and Discover's operations are subsumed in, and dwarfed by, the discussions of the parents' main businesses—investment banking, global, clearing, asset management, all brokerage, etc. However, DLJ did announce that its online sub earned record revenues of $118 million last year, up 61 percent from 1997. Also, client assets in DLJ Direct nearly doubled to $9 billion. The average trades per day increased 87 percent in 1998 and kept growing in early 1999.

Schwab's online business is so integral to its discount operations that one would have to look at Schwab in its entirety. Schwab does, however, show that 58 percent of its revenue *trades* came from online last year, with an additional 8 percent done on its proprietary TeleBroker and VoiceBroker systems; only a third were done via traditional phone orders. More than half its mutual fund OneSource trades were also done online.

With half Schwab's revenue base coming from commissions (an additional 20 percent from mutual fund fees), online trading is a big contributor to the bottom line. Still, its principal trading, margin lending, and new capital markets activities are also big contributors, so a "pure online" profit margin or return on equity (ROE) is impossible to ascertain. However, its margins and ROE are higher than those of traditional firms (as discounter margins always were, even before online came around). Its 1-year profit and revenue growth were 29 percent and 19 percent, respectively, and its 5-year profit and revenue annual growth were 24 percent and 23 percent, respectively.

Certainly investors are betting that online will continue to be a success as evidenced by Schwab's, E*Trade's, and Ameritrade's huge market capitalization relative to firms many times their size. Waterhouse Securities, another multichannel discounter like Schwab, has just filed an S-1 statement for its initial public offering. Waterhouse's pro forma statements show strong growth in customer accounts, commissions, total revenue and profits. Revenues grew 20 percent last year, and after-tax profits rose 38 percent. Also, 53 percent of its daily trades came from online in the fiscal year ended January 31, a heavy showing since only 30 percent of its accounts are online.

This leaves just E*Trade and Ameritrade to look at as the only public, fully online firms. As mentioned, heavy advertising expenses from national marketing drives to build account bases produced a series of quarterly losses for E*Trade and Ameritrade. While Ameritrade is now showing profits from its successful drive, E*Trade is expected to remain in the red for the balance of its fiscal year ending this fall.

GOING FORWARD

As we noted, online trading has been as much an evolution of the discount brokerage business as a revolution in Internet-based e-commerce. It wasn't a giant leap from punching a few Touch-Tone buttons on your home or cell phone to switch your mutual fund mix to clicking a mouse to enter a limit order.

Going forward, online trading will expand far beyond its discounter roots, with all the benefits of Internet account access moving to both mainstream investors and mainstream brokerages. Within just the next few months, three of the biggest retail brokerages will morph their Internet view-only account services to limited online trading capability. Within a few years, online brokerage will be universal—no longer a question of who, how many, or when. The only real question left is which other industries are next in line for online in the new millennium?

CHAPTER 4

The Internet Revolution in the Brokerage Services Industry: An Unfinished Play in Three Acts

Carlos Otalvaro-Coronado, Chairman
WallStreet.E
Wall Street Electronica

Noah Otalvaro, President
Net International Inc.

Francisco Otalvaro, President
WallStreet.E
Wall Street Electronica

THE PLAYERS

Act I

The Pure Online Internet Brokers, which evolved into the Pioneering Online Firms

The Online Wanna-bes

The Established Traditional Full-Service Firms

All the other regional and local firms, including discount firms

The story line followed by each player in Act I was "My way is the way—the only way!"

Act II–Still Being Written

The players of Act I

Banks

Insurance companies

Other companies with traditional operations in the financial services area that
have caught the "online fever"

At the heart of the "survival" are the themes of convergence and metamorphosis.

Act III–To Be Written

The actors that get to play Act III will be the ones that are successful in understanding, learning, implementing, and executing the survival story line of Act II.

ACT I   MY WAY IS THE WAY–THE ONLY WAY!

Act I was played between 1994 and the end of 1999. Starting in about 1994 the
Web platform made it feasible to use the Internet to send out information to brokerage customers and to allow them to place trades online. During this period
many self-appointed industry experts were quoting all kinds of figures to support their (often diametrically opposed) views of the world—"Their way—the
only way!" Passionate reports were written, predicting that in a relatively short
time the whole world was going to be trading online and that the traditional
firms soon were going to be a thing of the past. Taking the opposite view and
fully "My way is the way—the only way," at the beginning of 1999 a leading
established Traditional Full-Service Firm made a big splash by stating: "Trading
online is hazardous to an investor's financial health. It is a fad that will soon disappear!"

In the euphoria of this period, many Pure Internet Online Brokers, fully convinced that "Their way was the way—the only way," justified burning substantial
quantities of cash to sing their own praises ("create a brand") and prognosticated
the demise of the other players. They were even successful in convincing Wall
Street that a new accounting concept they invented was sound: "Profits *before*
huge marketing expenses."

The barrage of reports about the phenomenal growth of the Pure Internet
Online Brokers, coupled with the disdain and lack of respect with which the established traditional firms were treated,[1] was to the established Traditional firms akin
to waving a cape before a bull. This ended Act I and set the stage for Act II.

---

[1] Even Wall Street was in on the act. At the beginning of 1999 the market gave a greater capitalization to
    Charles Schwab than to Merrill Lynch.

ACT II   EXTINCTION IS A CHOICE! DEATH OR SURVIVAL THROUGH CONVERGENCE AND METAMORPHOSIS

Act II began in the middle of 1999 when the bull made a surprising about-face, charging with sound and fury.

Act I belonged to the Pure Internet Online Brokers—which evolved into The Pioneering Online Firms. They had big visions and profits "before marketing expenses." The players that launched Act II were the leading pioneers of Act I and some of the more realistic traditional brokers that in 1999, when Charles Schwab bypassed Merrill Lynch in total capitalization, finally "got religion" and started promoting their online conversion and backing it up with substantial financial and human investment commitments.

The plot of Act II still is not entirely clear. It has gotten more complex as a result of the changes in the financial legislation that allow giant banks and insurance companies, as well as the little ones, to be players in the brokerage services industry. Obviously these changes also allow all former players in the brokerage industry to enter the banking and insurance arena—not an entirely good thing, given the complexities of these businesses and the size of some of the traditional players in them. As if the number of players were not already enough, in Act II other firms with divisions in one area or other of financial services, e.g., loans, mortgages, tax preparation, etc., have caught the online fever and are looking for ways to cross-sell brokerage services to their existing client bases.

At this time all the players in Act II are trying to learn and practice their parts that will enable them to masterfully play the survival script of Act II. Act II is the endgame! It is the last chance to choose between survival and extinction. To successfully go forward, "My way is the way" is *no longer the only way*! As a matter of fact, it is *not the way at all*!

Pure Internet Online Brokers and Established Traditional Full-Service Firms, including the newest players (banks, insurance companies, and others), come face-to-face with the challenges of convergence and metamorphosis. Either they must converge their core competencies with those of other organizations in the financial services that have complementary ones, or they must metamorphose their organizations to execute and implement the business models that bring together the high-tech services of the Pioneering Pure Internet Online Brokers and the high-touch services of the Established Traditional Full-Service Firms.

The successful and profitable survivors will be those who implement the integration of technology into the traditional structure of a customer-service-obsessed organization. Though this concept sounds simple, making it work (implementing it and executing it) is a formidable challenge both for the Established Traditional Firms and for the Pure Internet Brokers. Yet the players must master the "high-tech/high-touch" theme in order not to lose the customers that will only do business with the customer-centric organizations that will star in Act III.

ACT III   DARWINISM—THE MOVING FORCE BEHIND
THE EVOLUTION TO THE CUSTOMER-CENTRIC ORGANIZATION

The firms that will navigate successfully the survival story line of Act II and thus get to be players in Act III are those that accept, implement, and execute a business model that integrates the best of "digital" Darwinism, the most valuable asset of the Pioneering Pure Internet Online Brokers, with the best of the "Organizational" Darwinism, the most valuable asset of the Established Traditional Firms.

The Pioneering Pure Internet Online Brokers gained an extremely valuable technological advantage while they had the time between 1988 and 1999 to play with and develop the most advanced technology for information and trading systems. These pioneers had the windfall of being in the right place at the right time— they had the technology in place when the Big Bang of the Web hit! They were able to benefit overnight from one of the great events in our history—the wide availability of the Web platform.

The Web platform made possible the widespread dissemination of technology that, up to that point, was "bottled" and being delivered to mostly techno-savvy investors through dial-ups or CD-ROMs. Now, complete packages of information and support services were made directly available to a widespread universe of individual investors through a more user-friendly medium.

And thus the Pure Internet Online Brokers were born. Because the Web was so easy to use, it made it possible for these firms to start serving a geometrically growing number of online investors. Copycat Online Wanna-be brokers with no digital Darwinism behind them proliferated. The media, the analysts, and all kinds of overnight "experts" and know-it-all consultants kept making ever-growing projections that in a few years the whole world would consist exclusively of online investors and traders and that the Established Traditional Firms were seeing their last days.

Naturally all this hype upset the Established Traditional Firms, which in the final analysis were beneficiaries of the organizational Darwinism that the Pure Internet Online Brokers had not had time to experience. As a result of this organizational Darwinism, the Established Traditional Firms had years of experience creating solid managerial infrastructures, financial reserves, and brand names.

Most important these firms had solid profits, before and *after* marketing expenses, that allowed them to switch gears and move from denouncing the benefits of online trading to aggressively and successfully promoting it as a value-added service to their advisory function.

This about-face of the traditional powerhouses in the brokerage business caught all the other players in the financial services industry completely by surprise and changed the script they were comfortably playing. As noted earlier, it opened Act II, which has a story line of survival.

The players in Act II that stand the best chance of successfully playing the survival script are:

The leading Established Traditional Brokerage Firms

The Pioneering Internet Online Brokers

Aggressive Money Centers and International Banks

First-Line Investment Banking Firms

Other Powerhouses with traditional financial services units—e.g., GE

Those with a reasonable chance of surviving include:

Regional Banks and Insurance Companies

Those with the poorest chance are:

All the other players in Act I:

Second-tier traditional brokers

Wanna-be online brokers

Non-Schwab traditional discount brokers

The Leading Established Traditional Brokerage Firms stand the best chance to survive Act II and be the stars of Act III. That's because they:

- Have *money, money, money!*—money from "profits after marketing expenses," money from reserves built up from years of profitable full-commission transaction-based business, and money with which they can bury their mistakes until they get it right!
- Benefit from the organizational Darwinism as a result of which they have super brand names and solid managerial and marketing infrastructures, which all other players "would die for."

However, even though they have money, valuable brand names, and managerial and marketing infrastructures in place, the Leading Established Traditional Firms are not a sure thing. They only stand the best chance of successfully surviving Act II and going on to play in Act III, the operative word being *chance*.

Their two biggest challenges to playing masterfully the survival script are:

Transitioning their organizations from a transaction-based commission business to a fee-only–based advisory business

Pruning/and or retraining their managers, never exactly considered a group of cutting edge thinkers, so they can function efficiently and contribute to the success of the customer-centric organizations that will be the players in Act III

To accomplish their transition from a transaction-based commission business to an advisory-fee-only enterprise, the Established Traditional Firms have used a considerable amount of their reserves and profits from traditional operations to put in place—through mergers, acquisitions and in-house development—the technology of the Pioneering Pure Internet Online Brokers and merge it into their existing organization. However, for this transition to be successfully accomplished, the Traditional Firms are faced with the very difficult task of dealing with the nature of one of their most valuable assets—the people (stockbrokers, insurance salespeople, etc.) who have been generating the high commissions. The problem is that in order to successfully play in Act III, these commissions have to be substantially reduced or eliminated.

For the Established Traditional Firms, one of the conflicts in the survival script they are playing in Act II revolves around their stockbrokers. The firms must try to convert the entrepreneurial attitude of their best brokers, who are ill accustomed to receiving high commissions for just being at the right place at the right time, to that of salaried employees who get their remuneration as a percentage of the, for example, 1 percent advisory fee the firms collect from client assets that the brokers are now expected to "work hard" gathering.

The best brokers of these firms caught in this situation are not happy campers. If they stay with their firms, their income from transaction-based commissions either disappears or is substantially reduced. To equal their previous income from a percentage of the advisory fee the firm is charging requires them to work gathering assets at a pace they never have been used to. Worst of all, the advisory relationship into which they put their clients is very difficult to break if they decide to move to another firm or go out on their own.

In effect the firms are locking in customers with their broad range of advisory, financial planning, and portfolio management services, relegating the former "diva" brokers to salaried "order takers."

Consequently, before it is too late, these most valuable assets of the Leading Established Traditional Firms are opting to leave those firms and establish their own advisory practices supported by a firm, such as WallStreet Electronica Inc., that specializes in backing up independent providers of financial services with proprietary "turnkey" online multiple account management and information systems. This enables them new enterprises to delight their customers by harnessing technology for the single-minded purpose of improving the customer experience and gaining long-term customer loyalty. After losing these top producers, the Traditional Established Firms will be left with the less entrepreneurial, more docile, former divas, most of whom will be unhappy salaried employees.

On the other hand, the happier salaried employees of the formerly Pure Internet Online Firms are acting the survival script of Act II by playing the theme, "moving up the food chain." To move up the food chain, the Pure Internet Online Firms that will get to be players in Act III have to complement their digital Darwinism by putting in place—through mergers, acquisitions, or in-house development—the infrastructure that converts them into the customer-centric organizations. These are organizations in which human customer relations management

(HCRM), and not just electronic customer relation management (ECRM), is a guiding principle that informs all their actions.

The other huge challenge that the Leading Established Traditional Brokers face in successfully playing Act II is pruning from their organizations the layers of managers who will be "dead wood" in the customer-centric organizations that require having strong technology skills. Once again, because of the money they have from profits after marketing expenses, as well as from accumulated reserves, the Leading Traditional Firms have the best chance of clearing from their structure the dead-wood managers who would kill the chances of the firm successfully surviving Act II.

The other players in Act II that have the best chance of surviving are the Pioneering Internet Brokers. These are the firms that have been consistently included for the past 5 years in *Barron's* "Annual Review of the Top Online Brokers." As a result of the digital Darwinism they have lived, they have proprietary technology that is a valuable "net currency" with which they already have made or can make survival deals when being acquired by Leading Established Brokers, banks, and insurance companies—businesses that have *real money* but have neither the time nor the human assets to develop the technology needed to survive.

The Pioneering Online Brokers may also use their net currency effectively in order to try to develop in-house, or acquire through mergers and acquisitions, core competencies in advisory services, banking, insurance, money management, etc., that will complement the technology they have in place and thus allow them to metamorphose into the customer-centric organizations that will play in Act III. In executing and implementing this metamorphosis, these firms have the advantage of being able to get to play Act III much faster than other Act II players since they do not have to go through the cumbersome process of cleaning out dead wood from their management structure.

In the struggle to survive Act II, Leading Established Traditional Firms and pioneering Internet Online Brokers should observe how Merrill and Schwab have been playing the themes of convergence and metamorphosis in order to survive. Although Merrill Lynch is not going to become Schwab and Schwab is not going to become Merrill Lynch, to get to play in Act III, Schwab has been metamorphosing by expanding its services up the food chain, using a core of salaried asset gatherers, opening more brick-and-mortar centers, and covering all bases through self-clearing and acquisitions of U.S. Trust and Cyber Trade. Merrill, in turn, has been restructuring its business to converge with the model that Schwab has implemented with more success than any other company.

Since both are still figuring out how to best play Act II, others should closely watch this duo and reconfigure their performance according to how successful Merrill and Schwab are. For example, it is an interesting and telling fact that in the first quarter of 2000 Schwab, in spite of Merrill's marketing prowess, gathered twice as many new assets as Merrill. This seems to confirm the fact that

Established Traditional Brokerage Firms are going to have a difficult time converting their diva brokers into effective, salaried asset gatherers.

ACT III   THE CUSTOMER WRITES THE
SCRIPT—ERGO, CUSTOMER CENTRICITY

The script of Act III will be written by the customer, not by the providers of financial services, as was the case of scripts for Acts I and II. Understanding this fact is the key to surviving Act II and becoming a successful player in Act III. It is the customer who now makes the calls. The possibility exists for scripts that feature a story line with a double theme of customer-centered organizations and customer-centric relationships, and each of these requires a different set of actors.

Most of the Leading Traditional Brokers and the Pioneering Internet Online Brokers are opting for the theme of the customer-centric organizations. They have the assets: net currency and real money that will allow them to put in place the best ECRM systems to "mass-customize" their interaction with the "masses" that are the customer base for the "impersonal" mass-customized service.

Second-tier traditional brokers, Wanna-be Online brokers, and Non-Schwab traditional discount brokers, on the other hand, do not have the assets—the net currency and real money—to restructure their organizations in order to effectively compete against the superpower customer-centric organizations. To survive they must reconfigure themselves and/or their organizations to be able to provide effective personal customer-centric relationships to specific market niches, not to the masses. They must understand that their "lifeboat" to survival is personal customization, not mass customization. Some of them will achieve this goal by adding key customer-sensitive associates, some by getting rid of personnel engrained in traditional ways that are at odds with surviving this sea change.

Since the customer is the one that writes the script for Act III, different players can choose the script they want to play according to the reconfiguration they have given to their enterprise as a result of having successfully survived Act II. Pure Internet Firms will play the script written by the day traders/gamblers. They will be the casino operations of the financial services industry. Powerhouse customer-centric organizations leveraging off their mass customization will play the script written by the masses to whom they are marketing with billion-dollar campaigns. Finally, for personal customer-centered entrepreneurs, Act III represents a unique opportunity for "boutique" providers of financial services to marry their HCRM skills with the best ECRM skills available in order to engage their customers by leveraging personalized customization with technology for the single-minded purpose of improving the customer experience and gaining long-term customer loyalty.

CHAPTER 5

The Internet Brokerage Industry

Ezra Zask, Executive Vice President
Advisor Software, Inc.
and
Visiting Lecturer
Bendheim Center for Finance
Princeton University

THE REVOLUTION IN THE BROKERAGE INDUSTRY

The Internet has profoundly altered the financial services industry, posing a challenge to established firms and untold opportunities to those able and willing to take advantage of the Web's capabilities. The Web's impact has been most dramatic in the brokerage industry. Online trading is not merely a high-tech version of traditional, broker-mediated trading. By providing investors with low-cost information and new communication and transaction capabilities, the Internet has allowed many investors to dispense with intermediaries (notably full-service brokers) and to interact directly with the marketplace, often with tools that were only available to professionals as recently as last year.

Armed with a 3-year head start in the Internet arena, online brokers have tried to undermine the Wall Street brokers' business model and source of profit as well-compensated intermediaries between clients and markets, continuing a trend that started with the growth of discount brokerage firms. This has led traditional brokers to undergo the most profound transformation since the discount brokerage revolution of the 1970s. The ongoing battle between online and traditional brokers had already changed both.

A version of this chapter was published by Berkshire Capital Corporation, New York, 2000.

The Growth of Online Trading

The growth of online trading started with the new order-handling rules introduced by the SEC in 1997 (the limit-order display rule and the market maker quote rule), which allowed alternative trading systems (ATSs) to capture public order flow going to the NASDAQ. These ATSs now include both 11 electronic communication networks (ECNs), which utilize price discovery, and 8 non-ECNATSs, which do not. By the end of 1999, ECNs accounted for one-third of the dollar volume and one-quarter of the share volume in NASDAQ trading. Three of the ECNs (Archipelago, Island, and Nextrade) have filed with the SEC for exchange status, and if granted, will compete directly with the NASDAQ. The elimination of Rule 390, which prohibits off-exchange trading of most NYSE-listed companies, will likely open the NYSE market to ECNs, which at the end of 1999 accounted for only 5 percent of NYSE volume. (See Table 5-1.)

According to a 1999 survey entitled "Equity Ownership in America," released by the Investment Company Institute and the Securities Industry Association (SIA), nearly half of all American households (around 49.2 million) now own equities either in mutual funds or individually (see Figure 5-1). Equity owners tend to be middle-aged with moderate income and assets. The typical equity owner is 47 years old, has household income of $60,000, and has household financial assets of $85,000. The majority of equity owners seek investment advice from financial services professionals. Although 64 percent said they rely on professional financial advisers when making equity purchases and sales decisions, 75 percent of investors closely follow the value of their investments.

While the outlook for growth in online trading is extremely promising, this growth will be slower than in the past and will be shared among online brokers, banks, Wall Street firms, mutual funds and insurance companies. Furthermore, there are clear risks to continued growth, especially any marked decline in the overall level of stock market activity. Finally, there will be clear winners and losers among the online trading firms as the industry undergoes a sustained consolidation.

According to a Securities Industry Association survey, online trading will account for 50 percent of retail stock market trades by 2003, up from 37 percent

TABLE 5-1

Securities Industry Statistics, Year-End 1999

NYSE average daily volume	809 million shares
NASDAQ average daily volume	1.1 billion shares
Revenues from mutual fund sales	$6.7 billion
Securities industry revenue	$183 billion

Source: SIA 2000 Securities Industry Fact Book.

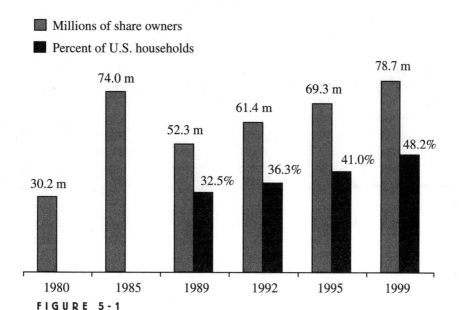

FIGURE 5-1

A steady rise in equity ownership.

in 1999. (Additionally, some 20 percent of trading in mutual fund shares is now online.) The SIA also estimates that 18 percent of stock buyers and sellers now use the Internet, compared with only 10 percent a year ago.

The average number of online trades per day has increased fivefold since 1997, and now exceeds 500,000. (See Figure 5-2.) The commission and related income from this activity have fueled the increased revenues of online trading firms.

Equally important is the increase in assets held in the accounts of online traders, projected to grow from between $375 billion and $500 billion at present to $1.5 trillion to $3 trillion in 2003. If these numbers are correct, online brokers, rather than banks or traditional brokers, will manage most of investors' money, marking a major secular change in the financial superstructure of the United States. It appears likely that banks will become more aggressive in online brokerage in order to maintain their asset bases.

Importantly, according to an SIA survey, investors who trade through the Internet tend to have more financial assets (an average of $246,300 versus $215,100 for full-service brokerage customers), trade more often (31.0 trades in the last year versus 13.5 for full-service clients), and have larger average brokerage account balances ($60,000 versus $50,000) than those who trade with brokers.

A number of factors will ensure the continued growth of online trading:

- While most of the 6 million customers who used discount brokerages in 1997 have switched to online trading, many more remain to be converted.

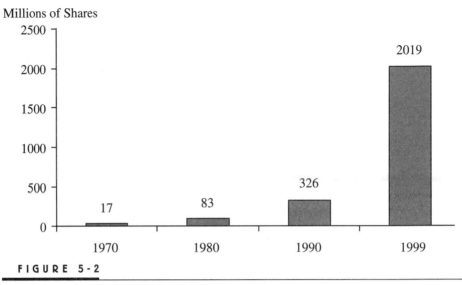

Millions of Shares

FIGURE 5-2

Daily share volume (on NYSE, Nasdaq, Amex, and Regionals).

- Technological advances, including wireless trading, interactive video, and broadband, will lead to greater use of all E-Finance, including online trading.
- The 80 million (or 50 percent of) American households that own stocks, directly or through mutual funds, represent a large pool for future online brokerage accounts.
- The 45–64 age group will comprise the dominant financial investors in the next decade. These investors tend to be wealthier and self-directed, favoring online equity trading.
- The growing internationalization of trading, with both foreigners tapping into the U.S. market (often online) and U.S. investors more readily buying and selling foreign shares, will also increase online trading activity and facilitate global, 24/7 (24 hours a day, 7 days a week) trading networks by ECNs, online brokers, and stock exchanges.
- Nearly 80 percent of all Internet households surf the Web for financial and account information and shopping, representing a large untapped pool of online traders. The younger generation of potential users are much more familiar with the Internet than their parents and even more likely to trade online.

Risk Factors in Future Online Trading Growth

Slower Growth

It is important to remember that the estimates for future growth of online trading assume continued increase in the overall level of equity trading. However, it seems unlikely that trading in equities will continue to grow in any straight-line fashion, especially if a long-awaited correction in the high-technology sector occurs. Given the importance of trading volume to the revenues and high share prices of online firms, a decline in this volume will have a dramatic effect on their share prices and valuations.

Most of the growth in online trading to date has resulted from converting the 6 million accounts that traded with offline discount brokers prior to 1997. These account holders were already experienced, self-directed traders who were quick to respond to low-cost online trading initiated by companies like E*Trade and Ameritrade. In addition, this growth occurred in the absence of meaningful competition from traditional brokers and during a period of rapidly growing stock market activity.

It is likely that the majority of active self-directed investors have already migrated to the Internet for their trading and that the transfer of additional accounts to the Internet will call for a different model. It is unlikely that the new online account openers will be as aggressive in trading as day traders or the early clients, especially if the stock market loses some of its luster, thereby placing considerable pressure on the online brokers in achieving profitability.

Charles Schwab, for example, estimates that 40 million households have sufficient assets to be of interest to the brokerage community. Only 6 to 7 million of these are truly self-directed in their investments, while 10 to 12 million are "delegators" who tend to use full-service brokers and investment managers. The remaining 20 million households are self-directed for some services and may delegate (or look for validation for) other areas of responsibility. Both the online brokers and the Wall Street firms are battling for this last group, especially for its younger and wealthier members. Moreover, this statistic underscores the likelihood that online brokers who can afford to provide a suite of products and services will emerge as the industry winners.

More Competition

The financial markets are efficient, to say the least, at producing competition when there are no legal impediments to entry into an attractive segment. This is likely to occur in online trading. While full-service brokers now control only 2 percent of online trading accounts, their inevitable growth will certainly come at the expense of online brokers. Equally important, while full-service brokers only have a 2 percent share of accounts, they have an 18 percent share of client assets, since their customers have a higher average net worth. This means that pure online brokers may see their share of brokerage accounts and assets decline substantially in the coming few years.

While online firms will continue to gain accounts in absolute terms, the rate of growth of online trading will probably decrease while the competition for these accounts will increase both within the online brokerage community and from offline firms.

VALUE DRIVERS IN THE ONLINE BROKERAGE INDUSTRY

The economics of the online brokerage industry are relatively simple because of the absence of fixed assets (bricks and mortar), relatively small personnel expenses, and a streamlined set of products and services. To date, the online brokers have been tightly focused on trading, although that will undoubtedly change as these firms continue to acquire and expand their service range. The key drivers responsible for profitability of online brokers include:

- *Income side*
  Transaction commissions and fees, which depend on overall stock market trading activity and the share of activity conducted online
  Interest income on margin lending less interest paid on account balances
  Referral and nontrading product income
- *Expense side*
  Account acquisition costs from marketing and sales or acquisition of competitors
  Transaction processing and back-office operations
  Development or acquisition of new products and services
  Technology, personnel, and (possibly) branch construction

Account Profitability

The key consideration here is the breakeven level at which the profitability of each account on a discounted cashflow basis makes the cost of acquiring accounts economically justifiable. There is little agreement about where the breakeven level is, which makes it difficult to value brokerage accounts or brokerage firms. However, the estimates of the industry leaders and many analysts are overly optimistic.

One analyst, for example, finds that each account is worth over $800 to E*Trade—that is the amount the company will earn from trading commissions and from the difference between the interest paid on deposit balances and the income charged on margin loans. This assumes that each account remains with the broker for 10 years and generates annual income of $212 (based on present account revenue). Since this firm's cost of acquiring each marginal client is around $400, the analyst argues that E*Trade has a business that can print money all day long. In fact, the analyst could have gone further and recommended that the broker make a cash gift of $200 for each new account and still pocket a handsome (albeit future) profit. E*Trade already offers $100 for new accounts. However, the restrictions and limitations on this prize limit its economic impact on the company.

As noted, the analysis assumes that each account will remain with the broker for 10 years and produce steady revenue of $212 for each of those years, expectations that we find unconvincing. The assumption of steady income over 10 years is based on the notion of account "stickiness," or unwillingness to leave a broker once a customer has signed up. If we have learned anything about the Internet economy, it is the danger of forecasting a steady state over 10 years. It is much more likely that account stickiness and income from each account will decline with increased competition and that the profitability of each account will similarly decline.

The squeeze on commissions will affect companies differently depending on the extent to which they rely on those commissions for income and profit. For example, Merrill Lynch's income from commissions is greater than that of Morgan Stanley Dean Witter, and therefore Merrill stands to lose more from the commission squeeze. Ameritrade gets 70 percent of its revenues from trading commissions, compared with around 57 percent for E*Trade. Schwab has been the most efficient in diversifying its revenue sources, with fully 53 percent of its revenues coming from sources other than trading commissions.

Many brokers' earnings from trading accounts are based largely on the difference between interest income from providing margin loans and the expense of paying interest on deposits. For example, interest income accounted for nearly 37 percent of Ameritrade's revenues in 1999. The importance of interest earnings arises from the fact that Ameritrade does not pay interest on credit balances under $1000 and pays only 2.75 percent for accounts over $1000, while charging prime plus 75 basis points for margin loans under $25,000 (and scaling down from there).

Ameritrade claims that its relationship between credit balances and debit balances has been constant over time. However, it is likely that the newer, more investment-oriented online traders will not be as active in using margin debt to finance investment. In addition, the competition for accounts (especially when banks enter the field) may well result in improved cash management products (including sweep investment accounts) that will reduce the credit balance income for all brokers.

The Commission-Free Gauntlet

The downward trend for average commission income from online trading will probably only get worse as competition for customers, accounts, and assets intensifies. As in most areas of high technology and the Internet, the trend is to reduce or eliminate any pockets of profit through competitive pricing. This is demonstrated by American Express's October surprise that it would offer free Web trading (plus $100) to customers with accounts over $100,000, following E*Trade's announcement in August that active traders would pay as little as $4.95 for some trades instead of the firm's usual rate of $14.95. (See Table 5-2.)

The willingness of brokers to reduce trading commissions and replace them with fees and minimum balances stems from a business model that sees these commissions as a "loss leader" to attract accounts and assets, especially from high-net-worth customers. According to this theory, the income earned from

TABLE 5-2

Free Trading Online

Company	Minimum Fee	Maximum Fee	Price per Trade	Minimum Assets
J.P. Morgan	$2500	Flat fee	First 24 free, then $30 each	$10,000
Merrill Lynch	$1500	1%	Free	None
Morgan Stanley Dean Witter	$1000	2.25%	Free	$50,000
PaineWebber	$1500	1.5%	Free	$100,000
Salomon Smith Barney	$750	1.5%	Free	$50,000
U.S. Bancorp Piper Jaffrey	$1500	2%	Free	None

deposit accounts and margin loans and the opportunity to provide ancillary financial services, including banking, funds management, and insurance, will eventually offset the low or negative income from trading.

Unfortunately, this business model calls for greatly increased expenditures on advertising, technology, service, and new analytical and information products, all of which will increase expenses in the short term while holding out an uncertain longer-term return. In addition, the evidence suggests that high-net-worth customers are the least likely to change brokers based on commission charges. This business model, when adopted by an entire industry, can only lead to lowered commission income for online brokers and, through competitive pricing, full-service brokers.

Advertising War Chests and Client Acquisition Costs

The prevailing trend for online brokers is to seek the maximum number of accounts possible, or in the words of one firm, "to grab millions of accounts now," in order to build a national and global franchise for online financial services. The major online brokers, led by Charles Schwab, E*Trade, TD Waterhouse, DLJdirect, and Ameritrade, are expected to spend $1 billion of the $1.7 billion they raised in 1999 in the next year to sign up new customers. This advertising spending exceeds the yearly advertising budgets of Ford Motor Company, McDonald's, and Burger King combined. This total is expected to be much higher when the yet-to-be revealed advertising budgets of the Wall Street brokers are factored in. E*Trade alone is expected to spend $300 million, or as much as Merrill Lynch, Morgan Stanley Dean Witter, and PaineWebber combined.

Clearly, the next phase of the growth of online trading—the conversion of full-service accounts or nontraders into online traders—will be much more expensive in terms of account acquisition than the previous phase, which was based on the conversion of self-directed traders and discount broker clients to the Internet.

While client acquisition costs in the early days of online trading were reportedly as little as $100 to $200, the expense is now closer to $400, and in some cases, closer to $600. Despite advertisements from online brokers hinting at an open-ended pool of self-directed security traders, the current target audience for online trading will be a tough sell, making account growth both less certain and more expensive than in the past, to the detriment of the online brokers' profitability.

It is important to note that some online trading brokers face a much lower account acquisition cost than others. For example, TD Waterhouse, which has a branch network and preexisting discount brokerage customers, pays about $200 to land new accounts, compared with $500 for E*trade.

A major goal of advertising is to develop an online financial brand that will serve as a platform for future delivery of financial services. Here the online brokers have substantial competition from established brands, including Merrill Lynch, Prudential, and American Express. By one estimate, it takes $300 million a year, for a number of years, to build a global online financial brand, making this strategy available to only a handful of firms. Nonetheless, it is clear that a few firms—notably E*Trade, Ameritrade, and DLJDirect—are quickly establishing themselves as brand leaders in the E-Finance arena.

THE COMING SHAKEOUT IN THE ONLINE BROKERAGE INDUSTRY

We believe that there will be continued consolidation of the online brokerage industry through mergers, acquisitions, and strategic alliances as a result of the industry's cost structure and excess capacity. Now, around 150 brokers offer Internet trading. Of these, as many as 50 have national ambitions and solid financial support, with many being the online offspring of traditional financial service firms: full-service brokers, discounters, banks, and mutual fund companies. However, the top 10 brokerages handle over 90 percent of online trades, while the top 5 alone account for 80 percent of this activity. This leaves 140 brokers vying for the remaining 10 percent.

The ease of equity, venture capital, and debt funding available to online financial firms has masked the overcapacity of brokerage firms. However, we believe that investors will eventually tire of the lack of profits of most of the online brokerage firms and that additional funding will become more and more difficult to obtain. At that point, the industry will be in for a period of increased consolidation. Indeed, as Figure 5-3 indicates, the stock market prices of Internet-based brokers have actually lagged behind those of the Wall Street firms since January 1999.

This consolidation, which will be spurred by the consolidation in financial industries brought on by the repeal of the Glass-Steagall Act, is comparable to that of the discount brokerage industry in the 1970s, 1980s, and 1990s, when dozens

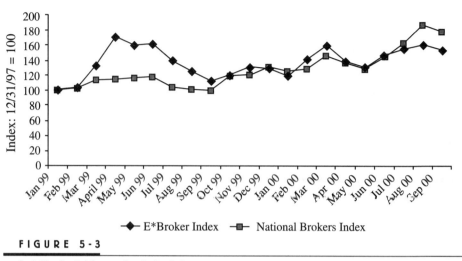

FIGURE 5-3

Berkshire Capital Corporation Broker Indexes.

of firms were acquired or merged. We believe that only those firms that have the technological and financial resources to compete or have a product or niche advantage will be able to survive. Many of the rest are sitting atop a "wasting asset" that needs to be capitalized through a merger, acquisition, or strategic alliance in the near future. However, a firm's ability to capitalize on this asset will depend on its technology, its customer niche, and the purchasers' alternative costs of account acquisition.

The Imperatives of Scale

The seeming ease of raising capital and starting a new online brokerage obscures the underlying trend: More and more, competing in this space will call for substantial resources for technology, advertising, brand recognition, and the ability to withstand any downturns in the stock market. This requirement for scale will limit the number of companies that can capture a profitable segment of the online consumer. The largest online and traditional brokers are building a lead and a market presence that may not be possible to overcome. While there will be an important role for niche players, the large share of the transactions will remain with a handful of the larger online brokers and those Wall Street brokers with resources to catch up to the current leaders.

The surviving firms will need deep pockets, a large and stable customer base, and diverse income sources, especially to survive any downturns in market activity. We are not certain that even the largest of the new e-brokers will be able to survive the coming competition without merging with each other or with traditional brokers. In addition, while the online brokers have been establishing name recognition, they still have a long way to go to catch up to the household names of the full-service brokers. Mergers and acquisitions may be the only way for these firms to develop the scale needed to catch up to the market leaders. For example, E*Trade, which has 1.6 million accounts, may need to consolidate to compete with Merrill Lynch, which has 9.0 million (traditional) accounts.

Traditional brokers will be tempted to acquire the Internet expertise and technological sophistication of the online brokers as an alternative to building these capabilities in house, often against the resistance of their own technical, management, and sales personnel. As noted earlier, many of the 150 online brokers are sitting on top of a wasting asset that needs to be capitalized through a merger, acquisition, or strategic alliance. Unless they possess a technological, client, or product edge, they are unlikely to survive future competition. Without these assets, it is difficult for a firm to differentiate itself from other vendors, given the commodity nature of the trading product. Full price transparency across the entire industry, available from numerous sources and advertising, makes it difficult for smaller firms to differentiate their products and services.

It is likely that larger firms will be interested in acquiring smaller companies that possess a technology, service offering, and/or customer niche. Examples would include options or futures capabilities, day trading or active clients, technical analysis, and real-time technology for integrating with exchanges and ECNs. The acquiring firms will need to evaluate the technological fit with their existing operation and the acquisition cost of new accounts versus the cost of acquiring accounts by other means.

The Valuation Discrepancy

A major obstacle in any mergers or acquisitions between Internet and traditional firms is the higher valuation given to Internet firms. While Internet firms are valued at multiples of 30 to 50 times earnings (down sharply from 60 to 300 times earnings in 1999), traditional brokers have multiples that average around 15 times earnings. Any traditional broker that attempts to acquire an Internet broker would have to pay an unacceptable premium and, given the low or negative earnings of the Internet firms, a significant dilution of the firm's earnings-per-share ratio after the acquisition.

Online firms tend to trade on a multiple of revenue, while full-service brokers trade based on a multiple of earnings. For example, Ameritrade's price-revenues ratio of 12.0 is (more or less) in line with Merrill Lynch's price-earnings ratio of 12.7. However, Ameritrade's price-earnings ratio of 327.8 bears no relation to Merrill Lynch's 12.7. The rationale is that once online brokers (and other Internet firms) become profitable, their profits will be a percentage of revenues.

One concern is that the high valuation of most online firms encourages Internet companies to spend more heavily on advertising than traditional brokers.

An e-broker that borrows money to advertise will likely see an increase in revenue and, as a result, higher share prices even if the interest expense of the borrowing leads to lower earnings. Traditional brokers, by contrast, take an immediate hit to their earnings and share prices by increased advertising spending where the pay-off may not show for several quarters.

M&A Strategies: Build, Buy, or Incubate

As long as Internet share prices maintain their substantial premium, M&A activity between online trading companies will probably follow the share-to-share swap that has been successful in a number of other Internet areas. We anticipate that there will be a number of these deals in the coming years between the largest of the online firms seeking to build scale and brand. Furthermore, the roll-up of the smaller players in the Internet area will also include a large stock component since few Internet firms can afford other purchase programs.

At present, large-scale mergers between Internet and traditional brokerage firms are unlikely given the wide difference in their valuation. However, because these mergers may make business sense, we foresee a number of possible solutions. The most likely is that the valuations of online and traditional brokerage firms will converge in the future by some combination of a steep decline in the valuation of online brokerage firms and an increase in the valuation of traditional brokerage firms with online businesses. Indications of this can be found in the recently announced AOL and Time Warner deal, which led to a marked decline in AOL's share price and valuation.

We expect that creative solutions will be developed to overcome the valuation issue and get on with the needed consolidation of the brokerage industry. One example is traditional firms offering tracking stock as a way of attaining Internet companies' valuation. A tracking stock is a publicly traded stock whose value is based on the balance sheet and income statement of a virtual entity that includes the Internet activities of the parent group. The best-known example in the financial services industry is DLJdirect, the Internet tracking stock of DLJ Inc.

Tracking stocks present a host of practical and legal issues. Having two separate, potentially competitive, companies reporting to the same board of directors may present an irresistible target for class-action law firms. Furthermore, there is the temptation of placing marketing expenses in the tracking company whose valuation is based on revenues rather than income. However, tracking stocks are presently the only way for a traditional firm to realize its Internet valuation, an essential means of providing incentives for talented personnel. These stocks also have the benefit of focusing a firm's Internet activity in one organizational entity.

We will also see more strategic alliances and investment of minority shareholdings by Wall Street and Internet firms as a way of gaining access to developing technology and markets. The transactions may involve smaller deals and start-up investments such as Merrill Lynch's acquisition of DE Shaw's technology group or investments in day trading firms and ECNs to gain access to trading technology. The options open to companies have expanded from build or buy to build, buy, or incubate.

Brokerage Business Models

Online brokerage firms are following four basic business models, depending on their client base and niche in the online brokerage space (see Figure 5-4). Broadly speaking, these business models are:

- *Online financial supermarkets or portals.* They combine banking, insurance, investment management, and brokerage under a single brand. Only Schwab, TD Waterhouse, and E*Trade are seriously attempting this strategy. The repeal of the Glass-Steagall Act may facilitate the move to a portal strategy among these brokers to protect their arena from the financial supermarkets.

- *Hybrid online brokers.* These brokers are able to compete at the discount price level but also provide value added services and advice that are attractive to high-net-worth investors. These brokers offer features normally associated with full-service brokers, including financial advisers, branches, research, and access to IPOs. Schwab, TD Waterhouse, Vanguard, and Fidelity are prime candidates here, while E*Trade and Ameritrade are striving to enter this space. (Schwab's proposed merger with U.S. Trust may take Schwab out of this category and into the full-service broker category.)

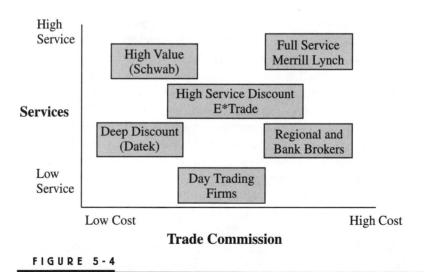

FIGURE 5-4

The competitive space for online brokerage.

- *Deep-discount brokers.* Deep-discount brokers offer low-cost transactions with minimal services for self-directed traders (FleetBoston, National Discount Brokers).
- *Niche online brokers.* They offer specialized technology or services to customers that demand specific credit, financing, or market access, including day traders, institutional firms, or other brokers (Raymond James, Datek, CyBerBroker, and Wall Street Electronica, whose strong options capabilities give them a competitive edge).

Diversified Product Offerings

Online brokers have developed two broad types of strategies in their quest for profitability: compete (firms that are determined to compete with the larger online and traditional brokers) and specialize (firms that are more narrowly focused on one or two customer segments and activities such as active traders). Firms that have chosen to specialize include the deep-discount and day trading firms that rely on trading technology, low-cost execution, and margin lending to attract and retain active traders.

The online brokers that have chosen to compete with full-service brokers and other financial companies have been developing increasingly sophisticated product and service capabilities (including cross-selling agreements) geared to a wide range of customers, including active traders, self-directed investors, long-term investors, and even day traders (defined as traders that average more than 31 transactions daily). In fact, several online firms have started offering investment banking services, including access to IPOs and research.

Table 5-3 is a sampling of the types of services being offered by online brokers, along with the customer groups they hope to attract with these services. The information and transaction services (i.e., wireless trading, live quotes) are of most interest to active traders, while investment management products are of most interest to self-directed and long-term investors. Cross-selling of banking, insurance, and credit products is geared to customers who may be looking for an integrated portal to meet many of their financial services needs.

The product offering strategy will undoubtedly advance online financial services technology and product development. However, it remains to be seen whether the business model of providing additional services in order to reduce the dependence on trading fees and commissions will actually lead to account profitability. To date, this widely adopted strategy has resulted in escalating expenses of providing services, most of which are not fully paid for by the client either directly or even indirectly with higher commissions and fees. Also, once a product is introduced, competition quickly turns it from an option into a necessity. At this time, only the day trading firms have been able to develop a business model where they are compensated for their non-trading products by charging a hefty fee for trading models and advice.

TABLE 5-3

Lining Up Services with Customers and Profitability

Service	Active Traders	Self-Directed Investor	Long-Term Investor
Account information	Timely, including margin	Timely	On demand or monthly
Market information	NASDAQ Level 2, live quotes	Live quotes	Daily (or monthly) quotes
Transaction execution	ECN interface	Low cost	Low cost
Analysis	Technical models	Stock research	Mutual fund
Education	Risk management	Investment basics	Asset allocation
Advice/asset Allocation/ Financial Planning	Direction, options	Stock recommendations	Asset allocation, financial planning
IPO access	Important	Somewhat important	Little importance
Banking, insurance	None	Potential client	Potential client

Online Investment and Asset-Management Services

Most brokers have articulated the strategy of providing money-management services to attract, retain, and profit from the assets in their online trading accounts. This strategy carries substantial risk because it brings online brokers into direct competition with full-service brokers, banks, and asset-management companies—both cyber- and terrestrial-based—that are determined to stake out the same space.

In order to attract and retain customers, online brokers are adding more services, many of which are typical of traditional brokers, including trust and financial planning. This trend appears to be leading to a hybrid broker model (best exemplified by TD Waterhouse, E*Trade, and DLJdirect, and especially by Schwab's proposed merger with U.S. Trust) that offers some contact with a human adviser as well as offering a wide range of investment and banking products.

The race to provide these services is driven by the importance of high-networth clients to the brokerage community. The full-service brokers' clients maintain an average of $310,000 in assets, compared with $137,000 for the hybrid brokers and $45,000 for the deep-discount brokers. This is a compelling reason for any firm to move closer to the full-service camp.

As technology advances, we expect that this will lead to some interesting experiments in providing online advice and funds management. These online advisers may well become a source of revenue as clients look for help in digesting and utilizing their online information, especially with higher-income clients that consistently express an interest in advice over low-cost execution. It is also likely that the younger generation of affluent consumer will be more technically proficient and may be interested in an online adviser they can utilize when they need specific problem-solving assistance and information.

In addition, online financial planning and money-management tools will continue to proliferate both as a free service and on a fee basis. William Sharpe's FinancialEngines.com, which provides a sophisticated portfolio allocation and optimization program to 401(k) investors for a mere $50 per year, may become a model for this area, especially if combined with human advisers who make the online tools more user friendly. A great deal of the competition among various types of brokerage firms will be over the 401(k) accounts that now make up a majority of mutual fund investor services.

The Click-and-Mortar Strategy

In some ways, the strategies of both online and full-service brokers may be converging such that we may need to change our terminology. An online broker that features branches, interactive video and audio expertise, extensive research capabilities, and add-on services that include funds management, financial planning, and banking can scarcely be called a discount broker. Similarly, full-service brokers that provide cut-rate (or free) execution and interactive video and audio expertise may begin to resemble the classic online broker.

Perhaps most telling in this convergence is the noted successes of Schwab and TD Waterhouse in using their branches to attract and retain accounts. (Up to 70 percent of Schwab's and 40 percent of TD Waterhouse's new customers come from their respective branch networks.) However, it remains to be seen whether an extensive branch network (other than a few branches in key locations) is justifiable given both the cost of maintaining this infrastructure and, especially, the developments in audio and video capabilities on the Internet that may be more compatible with customers than branch visits are. While we expect all the competitors for the higher end of the customer base to build highly visible showcase branches in key locations and metropolitan areas, we do not think this will lead to widespread expansion of branches.

International Strategy

The online brokerage firms are quickly putting together international strategies for capturing the growth of online (and individually directed) trading from Europe and Asia. Thus far, the effort has met with a small client base, stiff local competition, and legal and regulatory impediments. Taken as a whole, the international effort is unlikely, in our opinion, to offset the income squeeze in the United States and will not show much results for another 3 to 5 years. (For most of these firms, international trading is less than 5 percent of revenues.) However, some brokers are taking a stake in what will someday be a 24-hour global trading system with global investors and exchanges. Staking an early claim in this dream of the future has spurred some companies, especially Schwab, TD Waterhouse, E*Trade, and Ameritrade, to pursue aggressive international strategies.

Schwab is probably in the lead in Europe and Asia among American online brokers, having bought Share Link, the United Kingdom's largest online broker. TD Waterhouse is a close second with its purchase of U.K. online broker YorkSHARE and its 120,000 customers. E*Trade is also building a European presence with 42 percent owned E*Trade U.K. (which also covers Sweden, France, and Ireland). DLJdirect and Barclays are also a presence in the United Kingdom. However, the total online trading population of the United Kingdom is 800,000, compared with 8.5 million in the United States, while the number of U.K. Internet users at 12 million pales compared with the U.S. potential of 95 million. In addition, the United Kingdom has a 40 percent capital gains tax and 0.5 percent stamp tax on purchases, which may serve to limit the growth of online trading.

Ameritrade has cut deals with France's Cortal and Germany's Deutsche Bank to trade stocks in each other's country, while Fortrend Securities has launched a service to allow Australian investors to trade U.S. securities.

In general, the Far East, especially Hong Kong and Japan, is seen as the most promising area of growth for online trading. China and South Korea have recently allowed day trading of equity shares, with dramatic results in the latter and great potential in the former. Schwab, E*Trade, and TD Waterhouse have been especially aggressive in this region.

Financial Portals

A number of companies are attempting to become financial portals, one-stop sites where customers can meet all (or most) of their financial needs. While still at an early stage, this is clearly important since even partial success for a portal will come at the expense of online (as well as traditional) brokers. Portal strategies are visible from a number of sources, including mutual funds (Fidelity), insurance companies (Prudential and AIG), banks (Citicorp and Wells Fargo), full-service and online brokers (E*Trade, Schwab, TD Waterhouse, Merrill Lynch), and financial planning (American Express).

In addition to banks and brokerages, technology is making it possible for general portals (such as Yahoo, Microsoft Network, and AOL) and software companies (such as Quicken) to develop front-end systems designed to capture financial information and control of the customer. By gathering financial information from a variety of vendors, these portals may be able to consolidate and present a complete picture of an investor's finances, providing serious competition for brokers who can only present a partial picture.

It is certain that, as the restrictions of the Glass-Steagall Act disappear, there will be increased efforts by giant conglomerates to capture the portal marketplace, placing the smaller players at increased risk.

Internet Technology

Technology is sure to be a major, and very expensive, competitive factor and a source of differentiation for online brokerage firms, as shown by recent processing failures by Charles Schwab, E*Trade, and Ameritrade. The technological pressure is not helped by investors' expectations that their online brokers will never go down. (Otherwise, you may as well use a person to execute trades.)

E*Trade faces a class-action suit by customers that could not reach the firm by any means, while Schwab offered $500 in free commissions for trades placed at one of its 300 branches. Technology has become so important that Charles Schwab effectively acts as an Internet service provider.

There is a trade-off between expenditures on marketing and technological improvements. The more that is spent on marketing relative to technology, the more likely that service will suffer. In addition to their trading technology, online trading firms need to have a call center sufficient to cope with inevitable failure, as well as disaster recovery plans, backup plans, and duplicate data centers.

The importance of service and technological development is also indicated by Merrill Lynch's acquisition of DE Shaw's DESoFT for $25 million. Other firms that are strong in engineering talent are Datek, CyBerCorp, and Ameritrade. Smaller brokers are likely to outsource much of their technology to firms such as Reality Online.

Wireless access to information and trading will also become increasingly important as the 6 million people that access the Internet by wireless in 2000 grows to 484 million in 2005. A number of online trading firms have followed Schwab's example when it joined Ericsson to create wireless trading services using Ericsson's mobile phones.

Day Trading

Brokers that cater to active or day traders have developed a potentially profitable niche that may survive the coming consolidation of the industry. The best confirmation of this is the effort by larger online brokers, notably Schwab and E*Trade, to capture some of this traffic.

Day trading firms are ahead of many other brokers in providing customer interfaces and information and analysis tools. The fact that Softbank has invested in Tradescape.com, a day trading firm, is an indication of these firms' capabilities and future. Other top day trading firms are Tradescape, TradeCast, A. B. Watley, and Datek (which owns the Island ECN). Day traders are also an important source of liquidity for the marketplace, accounting for 11 percent of the NASDAQ activity in the third quarter of this year. It is conceivable that there will be a consolidation of deep-discount brokers and day trading firms, both in a quest for increased transaction volume.

Day traders (or on-site traders) are able to trade because of the NASDAQ Small Order Execution System (SOES) that allows small trades to be executed and unwound very quickly (often ahead of large orders) and the Order Handling Rule of 1997 that led to the establishment of ECNs. With these two pieces in place, brokers catering to day traders were able to implement sophisticated software systems that take maximum advantage of the NASDAQ and ECN technology. For example, CyBerCorp.com, which provides technology to trading firms, has a system (CyBerXchange) that is able to route trades to the quickest and most cost-effective ECN. The system, which could well be a model for all online brokers, automatically moves to the next vendor if its request is not handled in a timely fashion.

This should not deflect consideration from the continuing negative association of some day trading. The North American Securities Administrators Association, for example, states, "70% of public traders will not only lose but will lose everything they invest." The average day trader trades 8000 to 10,000 deals a year. This means that day traders need to generate returns of 56 percent just to cover the cost of commissions. The association concludes that this is "virtually a form of gambling" and blames some of the firms catering to day traders for misleading marketing and questionable loan schemes.

Government regulation will seek to curb day trading, which will cause serious problems for online brokers that derive a significant portion of their income from this segment. A first step has been taken by increasing the minimum account balance from $2000 to $25,000 for investors who make more than four day trades a week on margin. However, allowing day traders to borrow four times their account balance from brokers, up from two times previously, offset the effect of this action.

CHALLENGE AND RESPONSE: FULL-SERVICE BROKERS, BANKS, AND INVESTMENT COMPANY STRATEGIES

December 28, 1998, was a milestone date for Wall Street. On that day, investors decided that the market capitalization of Schwab and that of Merrill Lynch were roughly equal at $25 billion, despite the fact that Merrill had over $11 billion in equity compared with Schwab's $1.9 billion. Merrill Lynch's $1.5 trillion in assets and 18,500 financial consultants were also not considered sufficient to overcome Schwab's online capabilities. (In fact, investors saw them as a negative earnings factor.) The pressure on Wall Street firms intensified when Schwab's market cap reached $40.7 million against Merrill's $27.6 million a mere 5 months later.

Investors were clearly signaling that Wall Street brokers needed a viable Internet trading strategy or would face a serious loss of value. It was at this point that Wall Street firms were finally able to overcome internal resistance from brokers and began to adopt online strategies. Tellingly, the capitalization of Schwab and Merrill Lynch came into line again only after Merrill Lynch announced its aggressive new Internet plan. (Investors were more impressed by Morgan Stanley Dean Witter's Internet strategy, which promised a shorter implementation date.)

The Empire Strikes Back

The changes in the brokerage and trading industry over a mere 6 to 9 months have been astounding and unpredictable. Start-up companies such as E*Trade or discount firms quick to adopt the Internet looked like they would take over transaction processing from the established Wall Street firms. From virtually nowhere, the early entrees to online brokering captured one-third of the trading volume by the end of 1999. Furthermore, with online trading now accounting for 50 percent of retail equity trades, the importance of this space has become too much for the 800-pound gorillas to ignore.

The experience of the past 6 months has been profound and has literally turned our conceptions of the Internet world upside down. The importance of early leads and branding, for example, turns out to have been well overstated. Once the larger firms caught on to the business, many of the so-called obstacles (i.e., internal impediments, broker resistance, etc.) turned out to be chimerical, while many strengths were dramatically underplayed, including resources, name, customer base, technological sophistication, management skills, and cultural ability to change. In fact, the innovative solutions being applied by the major firms will spell some of the most interesting financial applications of the future.

Similarly, the original strategy of some online firms to develop brand names and then move upscale to capture assets, financial services, and value-added products has been stymied by the major firms' determination to capture the same space and to make online products available to hitherto taboo groups. Goldman Sachs and J.P. Morgan, for example, have been developing online strategies for high-networth individuals with $1 million or more, while Merrill Lynch offers proprietary research and unlimited trading for a $1500 annual fee.

The delayed response of the Wall Street brokers to the online brokers' challenge was perhaps predictable given their existing staff, culture, business model, and technology. Online trading would have meant cannibalizing their existing revenue streams from broker-managed trading commissions and alienating their brokers and sales reps. It was only when it became clear that a lack of an online trading capability would threaten their long-term viability did the Wall Street firms commit to an Internet strategy.

The five major retail brokerages—Merrill Lynch, PaineWebber, Salomon Smith Barney, Prudential Securities, and Morgan Stanley Dean Witter—are now committed to the Internet and have either rolled out or promised plans that offer extensive online trading services to most of their customers. The change is summarized by a statement from John Steffens, a vice chairman at Merrill Lynch & Co., that "the distinction between on-line and off-line services is rapidly fading away."

Clearly, all the firms competing in the brokerage space have adopted the notion that adding Internet-based features and services will be crucial in winning and retaining clients. According to TowerGroup, the technology budgets on Internet and Intranet products for securities firms jumped from $3.9 billion (or 3 percent of their technology budgets) to $18.4 billion (or 20 percent of their technology budgets). Among the features planned by the full-service firms are integrated financial portals, audio and video services, and portfolio evaluation services.

Wall Street firms clearly bring great resources to the battle with online brokers. Their broker and branch networks, brand names and reputations, earning power, access to IPOs, and research will make it especially difficult for online brokers to capture the real prize: high-net-worth clients.

To some extent, the key to the success of their strategies will depend on the extent to which they can reconcile the interests of their key constituencies, including both high-net-worth and less affluent clients, traditional brokers, technological departments, and management. While the Wall Street firms' Internet initiatives may not be able to reverse the course of the past 3 years, it will certainly slow the pace of client defection to online brokers and raise the cost of client acquisition for all.

The Broker "Problem" and Full-Service Brokerage

Full-service securities firms face some clear obstacles in the online trading arena, especially with regard to the extent to which they are willing to cannibalize their existing profitable brokerage business and possibly alienate their brokers and technology experts by providing open-ended online trading. This will become especially important as investors need less handholding and as online trading becomes more common, especially among their profitable high-net-worth clients.

The interim solution adopted by one bank, sharing the Internet transaction fees with brokers, will not make these brokers financially whole since a share of $29.95 is a long way off from a share of $250. It seems likely that there will need to be a transition of many of these brokers to "Internet brokers" (or e-brokers) or information facilitators, which requires a level of technological sophistication that is often absent among traditional brokers. We believe that the attempt to sort out these competing claims will prove to be a drain on resources and productivity for the next several years and may well prevent these firms from taking full advantage of the Internet's capabilities in the near term.

Commercial Banks, Mutual Funds, and Investment Management Companies

Commercial banks may become major competitors in the traditional and electronic brokerage businesses as a logical extension of their financial portal strategy and because of their strong market share in asset management. They have other advantages as well, including strong brand names, consumer trust and confidence, and a wide product base.

However, banks have thus far been relatively unsuccessful in cross-selling or developing multiproduct financial portals, never mind providing customers with a "seamless" way to use the Internet to go from traditional banking transactions to brokerage or asset management services. It would be difficult for most banks to jump into the online brokerage fray without an acquisition; and a number of large banks, including Bank of America, First Union and Bank One Corporation, the former Bankers Trust, and Bank of Boston, have acquired brokerages.

One example that may be a model of future commercial bank competition in this arena is the decision by FleetBoston to bring together its bank services and the brokerage services of recently acquired Quick & Reilly and SureTrade, its online brokerage unit. Customers use a single sign-on for Internet banking where they can move funds between their bank and brokerage accounts and view information on all of their accounts on one Web page. The service was started because Quick & Reilly found that 75 percent of their customers would open such an integrated account.

REGULATORY ISSUES

Government regulation threatens to impose burdens on both full-service brokers and online brokers. One example is the limitation imposed on the use of e-mail by the requirement that branch managers review all correspondence. On the other side, online brokers may face increased supervision as they branch into research, financial planning, and funds management.

This issue will become more important as more and more services are provided over the Internet. As brokerage firms provide an increasing amount of information and analysis on the Web, including interactive advisory services, the suitability requirement (the requirement that brokers know their clients' financial situation and risk tolerance and the suitability of any investment for that client) will become more of an issue. This is especially important in providing unsolicited information and analysis via the Internet.

While the industry's emphasis has been on technological improvements, the limits of online finance have become increasingly apparent in the form of outages and dropped connections (especially during busy times), so that the federal government's General Accounting Office has thrown down a challenge to online brokers to improve their service and technology rather than emphasize further growth. At the same time, the SEC has become increasingly aggressive about weeding out the increasing fraud and deception found in the Internet, with the threat of regulation of the Web a real possibility.

The SEC is also reviewing whether online advice should come under the publishers' exception to the Investment Adviser Act of 1940. The exception provides that an individual or investor does not have to register as an investment adviser if it is a regular publisher of financial information and does not offer targeted investment advice for compensation.

Regulatory efforts address a wide range of issues, including, but not limited to, moving to T+1 settlement, demutualization of exchanges, extended trading hours, decimal pricing, transparency, and market fragmentation. Compressing the settlement time from 3 days to 1 day will result in more efficient utilization of capital while minimizing operational and credit risks. The T+1 implementation plan will tackle institutional trade matching, electronic funds transfer, the elimination of certificates, electronic information storage and access, and global linkages.

The industry also began to formulate a strategy to address the plans of the NYSE and the NASD to convert to public ownership. Both marketplaces are taking these steps so that they can respond to increasing competition, particularly from ECNs, but conversion to for-profit structures raises important regulatory challenges. These and other issues relating to changes in market structure will continue to alter the landscape for both firms and investors in the years ahead.

ELECTRONIC COMMUNICATION NETWORKS AND THE EXCHANGES

ECNs have one-third of NASDAQ volume, but almost no Big Board volume because of two rules. First, users of the NASDAQ-ITS link must automatically execute orders in Big Board stocks received over the ITS, leaving them exposed to "double executions" if they receive more than one order for their posted stock quote. Second, users of the link need to post both buy and sell quotations. However, the latest changes in the rules exempt ECNs from both rules, and as a result, ECNs Bloomberg Tradebook, Brass Utility LLC (or BRUT ECN), and MarketXT now participate in the link. This is a follow-up to the NYSE withdrawal of Rule 390 that stated that stocks that traded before April 1979 could only be traded on its floor by NYSE members.

The symbiotic relationship between online trading and the electronic communications networks is reflected in the pattern of ownership of ECNs by brokers. The reason is straightforward: ECNs, which now control nearly 30 percent of the total trading volume of the NASDAQ, provide brokers with the liquidity and price transparency needed to service their retail client base. Brokers, in turn, provide ECNs with the volume they need to match buys and sells on their own books without the necessity of turning to the exchanges. For example, 80 percent of Island's deals are matched internally. It is this ability to match orders internally that makes ECNs independent of the NASDAQ's order flow and even trading hours. During the recent NASDAQ systems failure, the ECNs continued trading using their internal order flow. This liquidity also allows the ECNs to continue to trade after exchange hours.

The ECNs have made it possible for brokers to offer professional-level products and services to the retail client base. It is largely to guarantee access to this liquidity that brokers have been so eager to invest in or even start their own ECNs.

Because ECNs pool order flows from many brokers, they have a tremendous competitive advantage over the brokers whose individual transaction channels do not have the volume to achieve this internal transaction netting.

The ECN and stock exchange world is in a state of flux. The trend in the industry, actively encouraged by the SEC, is to create a global equity book that pools together order flow and information from myriad domestic and international ECNs and exchanges. The pressure toward creating this "central order book" will also increase pressure on the ECN community to consolidate, as indicated by the proposed merger between ECNs Strike and Brown. Consolidation will also be spurred by the extreme concentration of activity, with Island and Instinet controlling 85 percent of all ECN volume, and by the obvious economies of scale that larger ECNs enjoy in matching transactions on their own books. However, this consolidation may occur in fits and starts, given the low cost of entry to establish an ECN and the desire by traditional brokers and online brokers to own at least a share of an ECN.

Also waiting in the wings are the changes in NASDAQ and the electronic trading networks. The exchanges have been effectively subsidizing the profitability of the Wall Street community by providing members with free quotations. If and when NASDAQ becomes a profit-making entity, it is entirely possible that the brokers will find they are charged for quotations, escalating their cost of business. NASDAQ has also been aggressive in developing the systems and capabilities necessary to reach out directly to the retail public.

While the changes in the exchanges and the growth of ECNs have made it possible for online brokers to thrive, they also present some potential problems in the future. For example, stock market exchanges and ECNs can dramatically change their pricing structure so that they capture a larger portion of the commissions paid by the end users, which would create a major squeeze of brokers' commission revenues and profits. Another possibility is that exchanges and ECNs will offer direct services to retail end users, bypassing or competing with brokers. NASDAQ's newest computer system, for example, would allow up to 6 million Internet users to tap into its site at the same time.

A final challenge for online brokers will unfold as the system moves toward a central order book that provides all brokers with a single source of liquidity, information, and pricing. This would make it more difficult for brokers to differentiate their service on the basis of price or liquidity and place an additional emphasis on other product offerings.

APPENDIX: THE ECN MARKETPLACE

Instinet Corporation (www.instinet.com)

The largest ECN, this wholly owned subsidiary of Reuters Group, PLC, launched in 1969, has a membership on 18 exchanges and trades in 40 markets. Instinet provides trading research and has a large presence in the upstairs block trading market. It operates 24 hours a day, 7 days a week. In the mid-1980s, Instinet moved to the OTC market, where no central exchange existed. It became the de facto central order limit book for NASDAQ and began acquiring substantial market share. Instinet has a 14 percent stake in online investment bank W. R. Hambrecht & Co., which operates OpenIPO; and it has a 16 percent stake in Archipelago. In addition, it is part of a consortium that acquired a 54 percent stake in Tradepoint, a London-based electronic exchange. Most recently, Instinet formed a partnership with Stockholm, Sweden–based OM Technology. Instinet targets large buy-side firms and broker-dealers. Instinet has recently targeted the retail market by establishing relationships with online retail brokers.

Island (www.isld.com)

Launched in January 1997, Island is one of the four original ECNs—and currently the second largest. Datek is Island's majority owner, along with TA Associates and LVMH. Its operating hours are 7 a.m.–8 p.m. Island's founders realized that, with sufficient volume, they could match the orders prior to routing to SelectNet, the NASDAQ matching system. When the SEC began enforcing the Order Handling Rule of 1997, Island was launched to absorb all the unwanted NASDAQ limit orders from various market makers. At first, Island targeted orders that Instinet didn't want, namely retail order flow from online brokers and day traders. Island is one of the only two (the other being Instinet) true electronic matching engines in the ECN space. Island's auction system accepts orders from broker-dealers, and by following an automatic price-time priority rule, it can match orders virtually instantaneously. Island's main clients are sell-side firms, online brokers, day trading firms, and proprietary desks and firms.

Bloomberg TradeBook (www.bloomberg.com)

TradeBook, which started in 1996 and is also one of the four original ECNs, used its owners' buy-side subscriber base to become the third largest ECN. It has a joint venture with Investment Technology Group (ITG) and its electronic equity-crossing system, POSIT. Bloomberg combined technology from both TradeBook and POSIT to launch TradeBook Super ECN, which hopes to boost liquidity by incorporating POSIT's daily trading volume. It also formed a partnership with CLSA Global Emerging Markets to create Global TradeBook.

Archipelago (www.tradearca.com)

Launched in January 1997, Archipelago is owned by Merrill Lynch, Goldman Sachs, E*Trade, CNBC, Instinet, J.P. Morgan, Gerald Putnam, Townsend, and Southwest Securities. Archipelago was the first ECN to establish the "best-execution model," in which, if an order cannot be matched within Archipelago's internal book, the system "sweeps" the NASDAQ market makers and other ECNs for the best possible execution. Archipelago has links to the Pacific Stock Exchange, NYSE, Instinet, Island, and large NASDAQ market makers. Archipelago is also one of the members of the consortium that has a 54 percent stake in Tradepoint. In March, Archipelago formed a partnership with the Pacific Exchange. The agreement calls for Archipelago to provide the Pacific with a trading engine that will serve as the heart of its equity business, eventually phasing out the exchange's stock trading floors in Los Angeles and San Francisco. Archipelago targets large buy-side firms, proprietary traders, hedge funds, broker-dealers, and options market makers.

REDIBOOK (www.redi.com)

Originally owned by Spear, Leeds & Kellogg, REDIBook was launched in November 1997. In the summer of 1999, Charles Schwab, Fidelity and Donaldson, and Lufkin & Jenrette each purchased large chunks of the company. Then, in October 1999, PaineWebber Inc., Credit Suisse First Boston, Lehman Brothers, TD Waterhouse Group, and National Discount Brokers Group Inc. (NDB) all signed letters of intent to purchase minority stakes in REDIBook. REDIBook concentrates on institutional investors, hedge fund managers, day trading firms, individual traders, and options market makers.

BRUT (Brass Utility LLC)

BRUT is owned by Automated Securities Clearance Ltd, a division of SunGard Data Systems. In February 1999, BRUT merged with Strike Technologies to become the third largest ECN, using the BRUT name. The new ECN brought together 30 equity partners, including Bear Stearns, Bridge, Goldman Sachs, Herzog Heine Geduld, Knight/Trimark Group, Lehman Brothers, Merrill Lynch, Morgan Stanley Dean Witter, and Salomon Smith Barney. A recent report showed that trade volume on the BRUT ECN increased almost 90 percent during the fourth quarter of 1999 over the previous year. A large percentage of BRUT's volume comes from its group of financial institutions investors, and it also gets volume from Waterhouse, E*Trade, and Knight/Trimark. It is known as the "broker-friendly ECN." Not surprisingly, BRUT requires buy-side firms interested in receiving its service to be sponsored by a BRUT subscriber. BRUT promotes its low-cost pricing, which can be 90 percent lower than that of other ECNs.

Marketnxt

The latest ECN to enter the market and originally launched as Eclipse Trading, an after-hours trading system, Marketnxt began operating as an ECN in January

2000. In February 2000, Tradescape.com acquired the company in a $100 million stock deal. Minority owners also include Morgan Stanley, Salomon Smith Barney, Herzog Heine Geduld, Polaris Venture Partners, and Bernard L. Madoff Investment Securities. Its original customer base was professional traders and individual online investors, but the company is now looking to appeal to institutional clients, as well.

Attain

Owned by Rushmore Financial Services, Inc., the parent company of All-Tech Investment Group (a day trading firm), Attain began operations in February 1998, targeting broker-dealers, banks, and hedge funds. Attain can be accessed via the Internet and a modem, so subscribers can avoid fees for hardware and monthly service. In addition, Attain has no minimum transaction requirements.

NexTrade (www.invest2000.com)

Owned by Professional Investment Management, NexTrade became an ECN in November 1998. NexTrade has applied to the SEC to become a for-profit stock exchange. In anticipation of gaining exchange status, NexTrade is teaming with BEA systems to build a high-volume stock trading system. NexTrade has also entered into an agreement with Dreyfus Brokerage Services to provide Dreyfus customers with market access, trade executions, and technology. NexTrade also has formed partnerships with GlobalNet and Valhalla Forex to launch Matchbook FX, LLC, an institutional foreign exchange system based on the same technology running the NexTrade ECN. Consequently, NexTrade will become the first ECN to offer foreign exchange trading. NexTrade targets all financial institutions, including the buy-side firms, online brokerage firms, and traditional broker-dealers.

CHAPTER 6

Online Fixed-Income Trading

Robert Knox
Senior Vice President
Zions First National Bank

In 1987, Tom Wolfe wrote a best-selling novel entitled *Bonfire of the Vanities*. The hero of this book was Sherman McCoy, who was a successful Wall Street bond trader with a penchant for doing stupid things. Wolfe created Sherman and called him a "master of the universe." In the mid-eighties, bonds were seen as the tool with which global financial power was controlled. Sherman, as a caricature of the times, was Wolfe's foil by which he exposed not only the narcissistic decadence of the New York power brokers, but also the hypocrisy that most of these people exhibited. Bond trading, oddly enough, was the leitmotif that Wolfe chose to tie his story together.

Wolfe succeeded in capturing the pulse beat of bond trading. The extent of the detail he brings to his book confirms the thoroughness of his research on the subject of bonds. Why were bonds so important during the time of Sherman McCoy's ascendance into the world of the Wall Street elite? One reason was a depressed stock market that created, in hindsight, equity valuations that were ridiculously low by today's standards. Companies like Kolberg Kravis and Roberts and individuals like junk bond king Mike Milken recognized that bonds offered the most advantageous way to scoop up undervalued companies. Consequently, bond underwriters, lawyers, and traders possessed considerable power in global financial markets during this period. The easiest and most expeditious way, during these times, to buy a rival's business, or to finance growth in your own business, was to float a bond issue. In today's financial markets, the preferred method of buying a rival, or increasing the capitalization of your own company, would be to use equity.

Shortly after Clinton took office in early 1993, the President made it known that he was closely watching the "bonds markets" for its reaction to his policies. President Clinton also made it known that Alan Greenspan, even though originally a Reagan appointee, was his choice to keep running the Federal Reserve. James Carville, the Democratic campaign consultant and Clinton administration attack dog, spoke at a recent bond markets convention and confirmed the President's early preoccupation with the mood of the bond markets. Even though the economy by the time of Clinton's election was already on the road to recovery, the ravages of inflation were still fresh in the minds of many people, organizations, and institutions—including the Dow Jones averages. Any downturn in the 30-year U.S. Treasury bond during this period was considered a harbinger of inflation and the economic chaos that usually follows.

Sherman McCoy's perceived power came from the public's belief that whoever controlled the bond markets controlled the world's financial power. Also, bond markets were viewed as a secret and arcane world run by a mysterious society of people who only communicated with each other by way of a secret handshake. Most savvy individuals understood, or thought they understood, the stock markets, because stock quotes were available to everyone and magazines and newspapers gave stocks considerable coverage. Bonds, however, were a different matter. Bond prices were rarely published, and even when they were, they were hard to decipher.

An individual in Sherman McCoy's time, not unlike today, could have gone to his local newspaper and found a stock quote for almost any large equity issue. However, that individual would have found it extremely difficult to have located the same information for bonds. During times of high price volatility, similar to those that existed during the eighties, bond traders like Sherman were able to exert considerable influence over the "spreads"—i.e., their profit margins—at which their products traded. This fact came to public light in 1989 with what has since been referred to as the Salomon Brothers scandal, which involved a conspiracy within the firm to rig prices.

As a result of this scandal, an industry effort was undertaken to ensure that market participants had equal access to important price information. In the U.S. Treasury market, all of the primary dealers and the larger interdealer brokers, with assistance from The Bond Market Association (an industry trade association), formed GovPx, a jointly owned corporation whose sole purpose was to disseminate price information. GovPx was one of the early, though by no means the earliest, precursors of the current movement to online, real-time bond executions.

By the start of the second Clinton administration, any glamour remaining in the bond markets had been eclipsed by a soaring stock market. Bonds returned to their pre-1980s role as a place mostly for widows and orphans. CNBC, the successful all-day business news channel, employed only one full-time bond specialist who received limited airtime. More importantly, stocks were going electronic at warp speed, led by a discount broker by the name of Charles Schwab, who had the foresight to see the coming electronic revolution. Also, Instinet, a subsidiary of Reuters, was running an electronic exchange in stocks which had already taken a significant share of transactions previously executed by the traditional exchanges. It was not long before imitators, such as E*Trade and Ameritrade, were attracting large numbers of retail stock clients. Companies like Island, Datek, and Archipelago were successfully adopting Instinet's formula.

Ironically, the bond markets introduced some of the first innovations that became the basis for today's online trading revolution. In the early 1970s, Cantor Fitzgerald, a relatively unknown brokerage firm, partnered with Telerate, a newly formed company whose intention was to disseminate market information over a private communications network. While rudimentary by today's standards, Telerate collected price information from numerous sources, which was fed into a computer and then broadcast over a private telephone network to a terminal on the client's desk. While much of the information that Telerate broadcast was nothing more than rehashed news and price information that was available to any news service, Telerate's partnership with Cantor Fitzgerald allowed the client to receive real-time U.S. Treasury prices. The client, once having a Telerate screen on his or her desk, was able to execute with Cantor Fitzgerald at the price displayed on the screen. The client for the first time was provided not only reliable price discovery, but also the means to exploit it. By providing both market content and a reliable platform on which to execute U.S. Treasury transactions, Cantor Fitzgerald and Telerate established a franchise that to this day prospers. Oddly, Cantor and Telerate never took their product to the next logical step until after several other competitors entered the market.

While Cantor and Telerate were bathing in the glory of their success, a little-known bond trader had left his job at Salomon Brothers—one of the Goliaths of the bond trading industry. Hardly impoverished when he left Salomon Brothers, having received an approximately $10 million severance package, he chose to start an information company for bond traders. At the core of his business plan was the belief that bond professionals were looking for more in their electronic information service than the automated newspaper offered by Telerate. Out of this belief arose an interactive screen-driven system that allowed the user not only to gather market information but also to work with the information in real time using an array of sophisticated analytical tools. Michael Bloomberg's creation, simply known as Bloomberg, changed forever the fixed-income business.[1]

Bloomberg recognized that bond professionals had needs that were not being addressed by other systems. While Telerate and Cantor's live trading screens continued to attract users, their news and content service fell out of favor as a result of Bloomberg's success. Bloomberg's business plan was as simple as

---

[1] Michael Bloomberg and Matthew Winkler, *Bloomberg by Bloomberg*, John Wiley & Son, New York, 1997.

it was unique. While the Telerate business model was, in effect, an electronic magazine, wherein the users paid a subscription fee and content providers purchased pages upon which to advertise their wares, Bloomberg's plan was simply to attract as many subscribers as possible to his service. Unlike Telerate, which not only charged a basic subscription fee but attempted to sell a plethora of add-ons, Bloomberg allowed you on its system for a basic fee and made no attempt to sell additional services. Even though Bloomberg sold some advertising, its business model did not rely on it, and anyone with something good was invited onto the system without charge. Moreover, Bloomberg devoted considerably more resources to the creation of a robust database management system, which resulted in simpler and more intuitive navigation through the mass of information available. Bloomberg's data management software had the capability not only to assist in finding a particular security, but also to provide comparative statistics once the security was found. Finally, any Bloomberg user was given free e-mail privileges within the Bloomberg network, so he or she could communicate with anyone else who was also on Bloomberg's system. While today free e-mail privileges are available almost anywhere, 10 years ago this feature was near revolutionary.

What was unappreciated at the time about the Bloomberg system, and especially its e-mail feature, was that it may have represented one of the first accidental but successful attempts at online bond trading. Buyers and sellers, many of whom were previously unknown to each other, found themselves exchanging e-mails about securities that they wished to either buy or sell. These e-mail exchanges frequently resulted in completed transactions.

Bloomberg had another edge over Telerate that arose out of the exclusive contractual arrangement that existed between Telerate and Cantor Fitzgerald. Telerate, apparently, was severely limited in its ability to enter into a market-making arrangement with anyone but Cantor Fitzgerald. The result was that as dealers started to develop their own proprietary electronic trading systems, they were unable to distribute their quotes over Telerate without approval from Cantor Fitzgerald. No such restriction existed at Bloomberg. Consequently, Bloomberg started to carry and support the proprietary trading systems of CS First Boston, Deutsche Bank, and others.[2] Moreover, Bloomberg's systems had fully interactive capability, whereas Telerate's did not.

Another sector of the market was interested in automating transaction flows. The interdealer brokers—firms that trade exclusively with other dealers—recognized that faster delivery of quotes to their customers could increase their transaction revenues while lowering their costs. By the early 1980s, all of the interdealer

---

[2] Telerate and Cantor Fitzgerald were privately owned companies at the time, and the details of their contractual arrangement are unknown. Consequently, it is speculation as to why Telerate and Cantor denied access to other new electronic systems seeking a place on Telerate's platform.

brokers had their "green screens" in all the major Wall Street investment houses. These were computer-driven private networks that allowed the interdealer brokers to assemble the best bids and offers being submitted by their dealer clients for a multitude of securities. These screens were not interactive, but were invaluable to the users, who for the first time could watch and monitor several hundred security prices simultaneously. While a user could not interact directly with the screen, he or she only had to pick up a telephone to execute a displayed quote, which the brokers had committed to honor.

During the eighties, different forces were driving the equity markets in a similar direction to bonds. Fixed commission rates were a thing of the past, and the over-the-counter market was offering serious competition to the established exchanges. Major differences exist between the equity markets and the bond markets in the way they conduct their business. To this day, controversy abounds over these differences. The equity markets, encouraged by the Securities and Exchange Commission (SEC) and the National Association of Securities Dealers (NASD), believe in a national market system as embodied in the NASDAQ. The bond dealers believe that a national market system for bonds would pose a major setback for bond liquidity—i.e., the market for bonds would shrink as a result of a national market system.

Until the over-the-counter market started to emerge as a major force, stocks were supported almost exclusively by a specialist system, whereas bonds were traded through a network of market makers. Since for stocks like General Electric, IBM, General Motors, and Ford there was only one specialist, there was only one place and hence one price at which these stocks could be traded. With bonds, however, there were, and continue to be, sometimes numerous market makers, each quoting different prices for the same bond. Most bond market professionals, as well as their trade associations, believe that the regulators should not try to "fix what ain't broke." While a national market system may currently work for equities, bonds have characteristics that do not lend themselves to a national market system.

Because of the importance of U.S. Treasury securities to the market, the Federal Reserve Bank developed a network of "primary dealers" whose responsibility is to maintain markets in Treasury debt. Currently there are 25 "primary dealers," each of whom is expected to maintain independent markets in every outstanding Treasury instrument. While the Federal Reserve Bank and the U.S. Treasury have never publicly weighed in on this issue, one imagines that they would oppose a national market system, at least as it applied to Treasury debt. Although a discussion of the merits between a national market system, as embodied by equity markets, and an over-the-counter system of market makers, as represented by the bonds markets, may seem somewhat arcane, the outcome of this debate will determine how bonds are traded online in the future.

Today, the equity markets have, without doubt, taken over the initiative as innovators in e-commerce. However, this may change, as the bond markets appear to have recognized that they must regain momentum in this area. Currently, there are in excess of 80 different online bond trading projects, according to The Bond Market Association, in various stages of development.[3] Moreover, various research organizations, including Greenwich Associates and the Tower Group, predict that within a few years 70 percent of bond transactions will be handled electronically.

In the equity markets, organizations like Island, Datek, and Archipelago have developed technology that has reduced the cost of a stock transaction to almost nothing. These organizations, which include Instinet, a Reuters subsidiary that was an early entrant into this market, have been rapidly gaining market share as the established exchanges, which now include NASDAQ, have attempted to block their success. Because of recent directives from the SEC, these organizations are called electronic communication networks, or ECNs. As a result, several of the bond trading systems under development attempt to imitate the ECN model, which raises fear among many within the bond industry that a national market system in bonds is just around the corner.

How do ECNs like Instinet or Archipelago differ from models currently employed in the bond markets? ECNs build their business by inviting anyone who wishes to participate to place a bid or offer in their order book. The ECNs expect to attract enough participants to provide a liquid market in every stock. By doing this, they hope to even attract more people so as to continue to grow their market share. The participants knowingly, or unknowingly, become the market maker in the particular stock being traded. In order to attract initial order flow, ECNs will go to great pains, including paying for orders. The stategy of paying for order flow is no different from that employed by a Las Vegas or Atlantic City gambling casino, which hires shills to make a blackjack table look prosperous in order to attract someone, especially an out-of-town tourist, looking to make a quick buck.

While bond markets involve market makers, bond traders would argue that their market-making functions differ radically from those of a market maker in equities. First, bond traders will tell you that making liquid markets in bonds involves considerably more capital than trading equities. At today's prices, it requires approximately $56,250 to buy 1000 shares of General Motors stock, whereas it will cost approximately $1,000,000 to buy 1000 General Motors bonds. Second, the major investment banking houses that make markets in bonds retain huge inventories in these securities to assure continuous liquid markets, whereas most equity firms are working orders for clients and do not hold large inventory positions. Third, the major investment houses in bonds are willing to fill orders in excess of their published markets for their better customers. Fourth, many bond issues are too small to support more than a few market makers. Finally, most bond traders would not leave orders in a national market order book for fear of losing

---

[3] *Annual Survey of Electronic Trading Systems*, The Bond Market Association.

control and say, inadvertently selling bonds to a competing market maker, only to discover it after the fact.

As we approach the end of the year 2001, bond trading systems can be divided into two types: (1) the proprietary system and (2) the consortia system. Most of the major investment houses—such as Goldman Sachs and Merrill Lynch—have proprietary systems that they make available to their best clients. These proprietary systems allow their clients the same buy and sell opportunities they would have if they called their sales representative. At the same time, many of these same firms have formed consortia with their global counterparts. These consortia are founded on the basis that their clients may demand, as they have done in equities, electronic platforms that allow "one-stop" comparison shopping rather than having to travel from system to system. As part of an overall risk management policy, the larger, global firms are investing in multiple solutions in order to assure themselves that they stay in the game. Goldman Sachs was featured in a recent *Forbes* magazine article in which it as much as admitted that many of the electronic platforms in which it currently had investments may not succeed.[4]

The Bond Market Association has published an annual survey since 1996 that catalogs all the major electronic trading systems that involve bonds or fixed-income securities. In second-quarter 2000, the association began to post this survey on its Website, which it has decided to update as often as necessary to keep the bond markets abreast of the changing landscape. This survey is available to anyone at www.bondmarkets.com. One of the most interesting things about this survey is how the list of bond trading firms entering the online market has grown—from fewer than 10 systems in 1996 to over 80 in 2000.

Many investors fail to appreciate how much bonds differ from equities. While less than 100,000 CUSIPs are assigned to various equity issues, more than 4 million CUSIPs represent various bond issues. The basic mathematical formula for pricing a bond is a present-value calculation that discounts the *cashflows* that a bond generates as well as any *principal* payments received until maturity. As *interest rates* fluctuate as a result of market expectations, the *price* at which buyers and sellers are willing to exchange a given bond will change. For U.S. Treasury securities, interest rate fluctuation is the sole determinant of their price since U.S. Treasury securities have no default risk. For all other bonds that trade in U.S. markets, credit becomes the other determinant of price. (U.S. investors looking to invest in foreign bonds face the additional risk of currency fluctuations.) Whereas weak linkages exist among equities issues, such as sector risk, bonds involve complex mathematical linkages that are driven by the yield curve and credit comparisons. Equity investors frequently switch between companies, as a result of favorable news or a glowing review by a respected analyst. Bond investors, on the other hand, are generally more interested in the yield a bond returns and the certainty to which they

---

[4] "Fear, Greed and Technology," *Forbes*, May 15, 2000, pp. 170–175.

can expect to be repaid. Consequently, bond investors will frequently focus more effort on analyzing the cashflow characteristics, as well as the underlying credit quality, as the primary determinants of their investment decision, than on worrying about what the company's next quarter's earnings are likely to be.

With the exception of municipal debt, of which approximately 34 percent is held by individuals, bond investing remains the domain of the professional investor. Bond mutual funds are the single largest investor in non–U.S. Treasury and federal agency debt. Individuals, many of whom hold investments in 401(k)s, pension plans, and mutual funds, indirectly own bonds by virtue of these holdings.

Any conversation among bond professionals today eventually ends up in a discussion about online bond trading and what it means for the future. The heart of the question depends on one's view of an old adage within the bond trading community that says, "Bonds are sold, not bought." As already mentioned, bonds, unlike stocks, do not usually embody a story. An individual may read a newspaper story about IBM or General Electric that leads him or her to believe that he or she should invest. This story may involve an earnings forecast, scuttlebutt about a management shakeup, or any number of things. Under these circumstances, the individual may either contact a broker or sign on to Schwab's or E*Trade's Website and execute a trade. However, bonds receive little, if any, news or media coverage, and even the most sophisticated investor is rarely aware—especially with some-where over 1.5 million different bonds outstanding—of everything that is available at any one time. Some argue that the Internet cannot replace the bond salesperson since it is the salesperson who arouses the interest in whatever bond is for sale at the time. Put another way: Will bonds sell themselves, especially on the Internet where there is not a live salesperson to push the buyer to a decision?

Currently, there are six distinct types of electronic trading systems for bonds in some stage of development. Each type of system has the same objective, which is to automate all, or some part, of the sales and underwriting function in the bond markets. Because of the newness of many of these systems, there are many over-laps between categories, and the categories themselves are subject to debate. The Bond Market Association, in fact, identifies only five categories rather than the six described below.

A *single-dealer* system is the most common system today. The single-dealer system is usually for the purpose of distributing a single firm's inventory to its established account base. Most of the major Wall Street firms either have a system in place or will shortly have one. Examples include Deutsche Bank's Autobahn Systems, Merrill Lynch's LMS System, Goldman Sach's Web ET, and Zions Bank's Govrate/Oddlot Machine.

Multidealer systems provide customers with a screen that displays competing quotes from numerous dealers. The customer selects the bond in which he or she has an interest, and the system displays an array of competing bids and offers, which are usually identified by the dealers making the bid or offer. These systems have become very popular, even though the technology involved is not as advanced as some of the other systems being offered to the market. Examples include Trade Web LLC, Bloomberg's Bond Trader (BBT), and Market Access.

The *ECN* or *order book* systems adopt a model widely used within the equity markets. These systems create order books into which any authorized party may submit a bid or offer. An order book prioritizes the bids and offers according to predetermined protocols, including best price and time at which the bid or offer was submitted. The systems also allow for *reserve orders* and order designations. The best example of a system based on an order book is Instinet's attempt to gain entrance into the fixed-income arena. While The Bond Market Association does not recognize the ECN or order book as a distinct type of electronic trading system, the association has created a category of system which it calls a *cross-matching* system. The line between the ECN and the cross-matching system is somewhat murky. What both systems have in common is their ability to facilitate trades without providing any *market-making* functionality. In contrast to single-dealer and multidealer systems, which are backed by traditional market makers, the ECN, order book or cross-matching system takes on no principal risk. It is these types of systems that raise the most concern about what the bond industry might look like in 5 or 10 years. Examples of cross-matching systems include Bond Desk, Bond Book, Bond Agent, and ValuBond.

Interdealer systems allow dealers to transact with each other anonymously through a broker's broker. Technologically these systems have been developed to automate the functions that were previously carried out by *voice brokers*. Interdealer systems must be able to handle high volumes of business, but have limited features and are less concerned about "look and feel" than they are about durability and reliability. In this category, The Bond Market Association includes Instinet's fixed-income system because, as of now, Instinet has limited its use to the larger Wall Street dealers. In reality, it is hard to imagine, based on Instinet's previously successful entries into equities and foreign exchange, that it intends to limit itself to the interdealer market. Examples include BrokerTec, Liberty Direct, and Garban ETC.

Inventory-matching systems are sites where most customers can post either inventory that they want to sell or items that they wish to buy. These systems, in effect, are bulletin boards where buyers and sellers can come together. Some of these systems appear to have been quite successful, in as much as they provide a no-risk way for buyers and sellers to seek one another out. Example include BondTrac, BondExpress, and Bloomberg's PICK system.

Auction systems are modeled after successful auction technology developed outside the securities industry—especially, FreeMarkets.com. These systems facilitate spot sourcing of securities that are not continuously available to the market. These systems are especially useful as part of the bond underwriting function where an issuer wishes to sell at one point in time without having to worry about aftermarket liquidity and other risks associated with market volatility. Examples include MuniAuction, Dalcomp, and Bloomberg's Municipal Auction System.

The prospect of regulatory overkill in online securities trading has raised major concerns in both the equity and fixed-income markets. Of paramount concern to the securities industry is that regulators will try to impose pre-Internet solutions on an industry that is moving at warp speed to rid itself of these burdens. The SEC has already proposed that any firm that is not a broker-dealer, but facilitates, in any manner, a securities transaction, must register either as an alternative trading system (ATS) or as an ECN.[5] While most industry professionals recognize that regulations must change as a result of the Internet, the fear is that the regulators, especially the SEC, will cast too broad a net that will impede necessary changes in the industry as a result of the Internet.

In June 2000, The Bond Market Association filed a comment letter with the SEC stating that the SEC should move beyond incremental steps to recognize the impacts of the Internet, especially as it applied to filing and publishing disclosure documents.[6] In this letter, the association stated, "The Association urges the Commission to take more far-reaching steps . . . to create a regulatory framework that provides both greater flexibility and certainty to investors, issuers and market intermediaries, thereby permitting them to take full advantage of ongoing developments in information technology."[7] In addition to the SEC, the NASD and the Municipal Standards Ruling Board (MSRB) have weighed in on many of these issues without a full understanding of what is at stake.

While the SEC's proposed regulations on the publishing of disclosure documents is illustrative of only one small part of the problem the Internet is creating for regulators, it is worthwhile to examine the issue in a little more detail. Currently, volumes of papers representing various types of required disclosure documents are being distributed through the mail and various expeditors, such as FedEx. Many of these documents, by the time they reach their destination, are out of date and end up in the "circular file." The Internet not only facilitates instant and, hence, timely delivery of these documents, but also saves the expense of wasted paper and needless postage. Moreover, an electronic document can be easily forwarded, which eliminates the need for multiple copies, and allows supporting documents to be included by use of hyperlinks. The SEC, however, does not appear to see it this way.

Another example of an overreaction by a regulator was the recent direct issuance by the city of Pittsburgh (Pennsylvania) to end buyers of a $50 million bond issue. In this case, the city of Pittsburgh chose to eliminate the traditional

---

[5] In some instances, broker-dealers, depending on the type of system they operate, must take on the additional regulatory burden of becoming an ATS or ECN.

[6] Letter from The Bond Market Association to the Securities and Exchange Commission, "Use of Electronic Media—File No. s7-11-00, June 21, 2000."

[7] Ibid., p. 2.

bond underwriter from the underwriting process of $50 million general obligation bonds, which saved the taxpayers of Pittsburgh substantial underwriting fees. Using MuniAuction, a Pittsburgh-based technology company, the city of Pittsburgh created an Internet auction in which all qualified bidders were invited to participate. Following the successful auctioning of the securities, there was considerable regulatory rumbling from the SEC, MSRB, and NASD about the legality of the auction because the city of Pittsburgh had failed to formally appoint an underwriter. Admittedly, there were valid regulatory issues raised in this instance, especially as these regulatory concerns apply to protection of the ultimate investor. Nevertheless, just as technology eventually eliminated telephone operators, and diesel locomotives eventually eliminated the need for firemen, the Internet will eventually do away with or substantially change the role of bond underwriters. Regulators must keep pace with the times.

What are the economic drivers that will affect the fixed-income and bond markets over the next 3 to 5 years? The Internet revolution in the securities industry is the result of the interrelationship among three factors: (1) rapidly improving telecommunications, (2) computational power that has kept pace with Moore's law, and (3) rapidly improving network and industry-specific software. There is no reason to believe—at least, for the next few years—that the pace of development in all three of these areas will abate.

Twenty-five years ago, a telephone was a technological marvel. Direct dialing with a touchpad, having to use an operator only on occasion, seemed to defy improvement. Then with the advent of the fax machine, it became possible to transmit documents over phone lines. Of course, we can now send data, documents, or voice files via e-mail and the Internet. The issues for the future in telecommunications will be bandwidth and switching speeds. How much we can widen the pipe—add more lanes to the information superhighway—will determine how efficient we can move data from point A to point B. The vigorous competition that currently exists among the global communications giants bodes well for continual and rapid improvement in this technology.

Innovations in wireless technology promise to help the securities industry. As our population continues to become more mobile, and as we move to virtual exchanges and 24-hour trading, portability will become more important. Currently, transmission speeds are too slow and the software that runs these devices has not been sufficiently developed to make handheld devices practical utilities.

Computation power is still relatively slow in comparison to what is needed, especially in the bond markets. Bond analytics require considerable computational power, and even though CPU power and clock speeds have soared, bond calculations are still not produced fast enough to satisfy many bond traders. Also, screen refresh rates can be annoyingly slow when you are trying to search through volumes of Internet pages.

The bond markets have fallen behind the equity markets in developing the common protocols necessary to efficiently exchange data. The Bond Market Association's Online Bond Steering Committee expects to have a proposal out by the fall of 2001 on common protocols. The association, and specifically the steering committee, is looking at the standard messaging protocols for the equity industry, already developed by the Financial Information Exchange (FIX), a nonprofit organization. The issue of protocols can be likened to a three-pronged appliance plug. Without a three-pronged plug, every appliance we brought home would have to be specifically retrofitted to match the wiring unique to our homes. As ridiculous as this may sound, that is the current state of affairs in the bond industry. Part of the problem goes back to the differences between bonds and equities. The FIX protocols, whether for bonds or equities, reside on a server and have standardized fields, so messages between servers can be passed on efficiently. Because bonds have more parameters than stocks, more data fields are required, and, consequently, writing the FIX protocols for bonds is considerably more difficult. Hundreds of millions of dollars a year are being spent by the bond markets trying to solve the problems that connectivity issues raise.

As we move away from issues of technology, it is important to remember just how interrelated connectivity, computational power, and software are to the ultimate success of all the systems that are at some stage of development. Just like building a three-legged stool, where all three legs must be the same length, so it is with building electronic trading systems. We must accept the assumption that telecommunications, computer power, and software will continue to grow at the same rate as in the past, if we are to believe that online trading, whether in stocks or bonds, will continue to point the way to the future.

Not since the seventies and the elimination of fixed commissions in the equity markets has the securities industry been confronted with more issues and threats to its survival. While it is difficult to prioritize the risks facing the securities industry, the high cost structures that exist within the industry have to rank up there on the list. Investment banking firms that specialize in bond trading require more equity capital than most stock trading firms, since they have to carry larger inventories. Larger inventories result in higher costs of capital. The one cost, besides capital charges, that stands out in most traditional security firms, regardless of whether they trade stocks or bonds, is the cost of compensation. Many of the best-managed brokerage firms pay out approximately 50 percent of total revenues as compensation, and there are many firms that pay out between 60 and 70 percent. Banks, by comparison—especially, the better-run ones—have cost structures where total expenses (including all compensations cost) are less than 50 percent of total revenues (net interest margin plus other fee-based revenues). In this regard, it should be considered more than a coincidence that banks recently have been aggressively buying or merging with brokerage firms.

As a result of higher-than-necessary cost structures, brokerage companies quickly realized that electronic trading offered substantial cost savings, especially in the area of compensation. Electronic trading systems have the potential to reduce compensation costs from where they are now—in excess of 50 percent of total revenues—down to as low as 35 to 40 percent of total revenues. Marginal producers will be replaced by the Internet, while top producers will have to work harder to stay even. Certain types of transactions—such as complex bond under-writings and private placements—may continue to require a conventional sales effort, but other transactions will very likely be relegated to a Web page. High-volume, low-margin transactions—such as U.S. Treasuries and commercial paper—will only be executable on the Internet. The Internet will replace the *low-value-added* sales representative in the same way ATMs have eliminated many bank tellers. (Many banks now assess a service charge if you want to be served by a bank teller rather than place your transaction through an ATM.)

As customers discover the benefits of the Internet, which will include lower fees and a wider array of choices, the customer's primary relationship will move to a *portal*, with the client's secondary relationship falling to a marketing repre-sentative or relationship manager. Michael Schrage, a professor at MIT, calls this "relationship technology." As more people move into the digital age, the expres-sion "information technology,"[8] which connotes a place where techies and geeks spend their idle hours, will be replaced by the concept of "relationship technolo-gy." Relationship technology directs the priorities of the firm toward improving the relationship with the client through technology.

For brokerage firms that are not afraid of the information revolution, tremen-dous opportunity awaits them. The Internet offers new distribution channels. As the investment in technology begins to take hold, new sources of equity capital will flow in as a result of the improved return on shareholders' equity. Brokerage hous-es will be better able to compete with banks as a result of increased investment in technology. Firms, on the other hand, that ignore the trend toward technology solu-tions will experience an exodus of capital and will either be absorbed by those firms that have successfully developed a technology strategy or go out of business.[9]

Marketing and branding will become more difficult as space on the Internet becomes more crowded. While we have already identified at least six different types of online bond trading systems, most of these systems fall into distinct marketing categories. Steven Kaplan, professor at the University of Chicago's Graduate School of Business, and Mohanbir Sawhney, professor at Northwestern University's Kellogg Graduate School of Management, in a recent article in the *Harvard Business Review*, explained how various Internet strategies fit into a business-to-business (B2B) matrix.[10] Kaplan and Sawhney base their article on nonfinancial services, but it is

---

[8] Michael Schrage, *The Relationship Revolution: Understanding the Essence of the Digital Age*, Merrill Lynch, New York, 1997.

[9] "Will the Web Eat Wall Street?" *Fortune*, Aug. 2, 1999, pp. 112–118.

[10] Kaplan and Sawhney, "E-hubs: The New B2B Marketplaces," *Harvard Business Review*, May-June 2000, pp. 97–103.

easy to extrapolate their findings. To start, most B2B sites involve some type of *operating inputs*. These inputs are broken into three categories: (1) maintenance, (2) repairs, and (3) operating goods. These MROs, as the authors refer to them, include everything from office supplies to spare parts, airline tickets, and services. In this context, a bond is an operating input. There are many real-life examples of bonds as operating inputs. The financing of a new factory or office building, a company issuing bonds to increase its long-term inventory needs, and a school district building, a new multipurpose building, are all possible uses of bonds as operating inputs.

Having set the stage by defining *operating inputs*, Kaplan and Sawhney have then created a two-by-two matrix into which they classify four categories of B2B hubs. They are (1) MRO hubs, (2) yield managers, (3) exchanges, and (4) catalog hubs. Although the authors have identified four possible marketing categories for inclusion in their B2B matrix, only three appear to apply to the bond markets. First, *MRO hubs* allow systematic sourcing of operating inputs. Bulletin board or catalog systems, like BondExpress and Bloomberg's PICK, are representative of this type of system. Municipal bonds with unique characteristics and smaller corporate issues are the best examples of this type of system. Second, *yield managers* enable spot sourcing of operating inputs. These are primarily auction systems. Systems like MuniAuction, Dalcomp, and Bloomberg represent this category. Finally, *exchanges* allow continuous spot sourcing of operating inputs or outputs. This is, by far, the place where the most investment is being made on behalf of Wall Street and the securities industry. Firms like TradeWeb, BrokerTec, Espeed, and Garban ETC are competing for this piece of the e-commerce market.

Whether your e-commerce strategy is to build an MRO hub, be a yield manager, or create an exchange, the marketing budgets will have to be quite large to develop the channels through which the products will flow. As has been seen in the dotcom frenzy, most of the dotcoms, including Amazon, Yahoo, and others, have spent more on marketing and advertising than they have on technology. The Internet is crowded and noisy and, therefore, a difficult medium through which to deliver a crisp message. With over 60 bond trading systems somewhere in development, and with a promise of more to come, it has become very hard to be heard over the din of the crowd. With multiple electronic platforms already in existence in bonds, it is very easy to switch between systems, especially if you find any reason to become dissatisfied with one of them. At this point, there is very little brand loyalty between systems.

Ironically, brokerage houses, especially the huge Wall Street firms, pride themselves on their risk-taking ability, and yet the risks that the Internet imposes are, in some cases, even larger than what some of these bigger firms can handle. Many of the gambles that are currently being taken by firms to gain what is referred to as "first-mover advantage" will turn out to be "dry holes." Many firms, before the Internet was understood, had built large and expensive private networks for their customers to use. Most of the systems have since been scrapped at substantial expense. A bigger risk is that new delivery channels will make the 60-odd firms listed in The Bond Market Association's survey obsolete before they ever get off the ground. *Liquidity aggregation* is already in the early stages of development within the commodity exchanges. Also, there is a movement afoot to link and combine exchanges, such as what occurred when the CBOT and Eurex announced their joint venture.

The risks raised by the threat of *regulatory arbitrage* have not been given much thought. One of the features of the Internet is its mobility. It is as easy to communicate with a network server in Bombay or Aruba as it is with one in New York City or London. Therefore, regulators may discover that Internet-based exchanges and trading sites are shopping for the most favorable regulatory haven. One does not have to go back too many years to remember that the Eurodollar market was created out of regulatory necessity. The authors Patrick Young and Thomas Theys, in their book *Capital Market Revolution*, discuss borderless markets and the potential for regulators to lose control as the result of overzealous enforcement.[11]

Another risk that looms over many of the firms now developing digital strategies is how to retain their traditional, or legacy, businesses while moving full speed ahead toward implementing an Internet strategy. In his best-selling book, *The Innovator's Dilemma*, Clayton Christensen poses this very question, which he tries to answer by looking at several real-life studies.[12] His conclusion is that some of the smartest companies, using some of the best information available, make the wrong decisions when it comes to technology. One of the cases he focuses on is technological developments in the disk-drive industry and how companies like IBM were outmaneuvered by smaller start-ups like Seagate Technologies. While the reasons are more complex than current space allows, one of the paramount reasons that IBM lost part of this market was because it listened to its customers, as conventional wisdom dictates. Meanwhile, companies like Seagate were taking risks that IBM was unwilling to explore, which included looking beyond what customers told them they wanted. Many customers are currently telling their investment bankers that they do not want electronic underwriting and bond trading. They say that they prefer the personal contact and refuse to use the Internet.

How this question is being handled differs from firm to firm. Some firms have chosen, in effect, to jettison their legacy businesses in favor of an Internet strategy. Charles Schwab made a decision some time ago that the Internet was the future of equity trading and implemented a strategy wherein it was willing to cannibalize its existing business in favor of online trading. As it turned out, Schwab has been very successful and retains a substantial percentage of its pre-Internet

---

[11] Patrick Young and Thomas Theys, *Capital Market Revolution: The Future of Markets in an Online World*, Financial Times/Prentice Hall, London, 1999, pp. 43–61.

[12] Clayton Christensen, *Innovator's Dilemma: When New Technologies Cause Great Firms to Fail*, Harvard Business School Press, Cambridge, MA, 1997.

customers. Espeed is a large interdealer broker with a large institutional following in the fixed-income arena. Espeed is a spin-off from Cantor Fitzgerald, which, as mentioned earlier, was an early innovator in the bond industry. Since being spun off to pursue a separate digital strategy, it has enjoyed considerable success.[13]

Most firms, like Goldman Sachs and Merrill Lynch, are currently trying to implement Internet strategies within their existing customer bases. The question, again, is can firms with established legacy businesses get to the Internet soon enough to attract the "early adopters" while holding on long enough to retain the "later arrivers"? Undoubtedly some will succeed and some will not. The question is, who are they?

Bonds differ from equities, and consequently it is unlikely that online bond trading and underwriting systems will develop along the same lines. Over the last 3 years, the number of online bond trading systems has grown from less that 10 to over 60 today. Many of these systems will succeed, but most will not. Goldman Sachs, which has invested in a number of different strategies, does not expect all of them to be around within the next 3 years.

Most fixed-income professionals believe that bond investors make their buy and sell decisions differently from equity investors. Bond are more complex than most equities, because they involve decisions that include (1) expectations about general levels of interest rates, (2) inflation expectations, (3) issues of relative credit quality, and (4) cashflow projections, which become extremely complex in the case of mortgage- and asset-backed securities.

Whereas equities find themselves traded in a national market system, most bond market participants, including the leading trade associations, do not favor a national market in bonds. There are currently six types of trading and underwriting systems being developed for the Internet. Each type addresses a different need within the bond industry. The development pace at which these systems come to market will depend on (1) network capacity and bandwidth, (2) computational power as measured by internal storage capability and clock speeds, and (3) the software necessary to make everything run.

Bond trading houses and investment banking firms will be driven as much by the cost savings the Internet promises as by the lure of the technology. High-volume, low-margin transactions will be moved to the Internet in the same fashion many banks have forced their customers to use ATMs instead of bank tellers. Early movers will be rewarded by lower capital costs, increased transaction volumes, and superior market position.

Bonds are issued for different purposes than equities. Marketing and branding of bond underwriting and trading services will look like that of any other business. As firms sort out their competitive advantages, these services will be distributed in a manner similar to the B2B matrix described by Kaplan and Sawhney.

---

[13] "The Everything Exchange," *Business* 2.0, Aug. 22, 2000, pp. 242–244.

Companies with significant legacy businesses will struggle with how to enter the digital world without losing their customers' loyalty. Some will attempt to handle both within the same entity, other will start new divisions, and some will start separate companies with hopes of avoiding channel conflicts. Some will succeed, and some won't.

Finally, regulation will throw a wild card into the maze of decisions that bond firms will have to make concerning their e-commerce strategies. Besides the larger issues surrounding global regulation of securities underwriting and trading on the Internet, there are the specific issues that affect bond underwriting and trading. The initiative by the regulators, especially the SEC, to force bonds into a national market system will be vigorously opposed by the industry. Disclosure rules must recognize the benefits of electronic media. Ultimately, should regulation become too onerous and lack the savvy necessary to compete in global markets, then you could a see migration of many of these systems, similar to the Eurodollar market in the seventies, to offshore jurisdictions where regulation is favorable.

Sherman McCoy was a creation of the eighties. His talents resided in his ability to have known the "right people" and to have been seen at the "right places." While he probably understood most of the complexities of bond analytics, it is unlikely he even knew how to reboot his computer, if he had one. If he had refined any skills, it was probably the appropriate tipping strategy at the Yale Club. The masters of the universe of the twenty-first century will probably be men and women with spike hair and nose rings, who prefer a chatroom to a telephone. You will be more likely to see them snowboarding in Snowbird, Utah, than hanging around the Yale or Harvard Club.

CHAPTER 7

The Democratization of the Foreign Exchange Market

Richard Olsen, Chairman
Olsen and Associates, Zurich, Switzerland

The foreign exchange market, with a daily transaction volume of $1.5 trillion,[1] is 50 times larger than all the equity markets combined and is essentially controlled by only 10 or so major banks. Typically, every trade is for $1 million or more, much larger than in any other market. Smaller trades are aggregated.

How is it possible that this huge market has remained the fiefdom of the large investors and traders? Will the Internet and predictive technologies change all this? We clearly expect so. It is estimated that the foreign echange (FX) market will grow within a few years from a transaction volume of $1.5 trillion per day to $10 trillion per day and will be fully automated, transacting currencies at a minuscule spread of 0.01 percent and lower.

HISTORY OF THE MODERN FOREIGN EXCHANGE MARKET

The story of the development of today's FX market is remarkable. In the 1970s, after three decades of government restrictions on foreign exchange transactions subsequent to the Second World War, the FX market became highly efficient in a short period of time. With the regime of fixed exchange rates being undermined and currencies allowed to float freely, the volume of currency trading grew quickly.

---

[1] All money is in U.S. dollars.

Initially, the market comprised a large number of market makers. As we will see, this was to change rapidly in the late 1990s.

The foreign exchange market is a huge over-the-counter market of professional market participants. It was the first market where traders traded with each other remotely; i.e., they never met in a central exchange, such as a futures exchange or stock market. The currency traders conducted their business initially via telex, then over the telephone in direct contact or through a broker, and later over electronic communication networks such as the Reuters or EBS dealing systems.

Few people realize that the modern foreign exchange market evolved from a kind of early Internet-type communications system. It was Reuters news agency that had the idea of using its computer network to create a bulletin board for banks to post their indicative market prices. Starting in the early seventies and continuing up to the eighties and nineties, banks could subscribe to an electronic service from Reuters, where they could publish price information and market comments in an electronic format.

It was a very simple kind of service, with pages only 10 lines long and 80 characters wide, but extremely effective. It allowed banks to broadcast their information in real time to a wide audience. In addition, Reuters utilized this platform to create a bulletin board showing the most recent update published by any one of its contributors. The bulletin board was an indication of the current price level and an important reference point in the price negotiations between banks.

Eventually, Reuters introduced a money dealing system that increased the efficiency of trading between banks. It was a kind of e-mail system that allowed banks to streamline the negotiating and processing of foreign exchange transactions. With increased efficiency, the speed of transactions increased. In this more competitive environment, large banks with strong internal customer bases had a competitive edge because they could withstand adverse price movements better than their smaller competitors. As a result, the smaller entities gradually withdrew from market making.

In the nineties, the structural changes in the foreign exchange markets had a major impact on price behavior. Early in the decade, market liquidity during extremely volatile price movements was—with few exceptions—almost continuous. Today, this has changed. Market liquidity is discontinuous; i.e., only small price shocks are required to make market liquidity disappear. When the price movements stabilize again, liquidity reappears and markets return to normal working order.

This behavior pattern is highly disturbing. It increases the risk of exceptionally large price shocks such as the collapse of the Japanese yen in 1998. In this event, market making in the yen was discontinuous whenever there was an above-average price movement, with market liquidity disappearing. As soon as external circumstances led to large sell orders, the orders could not be accommodated due to the lack of liquidity. This, in turn, triggered additional sale orders, which further undermined the currency. Thus, the meltdown.

In our view, today's foreign exchange markets are extremely fragile. The reason for this is quite simple. The mergers between banks, and the closing of smaller dealing rooms within banks, have led to a reduction of overall "risk capital" allocated to market making. Simultaneously, there has been a dramatic increase in the volume of fundamentally driven FX transactions as a result of the rapid growth of international trade and global investing. To absorb the impact of these transactions, a high level of market liquidity is required. In the absence of this, the markets are extremely sensitive to small changes of supply and demand, leading to erratic price swings with intermittent market liquidity.

STRUCTURE OF THE FOREIGN EXCHANGE MARKET

The foreign exchange market is a two-tier market. On the one hand, there is a professional over-the-counter market for transactions larger than $1 million. This market functions very efficiently and operates 24 hours a day during the business week. It has a transaction volume of $1.5 trillion and offers a low spread of 0.03 percent during high-volume trading hours. This compares extremely favorably with other markets, such as the equity markets, where spreads of 0.7 percent and more are common. However, the professional market is exhibiting a degree of stress due to the continuing consolidation process within the banking industry and the reduction of dealing rooms per financial institution. Confronted with these realities, and the continued rapid growth of fundamentally driven transaction volume, the professional OTC market does not offer the same degree of liquidity as was available in the eighties and early nineties.

The second tier of the market covers currency transactions below $500,000. These transactions are not negotiated and are executed on proprietary transaction platforms. Typically, they are initiated as part of another transaction, such as the purchase of foreign stocks or the purchase of equipment or international travel. Unlike the highly efficient OTC market, this market segment is not efficient, and relatively large spreads are charged. Typical spreads are 0.5 percent, increasing up to 5 percent for credit card transactions. Because these transactions are executed in the context of other transactions, there is a high degree of "stickiness"; i.e., it is difficult for the customer to negotiate the price and select a preferred counterparty. The customer is kept hostage and has to accept the price offered. Needless to say, this second tier is highly lucrative for the banks offering the service.

Recently, a third tier has started to develop in which banks are implementing their proprietary transaction platforms for foreign exchange. With these platforms, they target transaction volumes of $100,000 and larger. The platforms are fully automated, and transactions are executed at a fixed premium over the current market price. Large transactions are negotiated and require manual intervention by the bank's trader. Banks are investing heavily to fill their platforms with contents, such as treasury applications, or updated market research.

Finally, there is also a fourth tier in development in which major banks are joining forces to create a joint transaction platform, such as FXAll. The unique selling proposition here is the competitiveness of the banks' market quotes. This is an attempt to extend the reach of the first tier and make it a generalized platform for business-to-business foreign exchange transactions.

My assessment: The two-tier nature of the foreign exchange markets is gradually being undermined. The institutions that in the past had to pay large spreads because they belonged to the second-tier group are getting access to significantly better transaction prices by joining the third or fourth tier. The question arises, will the foreign exchange market become a super ECN (electronic communication network) in the hands of the current incumbents, a handful of major banks?

For traders who have been participants in the foreign exchange markets over the past 20 years, these recent changes appear to be monumental. They are, however, nothing in comparison to what will happen in the future. The Internet and computing power in general will, in conjunction with predictive technologies, implode the foreign exchange market and transform it.

What are the driving forces of change?

THE INTERNET AND IDIOSYNCRASIES OF FINANCIAL MARKETS

The Internet has lowered the cost of handling and processing information by several orders of magnitude. This is a major driving force for change in the financial markets, the very purpose of which is to handle and process information.

In addition, many of the conventions in financial markets are completely outdated because they developed when the physical delivery of paper was the only means of written confirmation. This has resulted in the delivery date of foreign exchange transactions, i.e., the value date, being 2 business days after the transaction. Another example of the impact of legacy technology is interest rate payments, which are made only once a day, at the end of the business day.

With modern technology, nothing stands in the way of executing and settling transactions in real time and increasing the frequency of interest rate payments to an hourly or even minute-by-minute rate. However, existing players in the market have no interest in changing the existing idiosyncrasies because they are to the players' advantage and generate additional revenue. In addition, the idiosyncrasies are firmly embedded in their software systems, and established players in the foreign exchange markets cannot update these procedures without huge investments. This is, however, not the case for new ventures that build their systems from scratch and create an efficient platform. As soon as they become operational, they become powerful players with a strong momentum.

Oanda, an online company founded by Olsen and Associates, is in the process of launching a new foreign exchange market. Its FxExchange platform will initially be focused on small-scale transactions up to a size of $500,000. Its key features include:

- *Low average spread.* The average spread will be 0.01 percent, or approximately a third of the spread charged at peak trading times in the professional OTC market.

- *Continuous markets with 24/7 transaction capabilities.* Users will be able to trade at any time in the day, including weekends, when other markets are closed.

- *Incremental interest rate payments.* Interest rate payments will be made at hourly increments and later at higher frequencies. In the traditional foreign exchange market, investors can only take advantage of the interest rate premium if they keep their funds invested in the respective currency overnight. With Oanda, they can take advantage of any interest rate premiums during the course of 1 hour. These intraday interest rate payments lower the threshhold for getting investors to buy a currency that has a sales overhang, which will make Oanda attractive to countries whose currencies are under pressure. The payment frequency will also be attractive to corporate treasurers, who know that pennies add up.

PREDICTIVE TECHNOLOGIES

Oanda is capable of launching a new foreign exchange market because the company owns a "field of use" license for the Olsen market-making engine, for which a patent has been filed. This engine relies on predictive technologies for setting bid and ask prices and hedging market risk.

Olsen and Associates has pioneered predictive technologies during the course of a 15-year research-and-development effort in which an extensive high-frequency, tick-by-tick database of market-maker quotes and transaction prices has been created. The data have been analyzed, and a theory of heterogeneous markets has been developed that provides the foundation for the new technologies.

The hypothesis is simple: Unlike the approach of classical economics, where every market participant is assumed to be the same, the new theory emphasizes that market participants are different and, in particular, trade on different time scales. Using this approach it is possible to identify groups of market participants that have common trading patterns, which can be analyzed using high-frequency market data. With complex nonlinear indicators, the interaction patterns between these groups are mapped and probabilistic volatility and price forecasts generated. Using this information, the market-making engine is able to set continuous bid and ask prices and hedge any imbalances in incoming buy and sell orders.

By using predictive technologies it is possible to generate online forecasts and distribute them in a user-friendly, Web-based browser environment. These forecasts generate automatic research reports and are a substitute for, or at the very least an extension of, traditional research reports. In view of the high cost of providing continuously updated research, we anticipate that for established markets, such as the FX and interest rate markets, online forecasting services will become an important source of market information. In meteorology, large quantitative weather forecasting models have become standard. We anticipate a similar development in financial markets.

Figure 7-1 is a forecast graph for EUR/USD exchange rate. The cone indicates the 50 percent probability range of the future price movement.

EFFICIENCY OF FINANCIAL MARKETS

Financial markets are the lubricants of the fundamental economy. Without foreign exchange markets, international trading would suffer. If the foreign exchange markets are inefficient and spreads are large, then this adds dramatically to the cost of products. Essentially, the efficiency of financial markets is as important to the economy as the fuel efficiency of cars or the efficiency of any other critical technical device is.

The advent of the Internet and the development of predictive technologies will dramatically increase the efficiency of financial markets. To this end, it is our expectation that an automatic market-making engine will be significantly more effective in market making than traditional traders who rely on "gut" feeling. This is especially so because a market-making engine can be designed in such a way that the experience of traders can be input at a higher level, at which they supervise the operation of the engine.

Supported by an extremely efficient computing infrastructure for the processing and handling of transactions, the new foreign exchange market will have the

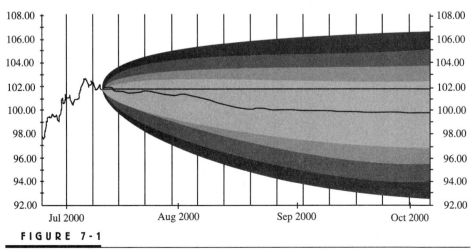

FIGURE 7-1

Forecast EUR-JPY (3-month horizon).

potential to transact huge volumes of currency transactions. We anticipate a dramatic growth of the FX market spurred by the Internet, international e-commerce, and access to the market by the small investor.

The small investor or day trader will be attracted to this market due to its efficiency and profit potential. The ratio of the spread between bid and ask and volatility determines the maximum profit potential of trading a particular market. For the new foreign exchange market to be launched by Oanda, this ratio is 1:1000, whereas traditional equity markets offer a ratio of 1:50. This measure makes the FX market 20 times more attractive to trade in than traditional equity markets. The incumbents will be under hard pressure to adapt to this changing environment. Those who resist will rapidly lose market share and find it extremely expensive to jump ship at a later stage.

In closing, we expect that the foreign exchange market will become a model for what will happen in the other financial markets in the future. There will be an ongoing democratization process, with everyone gaining access to an extremely efficient marketplace open for trades in any size and with microscopic spreads.

CHAPTER 8

The Future of Venture Capital

David Starr
Co-Founder of Vcapital and currently Client Partner at Culture Worx

Tim Draper of Draper Fisher Jurvetson dates the venture capital business back to the days of Columbus and Queen Isabella. But, in reality, the business has only been around for 43 years. Venture capital is no longer a profession of chance. Today's brightest MBA graduates now view the venture business as the preferred career of choice. Silicon Valley, flooded with venture capital, has certainly redefined American work culture. From dress codes to stock options, it has set the standard for what a work environment *should* be. Most of all, and more than any other industry, the venture capital business has produced tremendous wealth for a select group of entrepreneurs and investors with tremendous courage and foresight. These individuals took a chance and believed in a vision held by one or more individuals, who in some cases, were not old enough to drive a car.

America's investors have created, and in some cases incubated, companies that will forever change the way we work, communicate, and carry out our daily routines. In fact, venture capitalists have changed almost every single industry with their investments except one—their own. That is, until now. In the past year, several Web-based firms have penetrated the venture industry and are determined to alter the business that has resisted change for decades.

It is ironic that the venture business has remained largely the same since its inception. Nevertheless, change is constant and is a necessary force. The venture business is finally beginning to evolve, and current methods for deal sourcing, screening, and funding will change forever. Some experts believe that the Internet will shift the power to entrepreneurs. Others believe that the Web will bring a new level of efficiency to the process of raising venture capital. But one outcome is certain: Technology will force the venture capital business to change.

GARBAGE-IN–GARBAGE-OUT

Internet technology has had a unique effect on the venture capital business. While venture capitalists have enjoyed record returns from their investments in the Internet space, they have shied away from making investments in companies that combine the venture capital process with Internet technology. The question is why.

Prior to 1997, Web-based venture capital sites were nothing more than listing services, which are, essentially, electronic bulletin boards. Entrepreneurs were able to submit applications for investments and post them online, where they could be reviewed by interested users. For unsophisticated entrepreneurs, it was a plausible alternative to randomly calling venture firms to solicit meetings. However, for sophisticated entrepreneurs with capital-raising experience, listing services were not the answer.

Further, listing services met with significant opposition from venture capital firms. As Christine Comaford, a Silicon Valley venture capitalist, pointed out, "Do you really want to put your family jewels on a Website?" Nobody with an idea worth pitching would ever submit that idea to a public listing service. In addition, the notion of posting an idea for hundreds or even thousands of people to see was a sign to prospective investors that the entrepreneur was desperately shopping the deal. In venture capital circles, shopped-around deals are worth nothing because venture firms typically fund proprietary deals forwarded to them through trusted sources such as personal lawyers or accountants.

Not only did the bulletin boards fail to attract a surplus of quality deals, but there was also a lack of demand from the venture capital community to look at these opportunities. Simply put, the lack of confidentiality, coupled with the poor demand from investors to join these services, forced the best entrepreneurs and investors to conclude that venture capital is best practiced in the offline world. The result—most of the Web-based bulletin board services went out of business. This was a significant, unfortunate blow to the few online players who understood the investment space and foresaw the opportunities the Internet could provide.

NEW TALENT TO THE RESCUE

Given the poor reputation established by the first online "matchmakers," many questioned whether any courageous entrepreneurs would make a concerted effort to use the Web to bring a new level of efficiency to the venture capital process. A few daring entrepreneurs have emerged, bringing a new spirit and excitement to the practice of raising capital on the Web. What makes these upstarts different from their predecessors? They are not trying to guess what venture capitalists expect in a deal because they have all had prior experience—as either successful entrepreneurs or private equity investors. These individuals know the venture business inside and out and understand the fundamental rules of the game. They did not rush to the Internet to buy URLs like vc.com. Instead, they were more concerned about forming relationships with customers and studying ways to build successful business models.

The founders of the three most well-known firms—Garage.com, vcapital, and Offroad Capital—all have background experience in the venture business. Len Batterson of vcapital has enjoyed success as a venture capitalist and angel investor with Allstate and Batterson Venture Partners, respectively. Former Apple Computer evangelist Guy Kawasaki of Garage.com claims to have been offered the CEO position at Yahoo. And Stephen Pelletier of Offroad was an entrepreneur in residence at Benchmark Capital, a leading Silicon Valley venture firm. These pioneers of the Internet venture business will surely be remembered for their vision, as well as their ability to draw numerous new competitors to the scene, including Yazam, NVST, and University Angels. While the above firms employ vastly different business models and target different markets, they certainly do have one similarity—a belief that there is a demand and a market for entrepreneurs to raise capital on the Internet.

THE FUTURE

As the Internet becomes an integral part of everyday life, many wonder whether or not it will become a major component of the venture capital business. Will the Web transform the venture capital industry as it has done for so many other industries? With its ability to make commerce seamless and transparent, the Internet has forever changed the way we live and work—especially the way we buy. Simply stated, the Internet brings buyers and sellers together without the interference of brokers or intermediaries that so often dominate real-world transactions.

Businesses such as travel agencies will soon consolidate or possibly cease to exist because the virtual world has rendered them obsolete. How is this related to venture capital? Why is it important to consider the future of the venture capital industry in light of this fact? Certain industries require a third party to oversee transactions and relationships. In many cases, this need is generated when one of the parties involved does not understand the process in its entirety. Venture capital clearly fits this definition. Although a record number of entrepreneurs have experienced success while raising capital, the venture industry is very much an enigma to the general public. As David Cowan, the managing general partner of Bessemer Venture Partners explains, "[The venture business] used to be a cottage industry with loosely affiliated craftsmen working together." In the past, the ability to secure venture financing was based more on whom you knew rather than what you knew. Today, the industry is beginning to change, but most entrepreneurs still need direction when it comes to working with venture capitalists. Furthermore, the sheer difference in the number of entrepreneurs seeking capital and the small number of venture capital professionals making investments requires a filter between the two groups. While certain industries will thrive online, due to the elimination of a third party, the venture business will maintain gatekeepers to filter the endless flow of deals to the venture community.

THE ROLE OF THE GATEKEEPER

If the Internet needs a gatekeeper, what would its role be? What tasks and issues would a gatekeeper solve? With the right expertise, management talent and knowledge of the venture business, a gatekeeper should have the ability to eliminate several key inefficiencies using Web technology. Because the venture business is two-sided—entrepreneurs looking for capital and venture capitalists disbursing capital—the inefficiencies of both sides must be thoroughly examined and considered.

Value to Entrepreneurs

Entrepreneurs raising capital typically struggle with two issues—finding the right venture capitalists and expressing their investment opportunity in a way that is easily understood by all potential investors.

The Internet offers largely untapped potential to help entrepreneurs deal efficiently with the struggles of the capital-raising process. While it is true that most venture firms have begun to market themselves via the Web, many simply offer a general company pitch. Typically, an investor's Website pitch is very general and rarely separates the firm from other venture firms. The same is true of books about the venture capital industry. The lack of detailed information available in books and online is no fault of the authors or Web managers. The reality is, venture firms are very careful regarding the information they reveal to the public. Divulging too much information will result in a flood of business plans. And with massive amounts of information to review, uncovering the next Netscape or Yahoo becomes increasingly unlikely.

However, with the help of an Internet gatekeeper, venture firms can afford to divulge their prized investment criteria—provided the gatekeeper uses the information wisely. The Internet gatekeeper, armed with investment criteria information, can help thousands of entrepreneurs reach the right venture firms. And because information on the Internet can change in an instant, a shift in a firm's investment criteria can be reflected immediately. Obviously, this is not the case with venture capital–related books, which are updated annually at best.

Finding the right venture firm is only half the battle. With the economy moving at warp speed, today's bright idea can easily become yesterday's news. With only a limited amount of capital to invest and even less time to spend looking for quality deals, professionals opt to review summaries of business plans, rather than the plans themselves. This also allows them to quickly access the key elements and may convince the venture capitalist to look deeper. However, entrepreneurs often struggle with limiting their information to simply the most essential elements. They typically believe a 40-page document is not enough to tell their story, let alone a 2- or 3-page summary. An Internet gatekeeper with industry knowledge can help the entrepreneur understand the most important points to convey to investors. Essentially, the gatekeeper educates the market, which, in the long run, saves time for both entrepreneurs and investors.

Value to Venture Professionals

Venture capitalists are not without faults. Their main concerns center on the number of deals they see and the quality of those deals. Therefore, a trusted gatekeeper—whether online or offline—needs to ensure select, top-quality deal referrals that do not require extensive review. It may sound strange to be concerned about the number of deals referred to a venture firm at any given time, but the reality is that venture professionals are busy people. Their job description goes far beyond finding new opportunities. They participate on company boards of directors, offer management advice, and raise capital for the firm's portfolio companies and the firm itself. A typical venture capitalist does not have the bandwidth to review everything that is given to him or her, regardless of how great the deal is. A trusted gatekeeper must know the investment criteria of each investment firm so well that the number of deals referred remains small enough for the firm to feasibly manage, while precisely matching the firm's pre-specified investment criteria.

When referring deals, one must always take into consideration the issue of quality as well. Quality proves to be a very interesting term in the venture capital industry, with very diverse definitions across the venture capital community. However, there are specific criteria that all venture professionals seek in a quality deal. In some circles, they are referred to as "the four m's," magic, management, market and money.

> *Magic.* The company must visualize and be committed to its dream. What is it about the company that separates it from the competition? What is its competitive advantage? Is this competitive advantage sustainable?
>
> *Management.* The management team is perhaps the most important aspect of any investment opportunity. Intellectual property does not necessarily make great companies—but people do. Venture firms will tell you that they invest in people, not ideas.
>
> *Market.* The appropriate research, comprehension, and selection of the target industry, market, and potential competitors are critical to the potential success of any company. In order for a company to receive venture funding, it must operate in a large market that has the potential to reach mammoth proportions.

Money. The money factor is largely dependent on the factors above. Venture firms live and die by the numbers, and they must ensure that when all is said and done, the firm is looking for investments that will get them as close as possible to its desired rate of return.

No venture firm will dispute that the above factors are important. In fact, most venture firms also believe that quality only goes as far as their wallets do, meaning that quality is defined by the investments they choose to make. For example, the same deals cross the desks of multiple venture capitalists. One firm might view a particular deal as a quality deal and choose to invest. Another firm might view the same deal as substandard and choose to pass. Again, it should be the responsibility of the Internet gatekeeper to know the elements that make a particular deal desirable to one firm and undesirable to another.

This has much to do with the past experiences of the venture partners and the past portfolio companies these firms have funded. Today's technology has the ability to search and learn from past events and predict which deals may be appropriate for some firms and not for others. With these capabilities, a trusted gatekeeper could learn more about a venture firm's criteria each time the firm distributes funding. In time, that gatekeeper could know exactly the type of deals it should refer. The possibilities are clearly endless.

CHALLENGES

It is clear that the Internet can bring a new level of efficiency to the venture capital market. It is also clear that many challenges lie ahead for the Web-based venture capital space. If these challenges are overcome, entrepreneurs and venture capitalists alike will benefit immensely from the Internet, which will forever change the way the investment industry works.

MORE THAN JUST MONEY

To be successful in today's economy, a venture capital firm must provide far more than traditional capital. The element that separates plain old money from smart money is strategic, value-added services offered by investors—call them "IOU to IPO" services—such as accounting, legal, Web development, public relations, and most importantly human resources and recruiting. Most venture firms claim to provide these types of services, but only a few have organized their businesses to formally offer them. The cost of providing added services is high, and services are not the core business of venture capital firms.

How is this related to the online venture capital sourcing process? If one were to combine the venture capital process with the acquisition of services on the Web, it would save entrepreneurs time, money, and the hassle of finding the right partners. It would also help venture firms focus on their core business—providing money—and adapt to the new economy culture, in which services are added without having to pay any of the fixed costs associated with providing them. The aggregation of services with the venture industry is a natural phenomenon that should be incorporated into the fund-raising equation—an idea that is not lost on the early leaders in the Internet venture capital space.

SECURITY AND CONTROL

Security on the Internet has always been a hot topic. Stories of viruses spreading like wildfire from computer to computer have forced some entrepreneurs to shy away from the Internet-based fund-raising process. Although technical security concerns are warranted, most sophisticated entrepreneurs are concerned with a much larger issue—having their precious business plan displayed for the whole world to see. An entrepreneur's fear of this kind of security breach stems from practices by some early players who attempted to marry, or match, entrepreneurs with investors. This unsophisticated approach has hurt the online capital-raising industry, as most entrepreneurs wrongfully believe that all such sites work the same way—a plan is posted on the Web and any registered member of the site can view the information. It is unfortunate, but companies are still being formed today that believe this is an acceptable method of sourcing deals. Businesses engaging in the online capital business must have processes in place that guarantee airtight security. Most importantly, they must shift the control over the process, from the investor to equal influence from both the entrepreneur and the venture capitalist. Online capital businesses will only gain the trust of the entrepreneurial community with vital changes such as these.

In the offline world, smart entrepreneurs perform extensive research on potential investors and then decide which firms will receive their business plans, based on the investment criteria of each firm and their knowledge of the firm's track record. Raising venture money on the Web should be no different. Not only should entrepreneurs be able to perform fast, easy due diligence on potential investors, but they should also be able to decide for themselves which firms may view their plans and which ones may not. It is this flexibility and control that will separate the achievers from the failures in this new Internet space.

THE TRUST FACTOR

Whether you ask legendary Silicon Valley venture capitalist John Doerr or Jim Breyer or Lon Chow of Chicago's Apex Venture Partners, or virtually any venture capitalist in America, they will tell you the same thing. The venture business is based on relationships, trust, and human interaction. While the online space is clearly very efficient, it also, by its very nature, removes the human element from the equation. Venture firms argue that most of the deals they fund come to them via referrals from trusted sources, such as entrepreneurs they have funded in the past or service providers (accounts, lawyers, etc.) they trust. Most venture firms view entrepreneurs who use Web-based facilities as incapable of raising money the old-fashioned way. These entrepreneurs are branded "nonquality." This adverse selection phenomenon must be overcome if the online capital-raising business is to succeed.

How can the industry overcome this dilemma? The Web-based players must ensure that the online process mirrors the real world. Successful Web-based capital sources must create a "virtual venture community" that consists of all the key players in the real world that make the industry so unique. This community should include professional service providers, business schools, commercial bankers, and investment bankers, in addition to entrepreneurs and venture capital firms.

Though it may sound odd, Internet intermediaries in this industry can also overcome the trust factor by remaining relatively uninvolved in the deals themselves. The venture business has always been, and always will be, a face-to-face business. Smart Internet matchmakers will concentrate on making the introductory process more efficient and let the deal making take care of itself. They will also provide services to make the capital-raising process less confusing and time-intensive, including due diligence, industry reports, targeted content, multimedia presentations, and the ability to syndicate deals. The winner in the Internet space will offer a thoughtful mixture of these services, ultimately making the lives of entrepreneurs and investors much more efficient.

CONCLUSION

The greatest factor that will entice venture capitalists to use Web-based utilities is familiarity. The online process must mirror the real world. However, the world constantly changes, and so must the venture business. Like it or not, venture firms cannot stay "dinosaurs" forever.

Today, entrepreneurs have more access to information about the venture industry than ever before. Entrepreneurs are clearly well educated in regard to the valuations they can demand, and with an increasing number of business-to-business information sources, including publications like *Industry Standard* and Websites like Vcapital, their knowledge will only multiply. Informed entrepreneurs will know which venture firms best fit their opportunity and can be selective about revealing their deal.

Although venture firms are not panicking, they are scrambling to differentiate themselves in the eyes of this new breed of venture seekers. They see the balance of power slowly shifting. In fact, some venture firms are even rethinking their value propositions and deal sourcing strategies, recognizing the growing need for more than just capital.

NEW TRENDS EMERGING

Some venture firms have engaged in backward integration, forming their own incubators. Because the time to market has been so critical for Internet companies, venture firms are investing much earlier in the company's life cycle, finding that seed-stage investments often pay off quite handsomely. Bill Gross's ideaLab, CMGI, and Softbank are perfect examples of these types of industry success stories.

Other venture firms have engaged in vertical integration. Due to the market volatility, smart venture firms realized that the kind of valuations offered by the public markets over the last 5 years could not last forever. Forward-looking venture firms partnered with or formed their own distribution channels in order to raise capital for their portfolio companies. These new corporate entities, such as Epoch Partners and meVC, have utilized creative thinking to produce new ways to service their portfolios.

Yet another set of venture firms has engaged in horizontal integration, by partnering with professional service providers to provide value outside of monetary capital. A recent example is Bessemer Venture Partners' acquisition of Boston-based executive search firm Lexington Partners, which now offers core human resources functions to Bessemer's portfolio companies. Another example is Pennsylvania's Internet Capital Group (ICG) which offers services internally rather than by acquisition.

Given the recent developments in the venture community, some experts believe that this is the best time ever to be an entrepreneur. In truth, the best is yet to come. The venture business will be more exciting and competitive in the future. The public markets will certainly correct themselves, and companies that should receive venture financing will. Those that do not deserve capital will not get it. The laws that define who gets funding will not change, and Darwinian laws will prevail again. The smart entrepreneurs will receive as much money as they need, and the not-so-smart ones will continue to founder. The most exciting changes will occur within the venture firms themselves. Ironically, they have changed the world with their investments, but have yet to emerge from their own shell. The Internet will play a role in ensuring that these professionals catch up to the future. The very future that the capital providers themselves profess will dominate our daily lives from the time that we wake up to the time we go to sleep.

CHAPTER 9

Retail Internet Banking

Octavio Marenzi, Managing Director
Celent Communications

Isabella Cagnazzo Fonseca, Analyst
Celent Communications

Financial institutions are placing high emphasis on Internet banking initiatives. The year 2000 promises positive results for large and medium financial institutions striving to be early adopters of online technologies. As the online market expands and technology improves, offerings will become much more sophisticated. This chapter analyzes the drivers, business strategies, and trends for financial services providing online retail, wholesale, and brokerage technologies. It will be a source for financial institutions selecting or improving Internet technologies and for solution providers planning to enhance their offerings and remain strategic entities.

RETAIL INTERNET BANKING

Drivers for the Industry

The Internet represents an opportunity for the financial services industry to retain and expand customer relationships by cross-selling to existing customers and attracting new ones. Today, offering Internet banking has become a requirement for large financial institutions. Financial institutions that combine Internet technology and human interaction for sales and service will be at the forefront of innovation. Top banks have long since deployed Internet solutions and, in some cases, have moved on to second- or third-generation systems. While these large banks continue to offer ever-more sophisticated applications, an increasing number of smaller and medium-sized financial institutions are moving onto the Internet to accommodate heightened consumer interest.

The past 2 years have seen significant growth in the number of consumers venturing online to handle their banking needs (see Figure 9-1). Currently, there are over 6 million Internet banking consumers in the United States. While the rate of growth will slow to a more moderate pace over the next few years, adoption of the Internet as an interaction channel will remain quite strong. Customers will continue to realize the benefits and convenience of managing a variety of financial services needs online, including paying bills, applying for and checking the status of loans, viewing credit card statements, initiating brokerage transactions, etc. We anticipate that the number of Internet banking consumers will reach 16 million by 2003.

A significant number of banks are revisiting vendor selections made over the course of the past 2 years. Many banks find themselves dissatisfied and searching for new solutions that better fit their needs and requirements, highlighting the necessity for careful assessments of the available vendor applications.

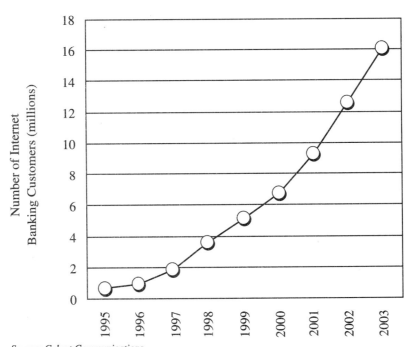

Source: Celent Communications

FIGURE 9-1

Number of online banking customers in the United States.

Business Strategies and Trends

Financial institutions looking to improve their Internet banking initiatives will focus not only on traditional services, but also on adding more advanced applications to their offerings. Different strategies are emerging to compete in this aggressive arena.

The vendor marketplace is quite congested and has led to stiff competition among firms on the basis of price, speed of deployment, flexibility, and availability of advanced applications, such as one-to-one marketing, aggregated account information, and personalized content. Table 9-1 lists the vendors of Internet banking technologies. Although the industry has undergone considerable consolidation in the past year, we believe further consolidation is imminent to make it a viable market for the remaining firms.

Many solutions include online transactions that span the financial services industry: basic banking, mortgages, loans, brokerages, and insurance. Consumers are no longer limited to simply reviewing their checking and savings account balances and to transferring funds back and forth between accounts. At the leading banks, consumers can apply for loans and mortgages, buy or sell stocks, obtain quotes for auto insurance, and view their credit card statements.

At the same time that the number and the range of financial products are increasing, the number of channels covered is also rising rapidly and going well beyond simple Web browsers. Advanced vendors are adding new channel access applications to support personal digital assistants (PDAs), mobile phones, and other wireless devices. Vendors that previously considered themselves to be pure Internet banking players are adding support for personal financial management tools, such as Quicken or Money, through OFX interfaces.

Another trend that has emerged is for vendors to offer both an in-house solution and a service bureau solution that runs at the company's data center. Running the system in a data center should allow the financial institution to get up and running quickly and at a relatively low cost typically. However, banks should be aware that some outsourcing services are neither fast nor inexpensive. A number of these application vendors provide an easy migration path for those banks that want to move the technology from the vendor's data center to internal deployment at the bank. Additionally, through internal development or partnerships, many vendors are also beginning to offer more sophisticated applications:

Financial planning tools. These interactive Web tools allow customers to share personal financial information and goals and to receive advice. For example, tools can suggest how much money parents should save per month in order to be able to send their children to college or what types of investments might be most appropriate for a couple that plan to retire in 10 years.

Financial alerts. Customers are able to set up electronic alerts when certain types of activity occur in their accounts. For example, a customer may request that an

TABLE 9-1

Vendors of Packaged Internet Banking Solutions

Technology Provider	Product	Technology	Number of live clients	Clients
Concentrex	Concentrex Online Customer Banking 1.0-1Q2000	Windows NT	0 (300)*	N/A
Corillian	Voyager	Windows NT, MS SQL	13	SunTrust, Citibank, Sanwa, Hibernia, Crestar, AmSouth
Digital Insight/nFront	AXIS Internet Banking	IBM AIX, Informix	435	West Coast Bancorp, Golden 1 Credit Union
	nHome (nFront)	Windows NT, MS SQL	144	Bancorp South
Home Account	Canopy		90	N/A
HomeCom	Personal Internet Banker	Windows NT, MS SQL	12	Georgia Power Federal Credit Union, Community American Credit Union
Intellidata	Interpose	IBM MVS, CICS	7	BB&T, Summit Bank, First Tennessee, Compass, National City, First Hawaiian/Bank of the West
Netzee	Internet Banking	Windows NT, MS SQL	400	N/A
Online Resources	Opus	Windows NT, MS SQL	408	California Federal, Dime Savings Bank, Riggs Bank
Q-up	Internet Banking System	Windows NT	211	Home National Bank, Pacific Mercantile Bank, Heartland Bank
S1	S1 Consumer Suite	HP UX, Informix	12 (in data center)	Huntington, SFNB
	Retail Banking	Windows NT, Oracle, Sybase, MS SQL, DB2	200	Wingspanbank.com, Chase
Sybase/HFN	Total Web Financial System	HP UX, Sun Solaris, Windows NT, Sybase	1 (7)*	Comerica, BB&T, Old Kent, First Hawaiian

Source: Vendors, Celent Communications estimates.
*The number in parentheses indicates the number for clients of its previously available application.

e-mail be sent to him if his checking account balance falls below $1000. Or a customer may establish an alert that sends a message to her beeper or mobile phone if one of her stocks falls below a certain price.

Aggregated accounts. Ideally, customers would like to see an aggregated picture of their financial accounts—savings accounts, mutual funds, loans and mortgages outstanding, etc.—in a single view. Applications have been developed which incorporate data from many different types of providers and present this to the customer.

Electronic check register. Similar to a checkbook, this application allows customers to keep track of checks they write electronically. This capability is integrated with the Internet banking solution.

Personalized content. This enables customers to view certain types of data and information upon log-in, according to personal preferences. Customers may choose from streaming stock quotes, news feeds, or the weather at a certain locale, etc.

Future Trends

The year 2000 will prove to be a very active year for Internet banking initiatives at financial institutions as well as for vendor selections. While a small number of banks are still developing their own internal Internet banking solutions, a majority of financial institutions have turned to outside providers. Typically, banks are buying off-the-shelf solutions because they lack the internal resources or expertise to create robust Internet solutions. Keeping pace with the dynamic marketplace, Internet banking vendors have evolved significantly over the past 18 months, and now offer a much broader array of products and services (see Figure 9-2).

While an overwhelming majority of the top banks in the United States offer Internet banking services to their customers (see Figure 9-3), small institutions are far less likely to be online. Less than a quarter of the banks with under $5 billion in assets currently offer Internet banking to their retail customers. Over the course of the next 2 years, we expect to see this change as an ever-increasing number of small banks and credit unions start to venture onto the Internet.

A number of ongoing trends are to be expected over the next 12 to 18 months. Banks will increasingly find themselves:

Supporting a larger number of electronic channels that extend beyond the Internet. These will include mobile telephones and personal digital assistants, as well as electronic devices that have not been seen outside of research labs.

Offering an ever-increasing range of transactions and financial products in a unified manner. Increasingly, consumers will expect to be able to access not only their checking and savings accounts, but also their mortgage, credit cards, personal loans, and brokerage services. Consumers will demand this functionality

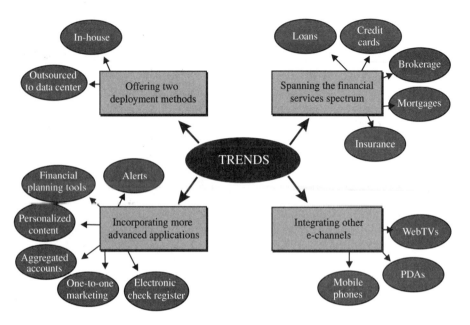

Source: Celent Communications

FIGURE 9-2

Trends in the Internet banking marketplace.

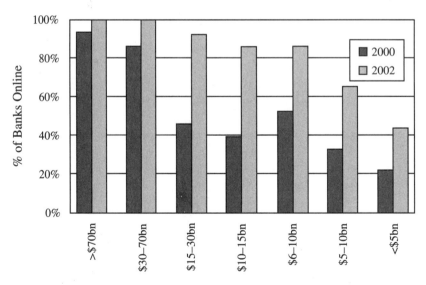

Assets of Banks

Source: Celent Communications

FIGURE 9-3

Penetration of financial institutions offering Internet banking.

through a single user name and password, and will expect to experience a uniform look and feel.

Engaging in one-to-one marketing activities. So far most banks have not been able to capitalize on the supposed benefits offered by the Internet. Lower transaction costs have been a seductive argument to bankers, but have proved to be elusive. Banks eager to use the Internet not only as a defensive mechanism, but as a proactive tool to gain more business, will turn to one-to-one marketing systems designed to actively sell new products to their clients.

Being forced to provide multifinancial institution reporting capabilities. A new breed of financial information aggregator that accesses a consumer's accounts at multiple financial institutions is appearing. A consumer is now able to sign up with an aggregator who then can, for example, collect information from the consumer's brokerage accounts at Merrill Lynch and Fidelity, bank accounts at Citibank, and life insurance policies at Met Life. All this information is then presented to the consumer at the aggregator's Website.

Expanding Internet offerings for consumers will be a requirement for financial institutions planning to remain competitive. Firms not engaging in the race will have consequences of a missed opportunity. Smaller institutions will venture online, following the early adopters.

WHOLESALE INTERNET BANKING

Drivers for the Industry

An explosion in the corporate Internet banking space is expected this year. With Y2K and the euro conversion behind them, banks have extra resources to deploy and money to invest. By the end of 2000, we expect that 25 percent of leading financial institutions worldwide will offer cash management and other corporate services via the Internet. That number is expected to climb to 50 percent by 2003. North America will lead the frenzy to adopt Internet solutions followed by Asia-Pacific (see Figure 9-4). European institutions will not embrace the Internet as quickly in the near term, as many have recently just finished implementing Windows-based systems.

Worldwide, financial institutions and their corporate clients have invested significantly in Windows-based technology in the past several years. While it is unlikely that these solutions or their DOS predecessors will disappear soon, the move toward browser-based corporate banking is inevitable. The added convenience and potential cost savings for both parties assure this trend.

Business Strategies and Trends

Solution providers have broadened their offerings, moving from basic cash management services to incorporating a wider array of corporate services as well as a

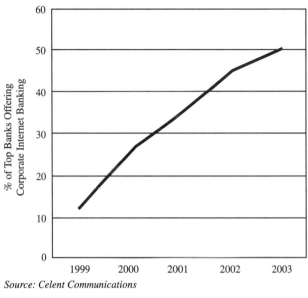

Source: Celent Communications

FIGURE 9-4

Penetration of corporate Internet banking at leading financial institutions.

new vision to help financial institutions and their corporate customers compete on the Internet. Table 9-2 lists the vendors of corporate Internet banking technologies. Vendors no longer are focusing on a single niche, but rather are concentrating their energies on providing a variety of services that can be integrated in a single delivery platform (see Figure 9-5).

Recently, there has been a trend toward delivering the vast array of corporate services via a single access point. Financial institutions and corporate clients alike see the advantage of maintaining a single Web-based system to handle financial services needs. Both sides will continue to move away from relying on stand-alone applications that support only one function, each of which may use a different access method—DOS, Windows, Internet. A single Internet system, which supports cash management, securities, foreign exchange, trade finance, EDI, and other corporate financial services, will simplify business. No longer will financial institutions be burdened with distributing updated copies of software to their clients or overwhelmed with incoming calls requesting installation support. Clients will benefit from the freedom to use any computer with a browser to access financial information and the need to remember only a single user name and password rather than one set for each system.

Another trend in the industry is for vendors to offer two deployment methods—in house at the financial institution and outsourced to a data center. In the past, most providers licensed their solutions to the financial institutions, which

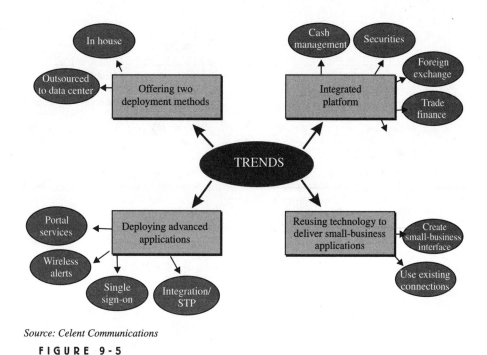

Source: Celent Communications

FIGURE 9-5

Trends in the corporate Internet banking marketplace.

maintained the application internally. A recent shift finds many vendors releasing an outsourced solution to meet the demands of financial institutions. Frequently, firms are anxious to deploy a browser-based system rapidly in order to capitalize on the early mover advantage. By first deploying the solution in the vendor's data center, firms are able to deploy quickly and to bring the solution in house when they have the appropriate resources in place to handle the migration. We do not anticipate that financial institutions that choose the outsourced mode primarily will use that method indefinitely. Rather, those firms will continually weigh the costs and make the decision most appropriate for their situation.

Leading vendors and financial institutions are also adding advanced applications to their systems:

Wireless alerts and notifications. Corporate treasurers may establish alerts, which will signal them on their mobile phones, PDAs, or pagers if a certain event occurs (e.g., the balance falls below a certain amount, an owned security moves dramatically up or down in the market, a wire needs approval, etc.). Currently, many of these types of notifications can be delivered via fax or e-mail. Going forward, clients will be able to take "action" via these channels. Mechanisms will be incorporated which allow treasurers to give their approval via their

TABLE 9-2

Vendors of Packaged Corporate Internet Banking Solutions

Technology Provider	Product	Technology	Number of live clients	Clients
Banklink	WebLink	Windows NT, Oracle	8	First United Bank & Trust
Bottomline Technologies	BankQuest	Sun Solaris, Windows NT, Oracle, MS SQL	5	State Street, Crédit Lyonnais, Standard Chartered
Brokat FS	Corporate Banking	Tandem, IBM AIX, Sun Solaris, Oracle	14	Huntington, Bank of Tokyo Mitsubishi NY, SunTrust, Union Bank of California
Credo Group	Fontis	Sun Solaris, Informix	6	United Bank of Egypt, Industrial Bank of Japan
Fundtech	WebACCESS, ACCESS.pro	IBM AIX, Oracle	8	Southtrust, First Security Bank, Frost National Bank, Republic National Bank
	Fundtech Banker for the Internet	Windows NT, MS SQL	15	N/A
Hamilton & Sullivan	H&S/Online Banking	Windows NT, MS SQL	4	N/A
Magnet Communications	iBank Suite	Windows NT	16	ABN Amro, Harris Bank, Manufacturer's Bank, Zions Bank, Bank of America, First Union
Politzer & Haney	Web Cash Manager	Windows NT, Oracle	46	Banco Popular, CoBank, Allfirst, Wells Fargo, Imperial Bank
S1	Corporate Suite	HP UX, Sun Solaris, IBM AIX	5	Firstar, CIBC, Fleet

Note: Not all clients are live. Some are in development, implementation, or testing.
Source: Celent Communications.

PDAs, and buttons will be included in e-mail notifications that enable clients to initiate a wire directly, for example. These advances will facilitate the process and streamline internal workflows.

Single sign-on. The ability to log on to the entire system is increasingly desired by corporate clients. Rather than maintaining numerous user names and passwords, clients will sign on once to the electronic banking solution and have access to all the company's financial needs that they are authorized to use. This can be accomplished by deploying the integrated Internet delivery platform discussed above and by deploying a separate front-end application that aggregates this information across product lines.

Integration and Straight-through processing. Tight integration between the company's electronic banking system and other back-office systems will bring numerous benefits to the client in the form of fewer errors, less time to process information, and cost savings. Many vendors are integrating the Internet solution with standard enterprise resource planning applications, workflow automation solutions, call center software, account reconciliation systems, etc., to enable straight-through processing at the corporate site.

Portal services. In order to add value to their financial services offering and to prevent disintermediation, financial institutions will begin to provide additional corporate services. They may deliver personalized content to the company's portal site or directly to the end user. This may consist of pertinent news, the company's updated stock portfolio profile, or other company-specific information, such as upcoming payroll information for the appropriate departments.

Another trend is for vendors and financial institutions to reuse their existing technology and connections to deliver customized solutions for small business customers. By rebundling core banking applications, re-creating user interfaces, and using existing links, firms are able to deliver valuable solutions to small business clients that meet their needs.

Future Trends

This is certain to be a dynamic year in the corporate banking space. Financial institutions will release Web-based cash management and corporate banking solutions in large numbers. While some will choose to develop the solution in house, the majority will look to vendor-provided products in order to implement the services in a shorter time frame. This high adoption rate will lead to browser-based cash management applications becoming commodities.

Vendors continue to improve their offerings to support a wide array of functions, and financial institutions continue to deploy these solutions with fervor, thus heating up the competitive environment. The successful financial institutions will provide additional services outside of the traditional cash management space (i.e., integrated trade finance, foreign exchange, and custody) as well as leading technologies that meet the specialized needs of their client base. Those advancements that should be on the radar screen include wireless alerts and notifications, single sign-on capabilities, integration and straight-through processing, and portal services. The largest financial institutions are especially well positioned to capitalize on the emerging business-to-business e-commerce marketplace.

Through their relationships with the largest corporate clients, the leading institutions have the opportunity to lead new initiatives (i.e., bill presentment, advanced payment mechanisms, procurement systems) to improve efficiency and save money.

INTERNET BROKERAGE
Drivers for the Industry

With the recent entrance of full-service brokerage firms, the competitive landscape of the online brokerage industry will undergo another dramatic transformation in the next 12 to 18 months. Larger brokerage firms with distinct brand names and a strong brick-and-mortar presence will triumph over the pure Internet players when mainstream investors—those Internet-novice investors seeking advice and guidance—finally join the online trading circles.

The last 3 years of phenomenal growth of the online brokerage industry was just the beginning. For the next 3 years, the online brokerage industry will continue its expansion unabated. Offering retail customers an online channel for trading has become a competitive requirement for brokerages, and may be a prerequisite for continued survival in the brokerage market. Consequently, brokerage firms of all sizes are scrambling to develop an online channel to their retail customers. Large banks with securities subsidiaries, as well, have begun to offer online brokerage as a component of their overall online financial services strategy. The window of opportunity for technology vendors is still wide open, however, as a significant percentage of firms have yet to roll out sophisticated transactional capability.

Most online brokerage solutions utilize a typical three-tier client-server architecture, with a Web server, an application server, and a database server, plus links to the back-office and market data servers. Vendors that offer turnkey online brokerage solutions provide a brokerage firm with all of the technological components necessary to give their retail customers the capability to trade securities via the Internet. Table 9-3 lists the vendors of Internet brokerage technologies.

Drawn in by decreasing transaction fees and increasingly sophisticated online research and financial planning tools, greater numbers of investors are signing up with online brokerage firms. The recent addition of full-service brokerage firms to the online brokerage market will further increase the total number of online investors. We expect to see an average annual growth rate of 46 percent over the next 3 years, with the number of online brokerage users expanding from 4.5 million in 1999 to 14 million by 2003 (see Figure 9-6).

Spending by financial institutions on brokerage technology will continue to increase throughout North America, Asia-Pacific, and Europe. We expect to see an overall annual growth rate of 10 percent through 2003, with spending increasing from approximately $825 million in 1998 to over $1200 million in 2001, reaching more than $1400 million by 2003. Spending in North America will increase from

TABLE 9-3

Vendors of Packaged Internet Brokerage Solutions

Technology Provider	Product	Technology	Number of live clients	Clients
AFS	Prospero	NT Sybase SQL Server	70	Wachovia Bank, PrimeVest, Stockwalk
digiTRADE	digiTRADE Retail Trading	Sun-Solaris Unify/Oracle	45	Citicorp Brokerage, First Union Brokerage, Bear Stearns, Quick and Reilly
Kingland	Financial Network System (FNS)	IBM AS/ 400e (core) NT (brochureware, auxiliary products) IBM DB2	40	Paine Webber CSC, Wit Capital
Reality Online	Reuters Electronic Broker	Any platform supporting Java2 standard Oracle	30	PaineWebber, Deutsche Bank Alex Brown, Instinet Retail, Wayne Hummer
S1	Consumer Investments	HP/UX Informix 9.2	1	Global financial services conglomerate
SunGard-EMS	BrokerWare	Solaris, AIX and SCO Oracle, ISAM, Ingress and proprietary	25	HSBC InvestDirect, the Montreal Exchange, Nesbitt Burns, Charles Schwab Canada and TD Waterhouse
TAHO	Online Retail Brokerage Integration Technology (ORBIT)	Windows NT, Solaris, AIX ObjectStore	1	U.S. clearing service provider
Vantra	Vantra Online Trading System (VOLTS)	Windows NT, Solaris Informix Unidata	50	American Express, Ernst & Co., Herzog, Heine, Geduld, Inc., Penson Financial Services

$375 million in 2000 to over $500 million in 2003. We expect to see spending in Europe rise from approximately $410 million in 1998 to $510 million by 2003. The real growth market, however, will be Asia-Pacific, where we expect to see an increase in brokerage technology spending from $190 million in 1998 to $450 million by 2003 (see Figure 9-7).

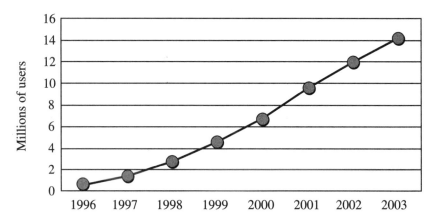

Source: Celent Communications

FIGURE 9-6

Projected annual growth of U.S. online brokerage users.

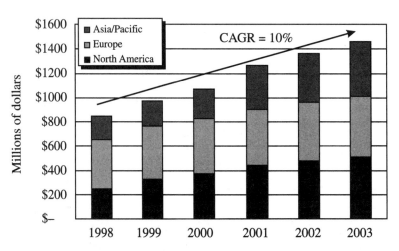

Source: Celent Communications

FIGURE 9-7

Projected FI Spending on online brokerage technology.

Business Strategies and Trends

As the number of online brokerages grows, the online brokerage market expands and becomes more mainstream, and technology improves, brokerage vendor offerings are becoming increasingly sophisticated (see Figure 9-8).

Range of Functionality

The range of functionality for retail investors is evolving from a simple trading interface that allows users to view their holdings to a more sophisticated interface including functionality such as:

Online account application and approval. Retail investors may apply for a brokerage account online and receive authorization to trade instantly.

Analytical tools. These interactive Web tools allow customers to perform sophisticated analysis of their holdings, such as benchmarking, risk measurement, and portfolio optimization. Tax lot tools and automatic cost basis calculation have also become standard parts of sophisticated vendor offerings. Additional value-added tools might allow investors to experiment with potential investment scenarios, through portfolio what-if calculations.

Financial alerts. Customers are able to set up electronic parameters to specify that alerts be sent to them when certain types of activity occur in the market. For

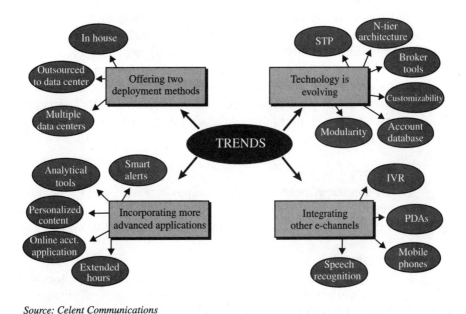

Source: Celent Communications

FIGURE 9-8

Trends in the Internet brokerage marketplace.

example, a customer may request that an e-mail be sent to him if the value of one of the securities he holds falls below a certain price, or if the price of a security the customer is interested in buying hits a specific threshold.

Improved content. Users are being provided with more significant research resources, as well as advanced market data such as free real-time quotes, streaming quotes, and Level 2 screen capability. Content has also become personalized, enabling customers to view certain types of data and information upon login, according to their personal preferences.

Extended hours trading. By partnering with firms such as MarketXT and REDIBook, online brokerage vendors are offering client firms the option to provide trading before and after market closing.

New Channels

At the same time that the range of functionality offered is increasing, the number of channels through which retail users can access their brokerage account is also expanding beyond simply Touch-Tone phones (IVR) and Web browsers. Advanced vendors are adding new channel access applications to support PDAs, mobile phones and other wireless devices, as well as natural language recognition trading engines.

Implementation Options

As the number and the type of clients change, the business strategy of successful vendors has to evolve so that they can service both small and large securities firms and banks. As a result, most vendors are positioning themselves as both a provider of high-end customized on-site applications and an application service provider (ASP), offering a cost-effective, full-featured, customizable service bureau solution that runs at the vendor's data center. The ASP trend reflects a new emphasis that extends beyond the application to include value-added services such as enhanced security, global connectivity, and guaranteed 24/7 uptime. Many vendors are also setting up multiple technology centers to ensure full redundancy and fail over capacity.

Technology

As the number of vendor implementations increases, and the number of retail customers using vendors systems also grows, scalability, operability, and reliability have become the key issues for brokerage technology solutions.

Architecture

Many vendors are transitioning from two- or three-tier architectures to n-tier distributed architectures that separate the specifics of the brokerage business from the specifics of the delivery channel. Separating the Web server, business logic, and data access facilitates moving information to and from the various resources involved, and provides for additional scalability and flexibility.

Customizability

Vendors are providing greater customizability of their solutions, moving away from "cookie cutter" customizations, which essentially replaced logos and buttons within a set template, to true branding. Most sophisticated solutions are set up with open APIs, as well, to allow for extensibility of the application, including a customized look and feel and integrating content.

Modularity

Vendors are providing increasingly "modular" solutions so that customers can pick and choose the functionality that they wish to provide.

Broker Tools

A year ago, only one or two vendors had developed Web-based modules for registered representatives to supplement their old desktops. Now, however, with the entrance of full-service brokerage firms into the online market, most vendors have expanded their online solutions to bring the registered representative into the online loop. Broker tools give brokers access to information from anywhere so that they are no longer tied to a 3270 terminal. Also, these tools can provide brokers and clients with the same view, which will increase the broker's ability to serve their clients.

Straight-Through Processing

Vendor solutions have improved in terms of their suitability checking and business rules. As a result, a greater percentage of orders are flowing automatically from the end user through the application to the back office. Greater implementation of straight-through processing (STP) is streamlining the business process, eliminating errors, and lowering the costs of each transaction.

Future Trends

We expect that the year 2001 will prove to be a year in which penetration of online brokerage continues to grow, but the vendor market consolidates. A number of ongoing trends will dominate the online brokerage space in the next 12 to 18 months. Over the course of the next 2 years, we expect to see a significant percentage of small firms establish an online presence. As full-service firms move online and existing discount firms position themselves to compete by offering advice-oriented functionality, we expect vendor solutions to show an increased emphasis on broker tools with expanded functionality, including interactive tools to allow brokers to provide better customer service. Vendor solutions will continue to support a larger number of electronic channels beyond the Internet, including mobile telephones and personal digital assistants. As uptime expectations and requirements increase, brokerage technology vendors that are unable to provide the minimum guaranteed uptime will be unable to remain competitive, leading to an increased vendor consolidation.

In the course of the next 3 years, we will see an explosion on Internet-related technologies in financial services. We expect the majority of brick-and-mortar companies to have an Internet presence in their area of expertise: retail banking, wholesale banking, or brokerage offerings. What started as a differentiator for financial institutions will be considered a common method to service customers. Internet banking technologies will continue to expand as the need for institutions to retain and expand relationships increases and online customers adopt these technologies. Financial institutions will be aggressive in their vendor selection as they find new strategies to remain at the leading edge.

CHAPTER 10

Online Banking

D. R. Grimes, CEO and Vice-Chairman
NetBank

NetBank was one of the world's first FDIC-insured federal savings banks to offer a full line of financial services through the Internet. Our mission, to profitably operate an Internet bank, has not changed since opening our virtual doors in 1996.

The founders of NetBank launched it with the belief that a bank could operate within a different business model—one that capitalized on the Internet as its principal delivery vehicle rather than expensive brick-and-mortar branches. Our banking experience indicated that by operating on the Internet, we could save over half of the non-interest expenses that a traditional bank incurs.

Our business model has also helped redefine an industry that had been practically unchanged for the past 10 decades. And for NetBank, our business model resulted in our being one of the fastest-growing banks in history and achieving our goal of profitability within a very short time.

Our strategy is focused and simple. Using the Internet as our service-delivery system, we offer customers in all 50 states convenience, higher interest income, and lower fees, along with personalized service. In doing so, we have the ability to attract deposits, which is obviously key to successful banking. This then allows us to invest accumulated deposits into earning assets at rates higher than the deposit yields.

One way of thinking about Internet banking is as an alternative banking model that uses the Internet for delivery services, but is not necessarily limited to the Internet. The whole point is that it is branchless banking, and it is a more efficient delivery system than the system associated with traditional banking.

For the last 100 years, banking has been a business where you went down to see the banker in a formal office. The bank had relatively small branches. In fact, branches have generally not grown in size in the last 50 years; they're smaller, and an increasing number staff only three or so employees. Those kinds of delivery systems are incredibly inefficient, because regardless of how much improvement you make in your ability to serve customers or how much technology you apply, there is no cost savings in a facility with only a few employees. The only way to get cost savings is to close the branches, which risks alienating your customers who are accustomed to visiting the branch. Fewer than 10 percent of the transactions in commercial banks are conducted in the branches, and it's been that way for at least 25 years. Yet branches are responsible for half the expenses in a bank. It's a fundamentally flawed system.

So traditional banks buy other banks and close the newly acquired bank's branch. That's the only cost savings they're getting, but they're not really bringing any cost savings out of their own organization.

REVENUES AND PROFITABILITY

We achieved profitability within 1 year of acquiring our bank charter and to date, have posted profits every quarter since. The significance of this achievement is twofold. First, we achieved this status within a very short period of time. Additionally, profitability is virtually unheard of in any e-commerce business, a trend we're pleased to say we're defying.

NetBank was always intended to be a profitable bank—an old-fashioned business, if you will. It was never our desire to prove that the technology works or to test a theory; these never entered the equation. Our goal was—and is—to be profitable.

One explanation for how we became profitable so quickly would be the efficiency of the Internet resulting in extremely low costs.

We have a lower cost for operations than traditional banks and yet we have this enormous potential market, reaching customers nationally and expatriates worldwide. The real challenge is growing as quickly as possible and managing this growth while running a profitable business. (See Figure 10-1.)

That's a key difference between NetBank (or the banking industry as a whole) and other companies that operate on the Internet; at least previously in other online business models, growth has been the only thing that seemed to matter. In some cases, the more customers acquired, the more money the company lost. Nobody seemed to be concerned about whether there was a profit or not, but things are changing now. A business is really not a business without a profit motive. And it's easier to make more money on every customer and add customers than it is to grow rapidly and then figure out how to make money, which is what some of these businesses do.

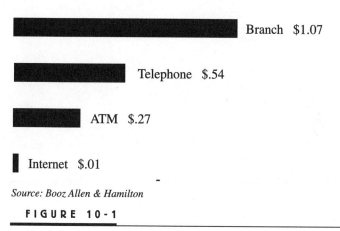

Branch $1.07

Telephone $.54

ATM $.27

Internet $.01

Source: Booz Allen & Hamilton

F I G U R E   1 0 - 1

Average cost per transaction by type.

Banking and financial services, however, have a huge advantage. The Internet applies across a much bigger piece of our total operations with digital fulfillment. Traditional companies have moved order taking to the Internet, but they haven't moved the operation to the Internet. You can order a book or a computer from the Internet, but you still have to warehouse and mail the book, or build and ship the computer once it's ordered. The biggest thing that we send in the mail is a free box of checks to the customer. We don't have inventory, warehouse, and distribution issues. The financial services industry remains very well positioned to grow on the Internet compared with businesses in general.

Our revenue levels are primarily dependent on interest margin because we are still at the stage where we are growing our deposit base rapidly. These margins are similar for us and for traditional thrifts. These revenues, combined with our lower expenses, have resulted in our achieving a profitable operation. (See Figure 10-2.)

In a sense, we are more like a bank or thrift from 25 or 30 years ago when deposit dollars were entering the banking system, not coming out like they have been for the last 20 years. I believe there are less funds invested in banking institutions today in large part because Fidelity Investments, as well as others, "demystified" mutual funds, making them available to the masses. People liked the idea of investing a relatively small amount of money and gaining ownership in a lot of companies; however, they didn't know how to withdraw their money from a mutual fund. It wasn't like withdrawing funds from a bank. So Fidelity used telephone systems to allow customers to transfer money between different funds and request withdrawals, generally making it easier for people to invest in mutual funds. That started a revolution in the whole brokerage and investment community. Contributing to this trend was Charles Schwab & Co., which offered significantly lower commissions with less personal contact. So instead of going to a brokerage

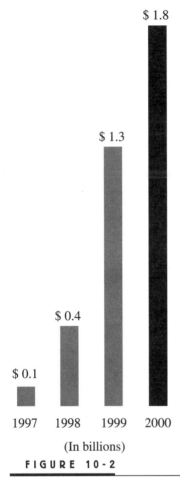

(In billions)

FIGURE 10-2

Growth in total assets.

firm and meeting with a broker, you researched stocks on your own, called in your investment, and mailed your check. For this less personalized service, a commission of less than $100 per trade was paid as opposed to several hundred per trade.

With these advances, people started to understand that they weren't limited to keeping their money in a no-interest checking account. They started investing in mutual funds, going to brokerage firms, and moving funds to cash management accounts. So the actual share of customers' deposit dollars that banks have is incredibly small today versus what it was 20 years ago. It's amazing how much erosion there has been.

NetBank is a throwback to the era when banks were actually growing deposits, and one reason for this is that, thanks to the Internet, our marketplace knows no geographic boundaries. As a result, we've been able to achieve some incredible growth numbers that no brick-and-mortar bank has ever come close to obtaining. (See Figure 10-3.)

CUSTOMERS

The bottom line is it's our customers who are making NetBank one the fastest-growing banks in the history of commerce. We have always shared with our customers the profits of Internet banking. For example, our checking account has no fees, offers unlimited check writing and free online bill-pay services, and requires no minimum balances to earn the stated interest rate, which is up to three times higher than the national average. There are no fine print or "teaser" rates. (See Figure 10-4.) Additionally, our customers are assured privacy, security, and insurance from the FDIC.

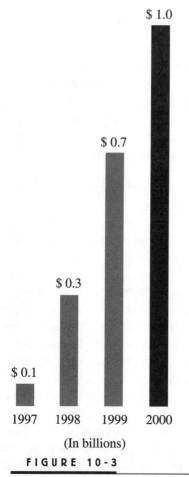

FIGURE 10-3

Growth in deposits.

Annual Percentage Yield (APY)

NetBank	3.05
National Average	.94

Monthly Service Charge

NetBank	$0
National Average	$9.59

Source: Bankrate.com, February 2001

FIGURE 10-4

NetBank's NetValue Checking vs. the competition.

There's also a market for those who embrace the concept of conducting their own transactions online and taking control of their banking experience.

We are proactive in seeking new products and services to empower customers to take as much control as possible. For example, we have a virtual safe deposit box for the secure online storage of valuable and confidential electronic documents. This unique product is just another innovative contribution to our full range of online financial and banking services.

Other customers are drawn to the convenience. For customers of traditional brick-and-mortar banks, it makes sense to pay bills online and bank online even if they're not earning a high deposit interest rate or paying low or no service charges because it's better than driving to the bank and standing in the teller line. Why would anyone do that for mundane transactions?

What we have learned is that we are attracting the top tier of Internet customers as NetBank customers, people who are comfortable with technology, who use the Internet for their other activities, and who tend to have higher average balances than typical bank customers. The typical NetBank checking and money market account customer is 37 to 41 years old and is a home owner. We find that our customers are primarily mobile professionals who are attractive long-term customers since they tend to be loyal. Based on our 4 years of experience, customers seem to be about 5 times less likely to move their checking account away from NetBank than from a traditional bank.

Our goal is to attract new customers to the convenience of banking online and to retain them. A brick-and-mortar bank with existing customers has two choices. It can try to provide existing customers with additional capabilities, such as Internet access, or it can try to attract new customers. But it has some difficulties with both. Since a traditional bank already has the expensive infrastructure of the branch system, its Internet activities are an additional expense—plus it is cannibalizing its own customer base. It must spend extra money in providing Internet access for its own customers. The customers who were in a branch yesterday are on the Internet today, and both of these delivery vehicles cost money. Until a traditional bank can offload a significant portion of its branch system operations, both options have disadvantages for a brick-and-mortar bank, and the bank has a challenge. It's not NetBank's challenge. In fact NetBank has been recognized in the industry for its outstanding value and customer service by Money.com, Gomez Advisors, *Smart Money*, *Worth* magazine, and *Upside Today*. (See Figure 10-5.)

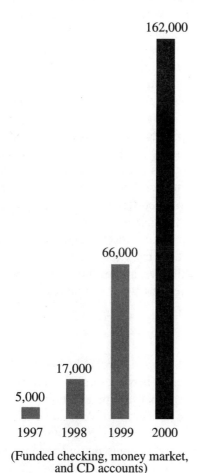

162,000

66,000

17,000

5,000

1997   1998   1999   2000

(Funded checking, money market,
     and CD accounts)

FIGURE   10-5

Account growth.

PRODUCTS AND SERVICES

Because we understand the value of the long-term customer relationship, we have focused our product development on those services that are appealing to the profile of customers we are drawing to our bank. For example, home equity products and mortgages are more attractive lending possibilities for us because of the demographics of our customers. While we offer a complete line of traditional banking services, we are constantly looking for services that go beyond what is expected so that our customers can continue to trust that we are a leader in technology.

It's critical that we implement cutting-edge technology to keep up with the demands and desires of our customers in terms of the products and services we offer. Whatever technology is available—wireless access, consolidated statements, plus whatever the future brings—our customers want and will have. We're adamant about providing our customers with the power to control their personal finances; we have to be in order to be competitive.

The other thing we have learned about our customers is that they like to have a sense of control over their financial affairs; that's why they're banking with NetBank, having left the world of traditional "banker's hours." Because of that, we offer robust self-service tools to allow them to manage their NetBank account from the beginning.

For example, once an online application is submitted, the applicant has the opportunity to log on to our site, check the status of the new account, and obtain instructions on banking with NetBank. As soon as the account is approved, the customer can consolidate their accounts at other institutions to be viewed alongside their NetBank accounts, then transfer funds into their NetBank account. When the supply of checks runs low, the customer can reorder them online. Our customers execute their own transfers online, receive and pay bills online, track their bill-pay history online, and view their canceled checks online. They welcome taking control of their finances, while we appreciate using the power of the Internet rather than human resources to satisfy our customers. (See Figure 10-6.)

MARKETING AND BRANDING

Can you spend $200 million and build a brand? Probably. But that may be inconsistent with running a profitable business. There are two economic drivers in terms of our branding: (1) significantly lower expenses operating on the Internet and (2) a significantly larger market that you can reach with your advertising dollars. The result on the marketing side is that we were able to get customers in all 50 states and grow at an incredible pace—accomplishments that were achieved as a result of sharing the cost advantage with our customers.

Our account acquisition costs are relatively low at $108 per customer as of the fourth quarter of 2000. Although we believe our acquisition costs per account

January	• NetBank account access through Yahoo! • Online safe deposit boxes
February	• Individual retirement accounts
March	• Online tax center, powered by H&R Block • NetBank eCare
April	• 24/7 customer support
May	• Online chat
June	• Upgraded online bill pay system • Online bill presentment
July	• Insurance products through Insurance.com
August	• NetBank checking accounts included on Ameritrade application • Instant funding for new NetBank checking or money market acounts • OFX support of Quicken
September	• Wireless account services
October	• Brokerage services through AmeriVest, an Ameritrade subsidiary • OFX support of Microsoft Money
November	• Membership in MAC ATM network • Online check images
December	• Online mortgage application with 10-minute approvals • Redesigned public Website • Account consolidation

FIGURE 10-6

Products and services introduced in 2000.

will increase over the next few years, the acquisition costs per dollar of deposits are still considerably less than those of traditional banks. (See Figure 10-7.)

The two disadvantages that we had being an Internet bank with no branches is that we had no physical presence and no existing customer base to draw from. As a result, we embarked on a challenge that's in essence foreign to the banking industry, which is marketing directly to consumers. We tried lots of different things, but consistently we found that Internet advertising in a variety of Web venues is best. We have complemented this with print advertising, radio, direct mail, direct e-mail, etc. So if you go back and look at what our marketing budget has

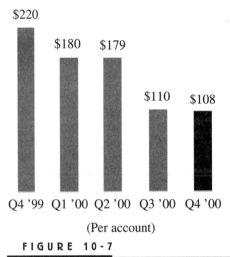

(Per account)

FIGURE 10-7

Account acquisition costs.

been as a percentage of our total expenses, it's always been very high compared with what it would be for a traditional bank.

It's not uncommon for management of traditional banks to be enthusiastic about doing business on the Internet, but they lack the expertise in marketing on the Web. It will take a change in the mindset of traditional bankers to think nationally or globally, plus there are different strategies involved in online advertising than in advertising elsewhere.

While Internet marketing has been very efficient for us, it has only been so because we have been very careful about measuring the results of that marketing. The Internet changes rapidly, and people change their Websites daily. Sometimes, those changes cause ads to be placed where they don't get the same traffic as before, or they may not appeal to the prospective customers as they did before. Essentially this means that for banner advertising, more than for any other form of marketing, you have to really stay on top of measuring results. If the results aren't there, we adjust immediately.

We have formed alliances with companies whose customers' profiles are similar to ours and who use the Internet to manage their finances. These affinity alliances have been mutually beneficial for our partners as well as for us. For example, our alliance with Ameritrade offers reciprocal services to customers of both companies. We offer banking services to their more than one million brokerage customers. And Ameritrade Holding Corporation, through its AmeriVest subsidiary, offers brokerage services to our expanding customer base. Such targeted approaches are proving to be a very successful marketing approach.

We have made an investment in brand advertising as well (although most of our marketing dollars have been spent more in an account acquisitions mode).

We've also been aggressive in public relations compared with most banks. Marketing, public relations, and investor relations together generated much attention, which led to growth, which earned us more attention. It has been an effective combination in building our brand.

Successful marketing seemed to make the difference in the phenomenal growth NetBank has experienced. Another bank with a similar model started about 18 months before we did, and we both paid almost the same rate on every account. Yet we dominated in terms of growth. Even with the other bank's significant head start, we had grown past that bank within a year, and we attribute that to our incredible success in marketing on the Internet.

While there is no doubt that you can build a brand simply by spending sufficient money to advertise it prominently, it is difficult to build a brand while you are running a profitable business.

COMPETITION

We believe the formula of customer convenience, a broad array of financial products and services, and low overhead gives us a competitive advantage over traditional brick-and-mortar banks. Plus since we have always been a pure Internet bank, we are more flexible and can change more quickly than the "click-and-brick" banks.

In order for our competitors to attract new customers, they have to give up focusing on serving a limited geographic area and be willing to do business in areas that are completely different from their home territory. They no longer can think about their primary delivery vehicle being a branch and drawing their customers from the relatively limited geographic area around that branch. Now they have to think about delivering services to people wherever they may be, whether it is while they are home or traveling. Customers want consistent services across the entire United States, if not around the world. And that is a difficult challenge for people who have always thought in very limited geographic terms.

Because of the explosion of the Internet, we face competition not only from brick-and-mortar banks, but from other financial services companies as well. In a sense, every company that is seeking to gain some share of a customer's assets is our competition. This could be a bank promoting a checking account or a stockbroker asking the customer to put the money in investments or a mutual fund. There is a tremendous amount of competition for that consumer's dollar. We are always sensitive to this.

However, banking remains a significant and serious part of everybody's overall financial portfolio. So we are going to continue to strive to be very competitive in the basic banking services, and we have found that people are responsive to that.

A company designed as an Internet company from the beginning can plan to offer products and services on a national basis. To a large extent, that ability to have customers distributed nationally helps insulate us from economic conditions that exist from time to time within one particular region. The big issue here is a mindset issue; it's a way of thinking, and it's a different way of thinking from what was successful in the past.

BUSINESS STRATEGIES

What will happen to the brick-and-mortar branches is more of the same thing that has happened to them in the last 20 years. When the brokerage companies began to take money out of the banking system by making it easy to invest in mutual funds, deposits began leaving the banking system. Since deposits weren't growing, loans were limited, resulting in their interest spread being fixed. Banks growing at 3 to 5 percent per year of internally generated growth don't fuel enough earnings increase to justify their stock value. One option was to grow by buying other banks, and it's likely we'll continue to see this trend of consolidation.

Other banks reacted by charging customers more and higher fees to conduct the same services they had always provided. Fee income, as a percentage of total bank income, has risen significantly in the last 20 years, and this trend will probably continue. Banks will charge higher ATM transaction fees, higher prices to conduct cash deposits—and so the more efficient transactions will leave the branches and go to the Internet and to electronic forms. For the services that remain—which will primarily be for that segment of the market that is unwilling to embrace technology or wants private banking services, trust services, or other specialized services—banks will be forced to charge higher and higher fees in order to continue their existence. Even today, you see some banks charging a customer to walk in and see a teller.

What does the future hold for brick-and-mortar banks? Most likely, they will become more specialized. Some banks will be very successful at supplying those high-end services. As people become more comfortable using technology and more demanding in getting a fair value for the services that they require, the survivors will be those that successfully market specialized, high-end services. Probably, checking accounts, bill payments, auto loans, savings accounts, home equity products, etc., will leave the branch system. A branch system is unnecessary to support these products. What remains will be a limited number of very complex, very expensive transactions.

Two issues will need to be addressed in the Internet banking industry. One is that we need to see more growth and more support for Internet banking. Competition for the customers' deposits is everywhere, including nonbanks that are opening banking companies and taking money out of the banking system, which is a detriment to the banking industry.

Most of the largest banks in the world today are not American, which wasn't true 20 years ago. These banks would love to have a large presence in the United

States, but without the Internet, it's very expensive to build that presence because they would have to build branches and offices, which are huge capital expenses. But with the power of the Internet, they theoretically could come into the United States and develop a significant presence.

There are nonbanks that want to enter into the banking services arena. Retailers are applying for banking charters; Sears is operating a credit card business. Insurance companies and others that haven't had banking capabilities before can look at the Internet and see ways to introduce those. So as an industry, we need to continue to promote and encourage the evolution of Internet banking in order to maintain our position as a leader in financial services. Banks are still trusted by people because the industry is so highly regulated and deposit accounts are insured. Our competitive advantage is that people will have more confidence in putting their banking dollars in a bank. As an industry, we need to take advantage of that now. We have to be aggressive about pursuing new customers and deposits. That's one challenge.

The other challenge is that the regulatory system that makes banking so strong is, just like all regulatory systems, very slow to change. Yet technology is moving ahead very rapidly, and a lot of the regulations and issues need to be reworked in order to totally support a banking model with a small number of physical offices and many customers in a broad geographic area.

The Internet bank is a challenge for the regulators. There is no argument that regulations are needed, and components such as community reinvestment are important. However, the laws and regulations must be updated to reflect the realities of the new banking industry.

TECHNOLOGY

First, we live in an era of incredibly rapid technological advancement. And yet of all the businesses that operate on the Internet today, the one that demands the highest level of security, privacy, and accuracy is the banking industry.

Most people come to the Internet initially to exchange e-mail, conduct research, shop for travel deals, etc. Then there are those who are slightly more involved in the Internet—those who are likely to buy a book or CD online. This level of involvement carries with it a comfort zone. After all, when you buy a book or CD online, you know exactly what you are getting; it's tangible. And it is not a significant investment, so even if something does go wrong, your credit card company will ensure you don't incur a loss. This is as far as some people have ventured on the Internet.

More adventuresome people will begin to invest online, which is very interesting because an individual now has the ability to see all the same research and information that professionals have had exclusive access to in the past. If you have enough time, you're able to study all the possibilities and make your decision, not unlike an individual's ability to research airfares and schedules, which only travel agents could do a few years ago.

But investing has one other characteristic that's really important. Most people view investment dollars as having some element of risk associated with them to start with. People are hoping the investment will rise in value, but it may not. Certainly most people are not willing to invest dollars that they must have in order to take care of their daily needs and life's requirements.

This is why banking is probably the last thing people do in terms of their evolution to conducting e-commerce on the Internet. Depositing a paycheck, paying the mortgage, etc., are serious issues, and people expect to incur minimal, if any, risk associated with such matters. Online transactions must be safe and predictable, and must be accompanied by the documentation that customers are accustomed to; otherwise, they are not willing to bank online.

Our industry operates in sharp contrast to other Internet industries. One major e-commerce company approached the Y2K event by announcing it would shut down for the long weekend. Banks can't simply not transact for a few days at a time.

In fact, the financial services industry—that is, banking, brokerages credit cards, lending, and so forth—did a lot of work in preparation for Y2K. As an industry, we should get an A+ for our performance during the transition to Y2K. There were no issues of any significance whatsoever. The reason for that is that we invested a tremendous amount of money and effort in testing and retesting and making absolutely sure that our customers had nothing to worry about. This is in great contrast to some of the Internet companies that shut down for the long weekend. We, as an industry, applied technology to prevent an event from being a problem.

There are lots of great new technologies directly affecting our industry that are amazing. Not only can individuals at home be connected to businesses, but businesses can be connected to other businesses. For example, items can be delivered over the Internet that used to have to be delivered physically, such as bills.

Basically, bill presentment over the Internet can be thought of as a technological solution replacing an important service provided by the U.S. Postal Service. With Internet bill presentment, companies such as credit card and gasoline companies process transactions and bill customers that live all over the country. Electronic bill presentment requires that a bill be delivered to a customer's address although it's an electronic address instead of a street address and Zip Code. But it's the same concept; the customer can be anywhere in the world. The idea that you can process and deliver a bill in a matter of minutes or seconds or hours electronically, and that a customer can see it, pay it, and store it electronically, is incredible.

In the early days of online bill paying, customers needed to enter account numbers, dates, and figures, all with a phone. Additionally, programs had to be written by the businesses and numbers translated: papers were still being prepared, shuffled, and stuffed. [Until the Internet (really NetBank), all bill payment systems were proprietary.] To pay a bill using one bank, the customer needed to use a certain phone number, but to pay using another bank, the customer had to dial another number. Then PCs were invented, allowing bill payment by typing on a keyboard or selecting something from a drop-down list.

Although the Internet has now solved the connectivity problem and the feedback problem, we still have the paper shuffling and filing issue. With electronic bill presentment, we can resolve that issue, too. Today, you can receive your bill electronically, pay it electronically, and file your bill electronically. You can still get paper, but you don't have to depend on it. That kind of technology, in many ways, is an example of the kind of things that the Internet is bringing to banking.

The Internet, which made universal connectivity possible, was a very important advance. In time, the Internet will be recognized as being more significant than the industrial revolution—perhaps even in our lifetime. Certainly, this era of the 1990s and early 2000s will be recognized as being one in which the most significant advancements in the history of humanity have taken place, at least in terms of conducting business and providing information, sharing information, and acting on that information.

The same research tools that people use to look for travel and information about medicine, etc., can also be applied to letting customers understand what's going on with their bank account. What's the status of a transaction that they have executed? One of the things that we spend a lot of money on is building capabilities into our offering that will allow customers to do their own customer service so that not only can they execute transactions themselves, but they can research those transactions when they have a question about them. That whole area is extremely interesting. It's not technology in the sense of hardware or programs, but it is a great example of using technology as a tool. These are important capabilities to give our customers, because people want to be in control of what affects them. They'd rather do that by logging on to the Internet than calling a person, plus they don't have to wait.

The companies that will be really successful on the Internet are those that do a good job of servicing on the Internet in addition to selling on the Internet. People will not only appreciate it; they will demand it. For example, Federal Express makes it easier and more convenient to track a package online than to call its toll-free number for the same information, which is easier still than talking to a person about it.

Some people believe that the first 25 years or so of the computer era were not necessarily years that contributed to greater productivity, but everyone seems to agree that the last decade has been enormously positive for productivity. The reason the economy is and has been doing so well is largely because of the Internet as a service delivery vehicle and the continued growth of information-related service businesses. Allowing people to take control to do their own research, transactions, and business on their own schedule in their own home is one of the major benefits of that.

As an Internet bank, we have to somehow walk a fine line between embracing this level of technological change and continuing to ensure security and confidence on behalf of our customers. While we're being asked to do bigger, better, faster, newer functions, we have to be extremely careful of the changes we implement because we're dealing with people's money. After all, when a person deposits a paycheck with you and asks you to pay the person's mortgage, that person is entrusting you with very serious matters in his or her life, and it must be done correctly. A dilemma we have is balancing the change of technology with the security and reliability that is required in banking; it's a balance not necessarily required in other industries.

THE FUTURE

Today, we're able to offer nearly all of the core transaction services over the Internet. We're also moving to offer other information services and products over the Internet as well as via a wireless system. We truly are going to solve the problem of consolidated financial reporting. This has been an issue in the banking industry for 30 years; it's been impossible to get a consolidated statement. But the Internet is finally making that available after all this time.

In keeping with this, the biggest change in products over the next 3 years will probably be the delivery of services that were once thought to be impossible to deliver over the Internet. Bandwidth on the Internet is increasing, better compression technologies are being developed, and the ability to deliver video and audio supplemented with live people, in both an audio and video sense, is being realized. We'll be able to deliver services with Internet banking such as private banking, trust services, and investment management. We're executing the basic banking functions today, but in the future we can provide the personalized services as well.

Pioneering this new banking business model—capitalizing on the Internet as a principal delivery vehicle system as opposed to brick-and-mortar banks—has been incredibly exciting. But as amazing as it's all been during the past few years, what's truly exhilarating is that there is much more to come. It's an exciting time for the financial services industry and for commerce as a whole, as the playing field has been dramatically changed thanks to the Internet.

CHAPTER 11

Internet-Based Bill Payment and Presentment

Gerhard Kschwendt, Senior Consultant
Dove Consulting

This chapter covers the emerging trends in electronic bill payment and presentment (EBPP) from the perspective of the two dominant markets today: business to consumer (B2C) and business to business (B2B).

EBPP is the electronic presentation of recurring bills, sent by billers to customers, and the corresponding payment for the goods and services. Electronic bills (e-bills) may or may not include advertising, disclosures, and regulatory information. While we often think of EBPP as a homogeneous topic, the B2C and B2B markets are in very different stages of maturity—both in terms of solutions offered and market acceptance of EBPP offerings and in their investment paths.

The B2C market, which is covered first in this overview, is an extension of the electronic bill payment business founded in the mid-1980s by CheckFree and other providers. While bill payment has grown significantly in the market, it is still dogged by infrastructure and acceptance hurdles resulting in high user fees, paper-based payments, and customer service errors. Early on, it was identified that the way to reduce errors and increase electronic payments was to submit bills electronically to the customer—hence, the industry's motivation for EBPP and the development of B2C EBPP that is largely based on the bill payment foundation. However, this approach is in the process of changing, as indicated by the emergence of consumer lockbox providers such as PayTrust and CyberBills, both of which are developing businesses based on consumer requirements for bill management and the future vision of an Internet-based payments system.

B2B EBPP has only recently begun to garner the attention of the market. B2B EBPP is not only about paying a bill—it is essentially a part of a high-volume trade document management process. Over the years, a number of technologies have been brought to bear to reduce the paper dependency of the U.S. payments industry, of which EDI is the most recent and obvious example. While a number of industries have made EDI a requirement for trade, it has largely underachieved in the market because of the costly network dependencies, complexity of the protocol, and steep implementation costs. What makes EBPP different is the ever-increasing pressure on U.S. businesses for business process efficiency coupled with Internet standards such as IFX and XML that standardize the exchange of information over cost-effective, open networks using common payments infrastructure.

It is logical to assume that the B2C and B2B EBPP markets and infrastructures will eventually merge based on the most efficient, most widely used infrastructure. We believe that the common EBPP infrastructure will revolve around standard Internet interfacing protocols for both bills and payments. What is unclear to us today is when this will happen, how it will happen, and who will emerge as the dominant players.

One thing is for certain—this is a high-risk high-opportunity market. Current market leaders have a distinct advantage based on infrastructure and market inefficiencies. The widespread adoption of EBPP will fuel new solutions that will inherently challenge leading infrastructure, payment, and consumer providers. The stakes for success are equally huge. Benefits resulting from more efficient billing processes and improved customer relationship management have the potential to reach hundreds of billions of dollars. Lehman Brothers, for instance, estimates potential savings from EBPP at $150 billion to $200 billion annually.[1]

BUSINESS TO CONSUMER EBPP

INTRODUCTION

EBPP adoption in the business-to-consumer market has the potential to generate significant benefits to both businesses and consumers, driven primarily by the large number of bills produced each year. Dove analysis suggests that the market for recurring payments is over 17 billion consumer-to-business transactions per year. Recurring payments include monthly utility, phone, and cable payments as well as membership fees and rental payments. Transactions are expected to grow at 6 percent each year. Key growth drivers include the overall growth of the U.S. population, accompanied by a big increase in the number of outstanding credit cards as well as a growing number of communication and entertainment accounts such as cell phones, pagers, Internet services, and cable TV subscriptions.

EBPP offers seemingly clear cost and productivity advantages to companies that implement it. The promise of eliminating the need to print, stuff, and mail

---

[1] *The Electronic Bill Presentment and Payment Handbook*, Mar. 14, 2000.

paper bills and statements, coupled with the potential transformation of payment processing, is leading many companies to investigate this option now that Y2K spending freezes are being lifted. Moreover, EBPP offers additional advantages that are harder to quantify, but provide even more potential such as more efficient customer service and the ability to target marketing offers more accurately, which can lead to greater customer retention rates and new revenue streams. EBPP has the potential to save billers and their customers tens of billions of dollars each year.[2] The savings could be even higher if we add nonrecurring bills, account statements, and transaction reports to the mix.

In the next 2 to 4 years, e-bill availability will increase significantly as major billers integrate electronic billing into their existing systems. By 2003, we expect 50 percent of consumer bills to be available for electronic presentment—up from 10 percent at the end of 2000. During the same time frame, the actual share of bills presented and paid electronically is expected to increase to 5 percent—up from the insignificant levels today (Table 11-1).

Consumer adoption of EBPP is currently hampered by lack of electronic bill availability and a poor overall value proposition to the customer. We predict that the consumer value proposition will be addressed by both billers and financial services providers eager to use EBPP as a lever for revenue growth. The future of B2C EBPP is driven by the relevance of electronic billing to customer relationship management on the biller's side and personal finance management on the consumer's side. Progressive and emerging EBPP infrastructure providers view this channel not as a transactional service requirement, but rather as a strategic anchor channel in developing customer service offerings across investments, banking, and insurance. Table 11-1 lists several characteristics of the B2C EBPP market and changes, which we are expecting to occur over the next couple of years.

LOW ADOPTION RATES

Internet-based bill payment and presentment has been widely characterized as the "killer application" of electronic retail banking. Industry insiders have predicted, for some time now, an explosive adoption by both businesses and households, but reality has lagged expectations. By the end of 2000, fewer than 10 percent of all consumer bills were available for EBPP, and less than 0.1 percent of all consumer bills were viewed and paid online.[3]

As Figure 11-1 indicates, it is important to distinguish between EBPP and online banking. EBPP is essentially a subset of online banking, which includes PC banking with dial-up access and Web banking. While we consider EBPP a critical

---

[2] Estimates based on cost savings of $1.00–$1.50 per consumer invoice.

[3] Dove estimates.

TABLE 11-1

Expected Developments in the EBPP Retail Environment

	2000		2003
Biller adoption	10% of bills	→	50% of bills
Customer adoption	Less than 0.1% of bills	→	5% of bills
Consumer value proposition	Stand-alone EBPP Add-on product to online banking	→	Fully integrated into online banking, or core feature of a new personal finance management product
Key issues	Consumers can't get all bills in one place Proliferation of intermediaries CheckFree is leading EBPP player	→	Business model becomes more efficient CheckFree will continue to be the leading player, but alternatives will emerge
Key functions	BSP/CSP/processors	→	Functions remain the same, but will be more integrated New players enter the field with more sophisticated and cost-efficient service offerings
Biller solution	In house	→	Outsourced
Role of banks	Banks host EBPP Banks outsource billing functions; billing is not a core competency	→	Billing function becomes highly relevant, but banks will continue to outsource
Where to invest	EBPP/billing software	→	System integrators

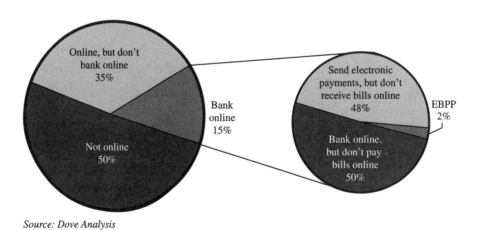

Source: Dove Analysis

FIGURE 11-1

EBPP adoption by U.S. households.

component of online banking, most banks offer online banking only with an electronic payment feature, but without e-bill presentment capability.

B2C EBPP BUSINESS MODEL

EBPP relies on a number of technology providers to produce an electronic invoice from the biller's legacy accounting system, present the bill on the customer's Website of choice, and finally route the payment from the consumer's bank account back to the biller's account (Figure 11-2 and Table 11-2).

Key infrastructure providers include bill service providers (BSPs), bill consolidators, and consumer service providers (CSPs). CSPs offer EBPP services to consumers, which include the presentment of e-bills and the ability for consumers to initiate electronic payments. Examples of CSPs include banks, brokerages, and portals such as Yahoo, AOL, Quicken, and MSN. Bill consolidators fulfill two fundamental functions: They collect e-bills from multiple billers and send them to the appropriate CSPs for presentment, but they also route consumer payments and remittance information to the biller and the biller's bank. BSPs help billers convert billing data to electronic documents, which will then be forwarded to bill consolidators or CSP sites for presentment to consumers.

Biller   BSP   Consolidator   CSP   Consumer

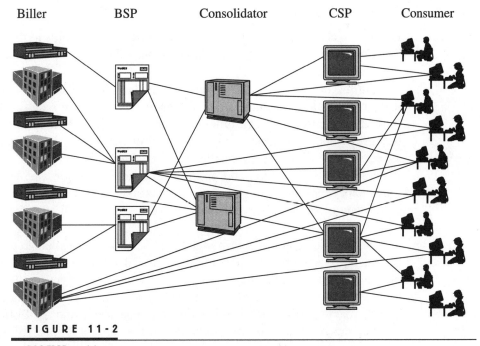

FIGURE 11-2

B2C EBPP model.

TABLE 11-2

Roles of BSPs, Consolidators, and CSPs

Type	Function/Role	Providers
Bill service providers	Convert billing data to electronic bills (e-bills), either from a billing system print stream or directly from the billing system	CheckFree edocs Avolent Pitney Bowes Princeton eCom
	Additional services include bill formatting, hosting of biller Websites and routing of consumer payments and remittance processing	
	BSP solutions come in two flavors. Billers can buy software from BSP vendors and implement the solution in house, or they can outsource all BSP functions	
Bill consolidators	Aggregate electronic bills, and route them directly to consumers or portals	CheckFree CyberBills PayTrust
	Aggregators also handle consumer payments and remittance processing	
Consumer service providers	Present electronic bills to consumers	Banks/Brokerages Portals Bill consolidators
	Additional services include basic customer care and payment initiation	

B2C EBPP DELIVERY MODELS

Billers can choose among four delivery models to present bills to their customers: The *direct model*, the *thick consolidator model*, the *thin consolidator model,* and the *consumer lockbox model.*

In the direct model, consumers access the biller's Website directly to view and pay their bills. Consumers dislike this model because it requires them to visit a different Website for each biller. Billers, on the other hand, prefer this model, because it allows them to completely control the display of the bill and most aspects of the billing cycle. The direct model gives billers the opportunity to service customers in real time and provide value-added service to enhance the customer experience and strengthen retention. Furthermore, the direct model provides better data protection, because it allows billers to keep all customer and billing data in house.

In the thick consolidator model, billers send all billing data to a CSP for presentment. Consumers benefit from this approach, because it allows them to access all their bills at a single site. However, consumers don't get real-time access to their accounts and have less self-service options available than under the direct model, making customer care less effective and less personal. Both companies without the resources to constantly manage a mission-critical billing site and billers that want go to market quickly can benefit from this model.

The thin consolidator model combines the benefits of the direct model and the thick consolidator model. Consumers can visit one site to view and pay all their bills, while billers retain control over much of the billing data, customer experience, and the overall relationship. Consumers access the CSP to view a summary of their bills. By clicking on a specific bill, customers are automatically connected with their biller's site, thus giving billers the same customer interaction benefits as the direct model. A future iteration of the thin consolidator model is e-mail billing, which is still under development. With this approach, billers would send the bill directly to the consumer's e-mail box or CSP, eliminating the need for consolidators.

The direct model and both consolidator models are biller-centric. Providers focus on signing up billers and serving their needs before targeting consumers. The consumer lockbox model takes the opposite approach by serving consumers before electronically linking billers into the process (Figure 11-3).

In the biller-centric consolidator model, consumers have to go to multiple locations to retrieve their bills. In the consumer-centric consumer lockbox model consumers go to one location to collect all their bills.

The consumer lockbox model is an emerging concept that is much more consumer-focused than the previous three delivery models. Companies such as CyberBills and PayTrust operate under this model, which is also referred to as the "scan and pay" model. It enables consumers to view every one of their bills electronically and handle payment and remittance processing. In addition, most consumer lockbox providers (CLPs) offer account aggregation services, which give consumers a much more holistic view of their financial situation. Consumers direct all bills (both paper and e-bills) to the CLPs, which will scan the bills and present them online back to consumers. Consumers review those bills and initiate payment through a preexisting bank account.

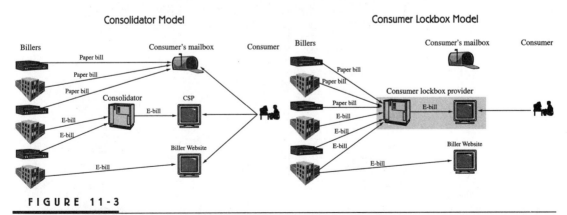

FIGURE 11-3

Biller-centric versus customer-centric delivery models. In the biller-centric consolidator model, consumers have to go to multiple locations to retrieve their bills. In the consumer-centric consumer lockbox model, consumers go to one location to collect all their bills.

The consumer lockbox model is based on the hypothesis that EBPP adoption will increase rapidly once a way is found around the chicken and egg dilemma that has plagued industry growth for some time: Billers are only willing to invest in electronic presentment once enough consumers have signed up to receive e-bills, and consumer will not convert to EBPP until most billers make electronic bills available.

Operating under the lockbox model is very costly due to the numerous paper-handling steps involved. In order to lower cost and stay price-competitive with the consolidator model, operators will have to drive conversion rates from paper to electronic presentment and payment.

The complexity in the marketplace is visualized in Figure 11-4. Several large billers such as First USA and Citi Credit Cards have adopted the direct model, while most banks, brokerages, and portals have opted for a consolidator or lock-box model. CLPs, which have the ability to present all consumer bills electronically, typically offer their services through their own portal sites, but are increasingly providing their services on a private-label basis to other portals. Bill consolidators generally "private-label" their technology to portals, banks, and brokerages. CheckFree also operates its own portal site, but that represents only a small portion of its overall business.

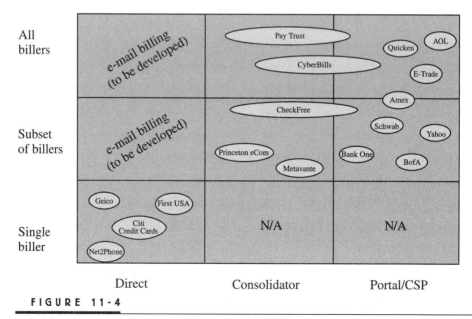

FIGURE 11-4

B2C EBPP billers and infrastructure providers.

B2C EBPP PROVIDER COMPETITIVE ENVIRONMENT

CheckFree is by far the largest EBPP infrastructure provider for consumer billing and payments. The company offers BSP services, bill consolidation, and payment processing under one roof. Consumers can pay their bills through the CheckFree portal site or through more than 300 CSP sites, most of which are banks.

Banks generally play a secondary role in EBPP. Only a few banks offer full EBPP today, including bill presentment. Those that offer the service typically out-source it to consolidators such as CheckFree. This fact is validated by CheckFree's acquisition of Bank of America's electronic billing and payment assets. What banks seem to be ignoring is a very real threat that by not controlling the EBPP process, they are in fact allowing new competitors into the financial services market. Internet portals, such as AOL and Quicken, and consumer lockbox operators, which rely on the same technology as banks, tend to be more customer-focused and have the potential to offer a more compelling bill payment and account management product.

B2C EBPP REVENUE STREAMS

Revenue potential varies significantly for the different EBPP infrastructure providers. Most of the revenue currently goes to the bill consolidators and CLPs. Figure 11-5 identifies major revenue streams in the flow between the key constituents.

Revenue flows mostly from consumers and billers to EBPP infrastructure providers, including BSPs, bill consolidators, and CSPs. Thicker lines indicate more and thinner lines less revenue potential.

CLPs capture the largest revenue streams, due to their bill delivery and management capabilities, which generates significant consumer value. As consumers experience those benefits, they will migrate in growing numbers to CLPs or banks and portals offering those services. While CLPs have the potential to generate significant revenues, their business model remains vulnerable due to the high cost of handling paper bills. Key to their success will be to effectively ally with BSPs to move all billers to electronic presentment as soon as possible.

Bill consolidators typically generate revenue from three sources: First, they receive a licensing fee from CSPs for providing them with the necessary technology to offer EBPP to their customers. In addition, CSPs pay a transaction fee for bill delivery and consumer payment processing. Consumers, who sign up directly with consolidators, are paying a monthly service fee and, in some cases, a transaction fee. Finally, BSPs or billers are paying consolidators to distribute bills to either CSPs or consumers.

BSPs generate licensing and transaction revenue from billers, but have to share a substantial portion of this revenue with consolidators. Banks, brokerages, and portals also rarely generate a profit from EBPP. While they receive account management fees from consumers and advertising revenue from billers and other

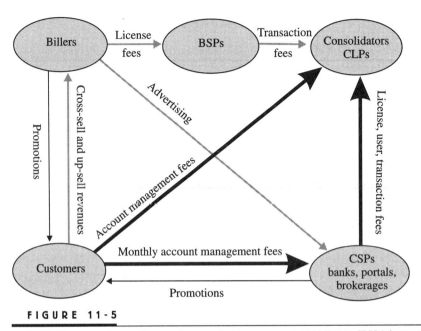

FIGURE 11-5

B2C EBPP revenue streams. Revenue flows mostly from consumers and billers to EBPP infrastructure providers, including BSPs, bill consolidators, and CSPs. Thicker lines indicate more and thinner lines less revenue potential.

e-commerce participants, they still have to share a substantial portion of revenues with consolidators or CLPs, which supply the EBPP infrastructure.

B2C EBPP GROWTH DRIVERS

Despite the significant potential for EBPP, current consumer adoption rates remain disappointingly low. Almost all B2C invoices are still presented on paper, and over 70 percent of invoices are paid using paper checks.[4]

Business metrics at CheckFree, the leading e-bill consolidator, paint a similar picture. Over the past 3 years the company has signed up over 220 of the country's largest billers, giving U.S. consumers the ability to receive over 1 billion electronic bills per year. But theory and actual customer adoption are two different stories. In December 2000, CheckFree processed more than 18 million payments, all of which were originated electronically. However, 40 percent of those payments had to be converted to paper checks and sent to recipients by mail, primarily because the receiving party was unable to accept electronic payments. On the presentment side, the adoption is at an even earlier stage, as CheckFree presented only 210,000 e-bills—a penetration rate of less than 0.1 percent.

---

[4] Other payment methods include payroll deduction, ACH, credit cards, money orders, cash, e-payments, etc.

One key reason is that Internet adoption—and more specifically online banking adoption—hasn't reached critical mass. Looking beyond those factors, there are a number of additional reasons that hamper adoption.

Customer convenience is probably the most critical factor, which existing business models don't address sufficiently. EBPP is currently offered as a stand-alone product by several portals or, in the case of banks and brokerages, as an add-on and without full integration into online banking. Another big problem that remains is that the vast majority of bills aren't yet available for electronic presentment. And finally, many major billers prefer the direct model, forcing customers to check multiple sites to pay their bills.

In addition, banks have not aggressively promoted EBPP as a value-added alternative to traditional presentment and payment. Moreover, many banks and portals charge some customers a monthly EBPP fee of up to $6 in addition to other banking fees.[5] Both fees and lack of promotions are currently limiting the momentum EBPP could gain through more extensive consumer trials.

In its current form, EBPP doesn't offer many consumers a compelling value proposition to switch their behavior. Fortunately, new and improved bill delivery models are evolving, promising lower cost and/or more consumer convenience.

BILLER VALUE PROPOSITION

Billers stand to gain significantly from EBPP, but also face a number of important challenges (Table 11-3). The biggest economic driver is the potential for cost savings. Benefits include the elimination of paper processing (invoice printing and handling); saved postage; a lower DSO;[6] more efficient payment processing, remittance, and posting; and the ability to better service customers. Various sources have estimated those potential savings anywhere between $1.00 to $1.50 per invoice—a major incentive, especially for large billers.

In addition to cost benefits, EBPP improves the ability of billers to strengthen customer relationships. Customer service improves as billers learn more about individual customer preferences and behavior. Billers can offer new value-added services that are delivered dynamically in real time. Furthermore, billers can increase revenues through cross-selling and targeted marketing campaigns that can be customized more accurately and have a much higher response rate than paper inserts that accompany most paper bills.

However, billers also recognize that they face higher overhead cost as long as they maintain two billing systems. Separate billing systems are necessary to support both EBPP and paper billing. Consequently, most small and medium-size billers look at current consumer adoption rates and opt not to invest in EBPP at this time.

---

[5] *U.S. News & World Report*, Mar. 6, 2000.

[6] Days of sales outstanding.

TABLE 11-3

Current Drivers and Barriers for B2C EBPP

Drivers	Barriers
1. Cost savings for billers	1. Internet and online banking adoption
2. EBPP-enabling technology	2. Consumer learning curve
3. Marketing opportunities	3. Lack of standards
4. Consumer demand	4. EBPP fees for consumers
5. Competition among billers	5. Overhead cost for billers

Other barriers include a confusing number of implementation options and evolving business models. Different vendors support different technology standards, which are not always compatible. There is also the organizational aspect of implementing and running EBPP as it integrates various corporate functions such as finance, customer care, marketing, and information technology into one product offering that's visible to the customer, requiring companies to figure out who should lead the effort.

In summary, EBPP can help billers lower cost, increase customer loyalty and retention though better service, and increase revenue through more focused cross-sell opportunities, but barriers remain high.

EBPP IS CREATING ATTRACTIVE INVESTMENT OPPORTUNITIES

The evolving EBPP market is creating significant opportunities for companies enabling the electronic billing and payment process. Value is currently being created by emerging technology providers with a vision for the future and the capabilities to create the technology that will drive adoption. A key question is whether banks, which are at the core of today's paper-based payment process, will also dominate electronic billing. Banks have a lot to lose—from customer relationships to lucrative biller cash management services. Early indications are that banks don't consider electronic billing a core competency, which leaves the door wide open for new entrants.

EBPP is a relatively new concept, and current business models have failed to generate widespread adoption. This situation paired with the significant market potential continues to attract new infrastructure providers with different business models such as the CLPs. Another factor facilitating market entry is that no single infrastructure provider has an entrenched or dominating market position that limits competition or innovation. In fact, provider roles are not always well defined and remain in flux. CheckFree, for instance, used to be a bill consolidator, but has recently expanded into the BSP market through its purchase of BlueGill Technologies. Now the company is also planning to offer consumer lockbox and account aggregation services.

When the market was in its nascent stages, infrastructure providers focused initially on the presentment side of the EBPP value chain, including bill creation and distribution. The target audience was primarily large billers with a preference for in-house solutions. In this market EBPP billing software providers and bill consolidators thrived.

Current efforts focus on two separate areas of the EBPP value chain: integrating the payment process into the biller's back-office systems and driving consumer adoption by allowing them to view and pay all their bills electronically. While the lockbox model is inherently less efficient, it gets at the crux of the adoption problem—consumers will only change their behavior and move to EBPP once the majority of bills become available online.

EXPECT MAJOR CHANGES

Going forward, we expect to see important changes in the business model, with technology providers focusing on new areas of the value chain. On the consumer side, EBPP will evolve from a stand-alone product to a core feature of a personal finance management product, which enables consumers to manage all their accounts and financial transactions from one central location. CLPs will drive most of the evolution in this area, creating a compelling value proposition for consumers and momentum to move bill management and payments online. Furthermore, bill consolidators and CLPs are enlisting a growing number of portals, banks, and brokerages for EBPP, making it more convenient for consumers to manage their finances from the Website(s) of choice.

As shown in Table 11-4, consumer demand for more convenient billing options, the need to distinguish service offerings in an increasingly competitive environment, and potential for cost savings will drive biller adoption rates higher. Emerging standards that lead to more interoperability among bill consolidators and lower implementation cost will also encourage a larger number of billers—especially medium-size and small corporations—to implement EBPP. Smaller companies tend to have less financial and technical resources than large corporations and also require less complex and cheaper EBPP solutions, resulting in slower growth

TABLE 11-4

Future Drivers for EBPP

Consumer demand
Cost savings for billers
Competition among billers
Revenue opportunities from cross-selling and advertising
Emerging standards

for in-house BSP software and a rapidly expanding demand for outsourced solutions. As both billers and CSPs increasingly look for a one-stop solution, BSPs will have to expand their service offering or merge with bill consolidators.

Growing biller adoption rates coupled with the need to integrate the payment process into the biller's back-office systems create opportunities for system integrators, which will become another increasingly crucial component of the EBPP implementation process. System integrators help companies link their billing engines to BSPs and integrate the flow of remittance information and payments data into their back-office systems. Their service is critical for companies without the necessary implementation resources and for billers that want to go to market quickly.

As we mentioned earlier, banks and portals are not expected to generate significant income from EBPP—a situation that will worsen in the years to come as competition drives down account management fees. However, some of the banks and portals will emerge as big winners in this area, by making up for the revenue loss and margin pressure through increasing advertising revenues from billers and other e-commerce participants.

CONCLUSION

Although B2C EBPP will experience dynamic growth over the next couple of years, it will take significantly longer to establish itself as a mass-market product. We currently estimate that by 2003, 50 percent of consumer bills will be available for electronic presentment, but only 5 percent of bills will actually be both viewed and paid by consumers. Increasing the adoption rates is both a demand- and supply-driven issue.

Most EBPP infrastructure providers are currently focusing on the supply side of the equation. Cost pressures, the emergence of technology standards, and more efficient business models are leading to growing adoption rates by large billers. At this time, smaller billers benefit less from a conversion to B2C EBPP since implementation and system integration costs outweigh recurring benefits from lower bill delivery expenses because of the lower number of electronic bills needed, coupled with ongoing requirements for paper bills for the majority of their customers.

In light of business adoption issues, consumer demand needs to be addressed for the B2C EBPP industry. Based on the current value proposition, there is currently little reason for consumers to sign up for EBPP, as sign-up rates generally show. Provider fee structures mean that consumers currently pay more for EBPP than for paper-based bill payment. In addition, consumers have to retrieve their bills from multiple locations. Over the next 5 years increased Internet bandwidth and electronic adoption will eventually spur demand for EBPP for up to 15 to 20 percent of U.S. households. However, in order to drive consumer adoption beyond that level, the industry has to offer more convenience and a stronger value proposition. We believe that the value proposition must approach a zero fee structure for consumers, coupled with the development of functionality in the EBPP software such as financial management tools that cannot be replicated in traditional formats.

The question still remains about how banks will react. The decision by banks to outsource payment and remittance functions to third parties has been a mixed blessing. Certainly from a cost and features perspective banks have benefited from their partnerships with providers such as CheckFree. However, as the market develops and EBPP takes on new relevance in the market, there is a potential threat on the horizon that outsourcing could eventually lead to loss of customers. Unless banks become more aggressive and completely integrate EBPP into their online banking products, third-party providers such as consumer and financial services portals could attract an increasing number of lucrative customers away from banks by offering consumers more value in EBPP and other products.

BUSINESS-TO-BUSINESS EBPP

INTRODUCTION

Over the last two years, B2B EBPP has emerged from the shadows of B2C EBPP in the minds of vendors and billing customers alike. In 1999, the size of U.S. business-to-business trade was $8.72 trillion.[7] In 1998, 43 billion checks were created by U.S. businesses.[8] While electronic funds transfer has been embraced by some businesses, 93 percent of B2B transactions were still based on paper invoices and payments. Considering that the round-trip cost of creating, sending, receiving, and administering paper transactions can amount to as much as $5 per invoice, the overall opportunity for EBPP in the United States is astounding. A 10 percent switch to electronic billing technology could potentially save all transaction participants $17+ billion annually.[9]

THE EBPP IMPERATIVE

Over the next 5 to 7 years, EBPP is expected to become the de facto payment process for U.S. businesses. While sharing many of the same players and system components as B2C EBPP, B2B EBPP has completely different market dynamics, value propositions, and market resistance issues. The key difference is that B2B EBPP describes both an electronification of the billing and payment process as well as the electronic distribution of the purchasing documentation. The true worth of B2B EBPP is not more convenient bill payment, but simplified trade. Therefore

---

[7] U.S. Department of Commerce, 2000.

[8] National Automated Clearing House Association, 1999.

[9] Round-trip includes biller, customer, and bank processing costs and fees. Estimated based on the estimated EBPP cost of about $1 and implied item savings of approximately $4.

B2B EBPP is part of the meta-initiative of electronic trade management that itself has significant growth drivers and acceptance issues.

Dove analysis suggests that there are five issues that differentiate B2B EBPP from B2C EBPP:

- *Volume.* The average business receives, processes, and sends thousands of bills per month. The scale of bills to be processed places a premium on processing and cost efficiency throughout the system.

- *Data Requirements.* B2B billing generally requires larger amounts of data and a greater number of data management options. Volume and granularity of data affect important customer features such as reporting, dispute management, and partial payment functionality.

- *Business Model.* The EBPP business model is being driven by savings from processing bills by both the biller and, unlike the B2C model, the customer. These cost savings have to be seen to be attainable in the short to mid-term.

- *Integration.* Integration of EBPP software into business processes and accounting systems is a major hurdle for biller and customer alike. A number of business processes are affected (e.g., payment authorization), and a number of new functions may be required (24/7 customer service, online dispute adjudication, partial payments, etc.) which themselves carry significant investments in capital, resources and operating resources.

- *Supply Chain Dependency.* In order for significant savings to be recognized by billers, all or most of their bills need to be converted to an electronic format. It is likely that by 2003–2005, large businesses will begin to require interfaces from suppliers. As we have seen in the auto parts and retail industries with their EDI implementations, businesses can be very aggressive in tying processing considerations to trading relationships.[10]

ADOPTION AND GROWTH DRIVERS

Market Sizing

The B2B EBPP market is in its nascent stages of growth.[11] While use is almost nonexistent now, most market analysts suggest that the market is poised for rapid and extensive growth in the next 5 years. Given electronic integration dependencies, B2B growth is contingent on both the billers' ability to create bills and the customers' ability to electronically receive and pay bills.

---

[10] For example, Wal-mart only contracts with suppliers that are EDI-enabled.

[11] DocSense (1999) has stated that the B2B EBPP transaction volume for 2000 is expected to be worth less than $10 million.

Because of B2B EBPP's requirements for integration, Dove analysis suggests that market growth will come in fits and starts as technology and infrastructure develop. During this period, we expect to see some latency in the small and mid-tier business adoption of EBPP solutions because of the markets' confusion over technology, business case, and customer impacts. Given that growth is dependent on the network effect,[12] or the number of other billers and customers willing to accept an electronic bill, we further believe that there are potential risks for delays in the growth of the EBPP market which will push relatively full adoption of B2B EBPP toward the 2010 time frame.

Dove analysis suggests, however, that the market impact of the B2B EBPP growth drivers, including electronic B2B markets (e-markets) and large corporate billing changeover to EBPP (described below), will be significant enough to drive the value of B2B EBPP transactions to a still relatively modest $200 billion[13] by 2003 (Figure 11-6).

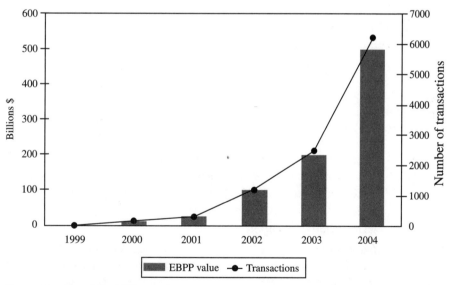

Source: Dove Consulting, 2000

F I G U R E   1 1 - 6

B2B EBPP growth.

---

[12] See Carl Shapiro and Hal R. Varian, *Information Rules: A Strategic Guide to the Network Economy*, Harvard Business School Press, Boston, 1998.

[13] Dove estimate based on B2B e-market sizing predictions, coupled with large corporate EBPP origination.

Growth Drivers

B2B EBPP growth is being driven by supply and demand factors that include:

1. Desire to reduce transaction and process costs for billing and trade
2. Large corporate adoption of electronic billing technologies that will place a premium on complete electronic interfaces
3. Rapid emergence of B2B electronic markets, trade, procurement, and shipping management
4. Packaged EBPP software offerings by banks and integration with cash management software
5. Heightened investment in payments and remittance management infrastructure that will reduce inefficiencies and improve product performance and cost
6. Introduction of standards-based data protocols (IFX and XML) and integration of standards within popular accounting and ERP programs that will increase the EBPP software choices for businesses

Reduced Costs of Business

The value proposition for B2B EBPP is driven by the promise of reduced costs for billers *and* customers—and the belief that the cost reductions will be *tangibly realized in the near term*. Cost reductions will be derived from three key areas:

- *Cost of paper management.* The cost of creating and managing the physical invoice and payment mechanisms will be reduced by developing electronic instruments and connections to accounting systems. Also implied is the reduction of errors and the resultant reduction in the administrative cost of error management between trading partners.
- *Cost of funds.* There will be a reduction in the cost of funds caused by delays since invoices will be processed faster. From a biller's perspective, this is seen as reducing the DSO (days of sales outstanding). From a customer's perspective, it is viewed as a proactive management of bills within incentives and terms offered by billers.
- *Data-based decision making.* Costs savings are implied by the better use of data for just-in-time delivery of inventory, better cash management, etc., within the business and between other third parties (i.e. banks, insurance, shipping). The savings are based on both administrative savings (FTE reduction) and savings that result from proactive management of resources enabled by timely and accurate information.[14]

---

[14] Similar to the ERP business model, the introduction of better trade documentation through electronic billing should allow customers tangible and intangible benefits associated with better information management and increased data on trade functions. Given the early stages of the industry, potential examples would include shipping management, trade financing, etc.

In addition to cost savings, Dove analysis (Table 11-5) suggests other potential data-driven benefits of EBPP for billers, such as the creation of sales channel capabilities, providing competitive barriers to entry and customer relationship. Likewise, in addition to heightened convenience for managing bills, the biller benefits may also apply to customers.

Large-Business Leadership

Both the scale and the diversity of large businesses force them to invest in electronic invoice and payments technology. Pressure from capital markets for cost management, coupled with large capital and resource pools, enables larger companies to make investments in electronic systems for long-term savings. Their role as the apex of the supply chain will force mid-size and small businesses to adopt EBPP technology.

Today the largest investors in EBPP technology solutions are ultralarge billers such as AT&T and ConEdison. While these investments are being made on the consumer side of their business, it is only a matter of time before business accounts are enabled with electronic presentment. Inevitably, large billers will begin to use their market power, incentives, and discounts to encourage business customers to switch to Internet-based billing.

Already, companies such as GM and FedEx are pushing Internet-based payment solutions in addition to their established EDI programs. We anticipate that billers will increasingly offer pricing and contract incentives to their business customers to embrace electronic billing technology. Dove research indicates that incentives and discounts will have a major effect on the B2B trade. With encouragement by their supply chain partners, we believe that small and mid-tier businesses will find themselves to be the biggest winners of B2B EBPP.

TABLE 11-5

EBPP Adoption Advantages

Biller	Customer
Cost reductions:	**Cost reductions:**
Streamlined paper and receipt cycle management	Reduces errors before and after billing payment
Reduced DSO	Heightens control of A/P and inventory
Customer service and dispute management	management and reduces cycle costs
Other advantages:	**Other advantages:**
Creates sales channel	Convenience
Enables database marketing and awards programs	Flexibility of payment terms
Creates a barrier to competition	Enables third-party financing options (escrow, letters of credit, factoring)

Increasing Influence of B2B e-Markets

The increasing relevance of electronic B2B markets is a key growth driver for EBPP. B2B marketplaces enable the purchase of goods and services by businesses across the Internet. U.S. B2B trade volume through e-markets (Figure 11-7) is forecast to grow to almost $3 trillion by 2004, while global B2B market growth is expected to reach $6 trillion in 2004.

E-market growth is being driven not only by the apparent increase in convenience, product choice, and transaction speed, but also by the cost savings associated with conducting trade negotiations and fulfillment electronically. A key barrier to the realization of these savings is the paper intensity of payment mechanisms; EBPP is a solution to this issue. As business volume switches to electronic markets, it will drive the growth of EBPP, not only because of payments management, but also because of increased order accuracy, thus reducing the costs of fulfillment and management. Further, the volume of trade and trading partners and the implicit geographic dispersion of the Internet further heighten the relevance of EBPP in the market for both cost and logistics management.

B2B EBPP More Relevant to Banks

In the United States especially, banks have the most to win and lose by the emergence of B2B EBPP. Banks occupy a pivotal position in encouraging B2B EBPP. Billing simply drives much of the banking cash management functions for traditional business, as well as holds the key to entry into trade finance, electronic procurement, and electronic market transaction management.

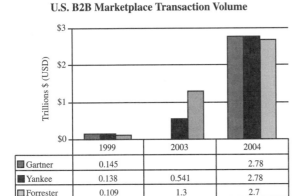

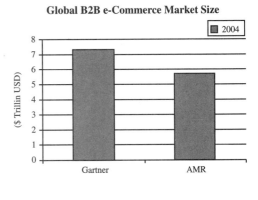

Source: Gartner Group, 2000; Yankee Group, 2000; Forrester Research, 2000; AMR Research, 2000.

FIGURE 11-7

According to major research houses, domestic e-market transactions will approach $3 trillion in 2004, representing approximately one-third of the overall U.S. B2B trade.

Banks that have announced investments in B2B EBPP products:

- PNC
- Mellon Bank
- Citibank
- Wells Fargo
- J.P. Morgan
- Chase

The banking industry's key advantage is the cash management software and the control of access points to the payment networks. While businesses have traditionally separated purchase from payment, with the electronic marketplace it is now possible to see a scenario where purchasing and payments are co-enabled. If that is the case, the business making the purchase defines the terms of purchase and chooses finance and payment options. From a strategic perspective, the cash management software becomes the point-of-payment control; therefore it is also the point of sales, the point of marketing and the point of financial services' product decision making for business accounts.

The size of the market and the relevance of payments to the account management process make the positioning of banks crucial in the next few years. While not all banks have addressed their B2B strategy, a number of players are looking to shore up their competencies in providing EBPP based on their inherent positional and resource advantages:

- Capital and resource availability and payments system expertise
- Control and ownership of cash management software
- Control of pricing for traditional bill payment mechanisms
- A market that favors direct billing models and direct payments, thus limiting the role of existing bill payment service providers

The banks that look to B2B EBPP as an offshoot of their current retail EBPP strategy are in a perilous position. As the B2B value chain morphs and shortens, the market's desire for payment efficiency will push out the least valuable value chain participants. On the surface, market efficiency poses little risk to banks, given the banks' relationships with businesses and the high barriers of entry associated with tight product relationships held by most businesses. However, given the EBPP integration issues, introduction into the market of nonbank-sponsored cash management tools and the cost drivers associated with the larger entry of electronic billing and supply procurement, we would suggest that in the mid-term the barriers of entry are false and that significant shifting of accounts is probable from banks that have not invested in EBPP. Further, it would be dangerous for U.S. banks to relinquish EBPP to third parties because EBPP decisions affect the greater relevance of the banks in terms of B2B services and payments management.

One of the key challenges for the industry will be the transition of their traditional cash management offerings as EBPP becomes more relevant to customers. For many banks, cash management revenues and customer relationships are a key component of their business banking franchise. Therefore, there will be significant internal friction within banks that have a legacy in cash management services such as lockbox. Without a defined electronic marketplace vision from senior bank managers, cost management and competing strategic visions will hamper many traditional cash management leaders in the banking industry as existing markets are favored at the expense of the future electronic marketplace.

Payments Infrastructure and Investment

According to Meridien Research, global spending on electronic payments products and infrastructure is estimated to be $5.6 billion in 2000 (Figure 11-8).[15] The expected investment in EBPP by banks and other providers is expected to surpass $1.5 billion. This level of investment will fuel further development of software, business solutions, and infrastructure and increase availability and overall value of solution offerings.

Market spending is being driven by both the perceived revenue opportunities based on the expected EBPP volume and the defensive posturing by banks that are concerned about the impacts of transaction and account erosion. As a result, there are significant opportunities for third parties and emerging players to create products and networks that will improve payment efficiency and processing. Not all of these entities will be bank-sponsored—we forecast that there will be significant pressure by banks and traditional players to radically enhance the payments infrastructure of the next 5 to 10 years.

IT Spending for E-Payments   IT Spending on E-Payments by Region

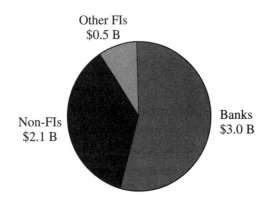
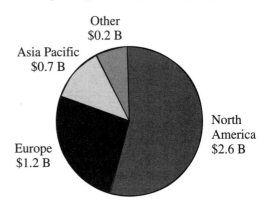

Source: Meridien Research, 2000.

FIGURE 11-8

Spending on global electronic payments products and infrastructure was approximately $5.6 billion in 2000.

---

[15] Dave Potterton and Sarah Ablett, *Top 10 Strategic IT Initiatives in e-Payment Services for the New Millennium*, February 2000, Meridien Research, 1999. www.meridien-research.com.

Open Standards Fuel Solution Availability

While standards have limited impact on consumer EBPP acceptance, they are vital for B2B trade. Scalability and interface issues dominate B2B EBPP—if the data are not transparent to biller, customer, and payment systems, an implementing business cannot eliminate processing costs. Standards are a major friction point in the industry to date. The introduction of standards fuels growth through reduced software costs and heightened solution availability.

Two standards are especially vital for EBPP:

- IFX (*interactive financial exchange*) specifies interfaces for all financial services transactions including EBPP. The introduction of IFX will enable investments in proprietary EBPP presentment to be utilized for subsequent generations of billing and payments technologies. At the time of writing, the IFX standard has just been published and will not likely be widely available in industry software until the mid-2001–2002 product years.
- The broader introduction of XML (*extended markup language*, on which IFX is based) and the extension of EDI standards on top of the XML protocol are also critical for the ongoing emergence of electronic trade. XML is becoming the standard for e-marketplaces, and its inherent flexibility and cross-platform capability further increase its relevance in the market.

The introduction of standards points the competitive environment of the EBPP industry away from solution dominance to solution compatibility. Compatibility of interfaces reduces the biller and customer investment risk as well as opens up greater potential for emerging players in the infrastructure and value-added services components of the solution. With compatibility and an increased value proposition associated with increased service, the barriers to EBPP adoption are reduced.

Barriers to Growth

Significant growth barriers still exist for mass rollout of B2B EBPP technology for both billers and customers alike (Table 11-6). The barriers to adoption can be summarized into three categories:

- Return on investment
- Paper inertia
- Business culture and practices

While the cost savings of EBPP are real, they are offset by the costs for integration and the indirect impacts of transforming business processes and systems. Foremost, the cost savings that have been promised to billers and customers must materialize in meaningful form and in a short time frame. From our perspective, the timing of the return from investing in EBPP is the major issue. It is unlikely that even by 2003, EBPP alone will create a positive return on investment for implementing

TABLE 11-6

Barriers to EBPP Adoption

Biller	Customer
Cost of customer service	System integration
Customer acceptance	Authorization and payment control
Paper billing requirement	Fraud prevention and accessibility
Security	Audit and tax requirement for original receipts
Scalability	Staff training
	Technology availability

businesses. Thus the expectations and business planners must be appropriately modified to see the longer-term benefits of the EBPP implementation.

Business dependence on paper documentation will not evaporate. As a result, businesses looking to EBPP will be forced to run both electronic and traditional billing mechanisms for the foreseeable future. This makes EBPP an extra layer of cost to most businesses instead of a replacement cost. However, paper and integration management issues open the way for third-party providers that can specialize in managing the paper-to-electronic document flow and vice versa, which may provide practical solutions to business customers.

There is also a collateral issue of cultural and process barriers. The introduction of electronic billing technology affects a number of processes and practices within a business environment. Given the largely human involvement in the current billing processes, we see a significant hurdle for businesses looking to implement and optimize billing practices. Our work to date in the field suggests that even one stream of the decision-making process such as billing and payments involves a number of business transformation, organization, and retraining issues. These issues are potentially messy and costly for those companies that have not planned in advance for the transformation to occur, particularly for those companies that think EBPP is a just a technology issue.

INVESTMENT OPPORTUNITIES: MANAGING THE COMPLEXITY

B2B EBPP Delivery Models

The longer-term EBPP solution winners will be those entities that are able to create or capture the most value and simultaneously reduce the overall cost of transacting commerce for businesses.

The cost of managing the paper flow between the ordering, accounts, billing, and payments functions is the primary motivator for billers and customers to adopt e-billing solutions. Because of the drive for efficiency, the most likely model for B2B

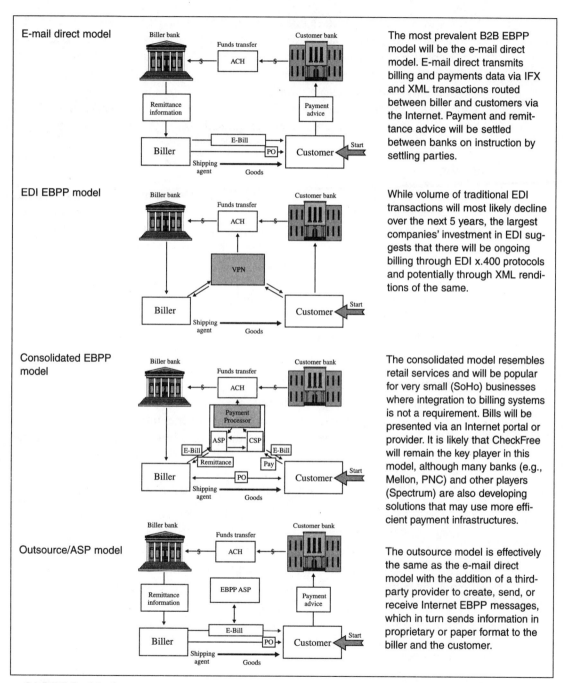

E-mail direct model

The most prevalent B2B EBPP model will be the e-mail direct model. E-mail direct transmits billing and payments data via IFX and XML transactions routed between biller and customers via the Internet. Payment and remittance advice will be settled between banks on instruction by settling parties.

EDI EBPP model

While volume of traditional EDI transactions will most likely decline over the next 5 years, the largest companies' investment in EDI suggests that there will be ongoing billing through EDI x.400 protocols and potentially through XML renditions of the same.

Consolidated EBPP model

The consolidated model resembles retail services and will be popular for very small (SoHo) businesses where integration to billing systems is not a requirement. Bills will be presented via an Internet portal or provider. It is likely that CheckFree will remain the key player in this model, although many banks (e.g., Mellon, PNC) and other players (Spectrum) are also developing solutions that may use more efficient payment infrastructures.

Outsource/ASP model

The outsource model is effectively the same as the e-mail direct model with the addition of a third-party provider to create, send, or receive Internet EBPP messages, which in turn sends information in proprietary or paper format to the biller and the customer.

FIGURE 11-9

There are a number of B2B EBPP delivery models in the market today. On the basis of current trends, Dove analysis indicates that e-mail direct will be the most prevalent model for B2B transactions. However, other models will coexist for various segments of the market based on needs sophistication (EDI) and billing volume.

EBPP will be e-mail direct (see Figure 11-9). The e-mail direct model sends complete billing advice directly to customers via the Internet or VPN mail. These mail messages are then read and processed automatically by customer accounts systems. Authorization and payment control are handled by the customer systems (potentially automatically), and payment and remittance advice are sent to the customer bank. On advice of the customer, the customer bank forwards payment information to the biller bank, which in turn notifies the biller in conjunction with the remittance details.

Constituent Analysis

There will be a number of a winners based on investment in EBPP technology, but it is too early to identify those winners outside of broad categorizations based on industry categories. We see today's provider environment as somewhat in flux, given the early stages of the industry, the growth drivers described above, and the relative immaturity of the vendor market.

Dove analysis suggests that there will be a trend toward service bureaus and integrated software packaging that will affect many of today's leading vendors. In the following section and in Table 11-7, we have outlined some of our best guesses on where the industry categories are going and which companies will be the likely winners.

Pure EBPP Software Providers

On the basis of our analysis, we do not feel that the EBPP software industry will be in a position to capitalize on its current investments in developing EBPP solutions. Given the overall cost of implementing many business billing systems and the relative age of those systems, we suspect that EBPP software will be integrated into the new generation of e-commerce and ERP software from providers such as Oracle or iPlanet—thereby marginalizing pure EBPP software makers.

- The EBPP software industry captures little overall additional value and is being commoditized by the introduction of standards, application service providers (ASPs), and banking payment software.
- Current EBPP software industry profits are being driven by implementation and system integration fees which we feel will face competitive pressure as the large system integrators enter the market.
- Industry competition, in-house development, and entrance of accounting software providers into the EBPP software space will keep competitive pressure on software prices.

System Integrators

System integrators that integrate EBPP software into the business systems and that realign resources within the company are vital. In short, the ability to create an

TABLE 11-7

Industry Investment Summary

	EBPP Software Providers	System Integrators	Service Bureau and ASPs	Payment Remittance Networks	Customer Service and Dispute Management
Functional description	Develop software to create, deliver, and receive bills over the Internet and sell to business clients	Integrate billing and business accounting software	Create operating environments to run and manage EBPP and/or accounting software	Manage current payment and remittance flow between banks and billing businesses	Manage call center and automatic trade arbitration software for billers
Investment summary	Relevance expected to diminish as offerings become commoditized by ERP, accounting software, and other emerging players. Leading providers will be bought outright or move into integrator or ASP roles	Between 2001 and 2003, system integrators will capture the most value for integrating EBPP software into businesses. Integration of other accounts systems will be primary driver	Expect number of providers to swell as market matures and businesses seek cost-effective processing options for EBPP. In the end, scale and solution functionality will dictate consolidation of players	B2B EBPP needs remittance and payment providers in short term. Players that are able to create highly efficient and scalable solutions will reap windfall. Pure retail players face daunting task to move to B2B market	Call center business model is high cost and transaction driven. It is currently unclear how much of a factor software-based assistance will cut management cost and profitability
Players to watch	CheckFree edocs EDS Avolent iPlanet Trisense BottomLine Technologies Pitney Bowes/ DocSense	IBM Accenture Deloitte Consulting Cap Gemini Ernst & Young KPMG EDS PriceWaterhouse Coopers	CheckFree edocs Derivion BCE Emergis PayTrust CyberBills Princeton eCom Billingzone	CheckFree Spectrum PayTrust CyberBills Metavante Princeton eCom	N/A

electronic bill can only be realized when all parties can create and receive billing and payment information.

Investments in integration by billers and customers are likely to range from under to $100,000 to over $1 million per instance. As a result, the development and investment in EBPP technology is focusing not only on the bill, but on the payment and remittance information flow and the strategy and operations to integrate it into a company's business. The system integrator value is increased if examples of ERP integration are examined. The involvement of an integrator to improve business functionality and its role as a sales and decision leader for software solutions gives it an ongoing, sustainable value proposition.

Service Bureaus

Dove analysis suggests that there is a significant opportunity for outsource and ASP models in the B2B EBPP space. A number of medium-size and small businesses will lag in integrating payment and billing systems into their accounts management process. For those companies, the industry's push toward EBPP will require them to contract with service providers in order to send, receive, and pay bills.

These service bureaus are able to perform a variety of functions on behalf of the company:

- Run ASP versions of accounts, payments, and billing software, thus completely divorcing themselves of the need to own, run, and operate their accounting systems.
- Run electronic bill-creation operations from business files, thus reducing the investment in creating duplicate billing infrastructure until a complete switchover can be made.
- Run operations that convert inbound bills to electronic information so that clients and suppliers can create an electronic interface with the company without requiring the company to invest in integration of billing systems.

Payment and Remittance Networks

The existing U.S. infrastructure for payment and remittance processing is a major stumbling block for EBPP providers. In order to cut costs, a B2B system has to seamlessly transform information from purchase through settlement—between biller, bank, and customer. Two issues dominate the remittance management field. First, U.S. payment networks cannot simultaneously carry payment and remittance instructions directly to biller systems. Second, most U.S. businesses are not equipped to handle electronic payments and remittance information.

On the retail side of the equation, players such as CheckFree have developed their business on transforming paper-based transactions into electronic forms—or, all too frequently, the other way around. Because of the volume and efficiency requirements demanded by businesses, this additional layer of processing is seen as a barrier to adoption. While the long-term role of a remittance processor is questionable, the mid-term role and value relevance are positive.

Customer Service and Dispute Management

An unknown in the market is the requirement for customer service and dispute management from biller sites. Dove experience in B2C EBPP and B2B commerce suggests that customer service expenditures will increase with B2B EBPP. The complexity of the transactions, the availability of real-time transaction data to customers, and shorter payment cycles will place a premium on real-time response between the customer and biller.

While most functions will be automated in time, we believe that many businesses will find themselves having to increase overall customer service through call centers (i.e., 24/7 service, multilingual service). In the long term, the addition of electronic self-service systems will offset the cost of introduction and significantly improve customer satisfaction. If consumer and B2B commerce businesses are a guide, customer service functions may eventually account for 25 percent of ongoing costs. While many companies will be able to leverage existing consumer call center support, many others will be forced to invest in building or outsourcing customer service functions. Again, scale and cost pressures may give rise to third-party companies that provide ongoing call center and Internet-based decision support, but at this time no players have created a dedicated customer service function for B2B EBPP.

CONCLUSION

The B2B EBPP industry is in the nascent stages of its development. To date, B2B EBPP has been thought of as an extension of B2C EBPP with the same business case and growth rationale. In fact, while B2B shares many of the same participants and issues with its B2C brethren, the primary issues affecting use—transaction growth, business case, and infrastructure development—are completely different.

B2B EBPP is an extension of the trade document process. It places a premium on the efficiency of managing workflow between two (or more) trading parties. Efficiency dictates tight, electronic integration of information between trading parties to meet significant thresholds for cost savings. As a result, the key to creating mass market is not only the number of billers online but the number of customers willing to accept electronic bills.

While B2C EBPP struggles with a value proposition to the customer, significant forces are at play that may make B2B EBPP a de facto standard in as little as 5 years. Chief among these factors is the rise of electronic B2B markets and the ongoing role of large corporations to digitize trade documentation. In this light, EBPP plays a supportive, yet vital role in the overall transformation of the economy to digital trade. In this case, it is the tail on a much larger, more important dog.

Among the vendors and providers in the B2B EBPP, banks have the most to gain and lose by how they choose to enter the market. Banks' investment in cash management products is a key enabler of EBPP, but may also turn out to be a stumbling block for those banks that are unwilling or unable to invest in the electronic trade process. Our analysis also indicates that system integrators and service bureaus will also be likely winners in the market over the next years as the market steps from its legacy environment to the electronic environment.

CHAPTER 12

Online Credit and Banking

Scott Gregory, Director
PriceWaterhouse Coopers Consulting

OVERVIEW OF MARKET DEVELOPMENTS

In recent years, the face of the consumer and small business lending market has changed dramatically as lenders have adopted new technologies designed to make lending processes faster and less objective, and as nontraditional lenders and mono-line banks have raised the level of competition. The Internet has further complicated the market by accelerating these trends as well as introducing new catalysts for change by:

- *Intensifying competition.* The Internet has provided a relatively cost-effective channel for delivering financial services that immediately provides national, or international, reach. Internet-based players have entered the market and are challenging the dominance and business models of "brick-and-mortar" finance providers. Without the barriers presented by potential cannibalization of other distribution channels, legacy technology systems, and limited brand risks presented by potential missteps, these competitors have been moving aggressively to gain market share and have established flexible business models that enable rapid reaction to changing market conditions. In addition, traditional financial services players have extended their market reach by embracing the capabilities of the Internet, either through a separate Internet-based subsidiary or by tying Internet delivery in with their existing organization, or both.

- *Educating and empowering consumers.* The Internet is bringing more knowledge and awareness of products to individuals and small businesses by making a wide range of information and financing options readily available to borrowers. Aggressive pricing by competitors seeking to build market presence, along with the availability of comparative information, has shifted much of the power in financing decisions from the credit provider to the consumer. This in turn is speeding commoditization of the market and the trend of decreasing margins on lending products.

- *Facilitating new business models.* The Internet has also made new business models possible that were not feasible in the physical world. For example, both consumers and businesses are now participating in electronic communities that facilitate trade between previously unknown, geographically dispersed counterparties. Whether the buying and selling occurs in a consumer-to-consumer or business-to-business environment, these trade-based communities require methods of financing purchases. The challenge faced by both traditional and nontraditional credit providers is to adapt existing products to support these new models, and to define new financing structures that support the real-time requirements of the online world.

The remainder of this chapter explores each of these areas, their impact on possible business strategies, and the skills that credit providers must have to win in this dynamic market.

INTENSIFYING COMPETITION

The nature of the Internet makes it possible for players in the credit market to rapidly establish broad market presence. The competitors are represented by "virtual" finance companies that have no brick-and-mortar presence and by arms of traditional companies that are utilizing the Internet to expand their reach.

The Internet-based lending market is experiencing explosive growth. As shown in Figure 12-1, recent market information from the Gartner Group indicates that over 13 million consumers entered online applications for credit in 1999. The majority of the applications to date have been for credit cards, but market analysts agree that the number of online applications and originations for more complex products, such as mortgages, will increase dramatically over the next 5 years. Current estimates are that only 0.5 to 1 percent of total mortgage originations occur online today, but the volume is expected to rise to approximately 10 to 15 percent by 2005.

The competitive intensity in the market has been characterized by a number of factors that are separating market leaders from also-rans. The primary trend has been the use of aggressive pricing structures by pure online players that are designed to build market presence and rapidly establish a base of customers that can then be mined for additional products and services. Examples include:

- Priceline.com lets consumers name their target rates for mortgages and cuts up to $1000 off closing costs.

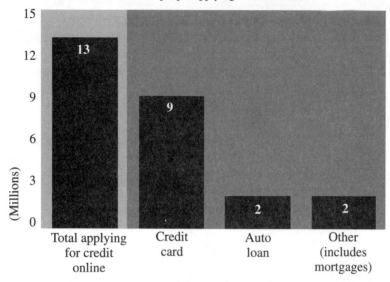

Credit cards lead online credit applications

Number of people applying for credit online

Source: Gartner Group

F I G U R E   1 2 - 1

Outside of the pure consumer online credit activity, the small business lending market has also seen increasing competition as lenders leverage credit-scoring techniques and technologies developed for the consumer market in combination with internet delivery to address the unique needs of this "near-consumer" market.

- iOwn.com doesn't charge an application fee for mortgages and offers 50 percent off origination fees.
- Peoplefirst.com quotes rates on auto loans that range from 0.5 to 2.5 percent lower than rates on comparable loans from banks.

Traditional market players have had to react accordingly by creating pricing structures that are in line with those of their new competitors. This has placed pressure on the profit margins of credit and financing products, especially products such as mortgages where high origination costs are difficult to reduce due to the complex nature of supporting processes.

As price competition accelerates the commoditization of the market, some lenders are responding with more personalized approaches to designing products and to providing service. Many of the most interesting innovations taking place in the market today are occurring in the credit card arena. NextCard is a leader in providing innovative personalization services for customers. As prospective customers go through the NextCard site, they are asked to structure their card by choosing features such as the interest rate, points programs, and annual fees. In

addition, customers are able to personalize the look and feel of their card by selecting a personal photograph, logo, etc., with which to mark the plastic. These
options are designed to increase customer loyalty and use of the cards. As indicated in Figure 12-2, NextCard's rapid growth in both number of customers and managed loans over the past year indicate that the company's approach to
personalizing products is popular with consumers.

Time-based competition has also been a critical factor in this market.
Lenders' Websites have rapidly moved from "brochureware" to transactional sites
with the ability to handle online applications, approval, and, in some cases, fulfillment. A consumer can now apply online for credit cards, auto loans, unsecured
lines of credit, mortgages, and other credit instruments. Rapid approval and fulfillment activity has been greatest in the credit card market. Virtually all of the
leading credit card providers give applicants the ability to apply and be approved
online. Usually the approval process takes less than 1 minute. In some instances,
such as with Click Citi cards, which are targeted toward online purchasers, fulfillment is instantaneous as well. An active card number is provided to the applicant
immediately after approval; no plastic is issued.

Changes are also occurring in other credit markets. Advanta's Business
Credit service for small businesses offers up to $100,000 credit online, and utilizes
a credit decision process that usually returns a response in less than 60 seconds.

As the ability to support rapid application, approval, and fulfillment of credit products increases, the face of the lending industry will undergo dramatic
change. The potential scope of change can be illustrated by using mortgage processing as an example. As shown in Figure 12-3, the mortgage process of the
future is likely to be vastly different from the process as it stands today. As these

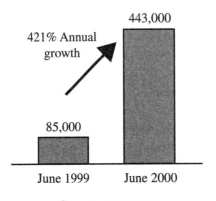
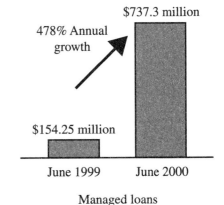

Source: NextCard 10K, August 14, 2000

FIGURE 12-2

NextCard's rapid growth.

Current State: 8–56 Days

Application   `0.25–0.5 day`

Preprocessing   `0.5–4 days`

Processing   `5–45 days`

Underwriting   `1–3 days`

Closing (also dependent on agreed closing date)   `1–3 days`

Future State: 7–21 Days

Application	Underwriting	Preclosing and Closing	Postclosing and Delivery
• Prequalification • Product selection • Application completion • Loan registration • Loan submission	• Credit report • Automated underwriting • **Commitment issuance** ↓ **Exception processing**	• Automated property valuation • Automated mortgage insurance U/W • Commitment condition compliance • Survey, title, insurance, etc. requests through EPN • Document preparation • Closing instructions • Funding authorization	• Postclosing document tracking • Servicing system setup • Loan package audit • Shipping
`0.25–0.5 day`	`2 min.–10 days`	`3–7 days`	`3–7 days`

Source: Tower Group

FIGURE 12-3

Mortage processing time compression.

changes occur, key players in today's process are likely to see their roles cut back or done away with altogether, with a corresponding decrease in cost to both the lender and the consumer (Figure 12-4).

Although the technology currently exists to enable these changes in the mortgage process, streamlining the process is not solely dependent on the underlying technology. For this future vision to come to fruition, other significant changes must occur. First, consumers must exhibit a greater willingness to conduct one of the largest financial transactions of their life with minimal face-to-face contact with a lender. Second, regulations must be changed to accommodate new processing approaches. Some significant barriers are beginning to fall, as evidenced by the passage of legislation to recognize digital signatures as valid for a wide range of financial contracts. However, substantial regulatory limitations—for example—the requirement for physical examination of some paperwork—still exist.

EDUCATING AND EMPOWERING CONSUMERS

The Internet has also served as a tremendous tool for educating those seeking credit. In the traditional financing model, the power in the relationship belonged to the lender. The borrower generally had the option of going to one or two lenders and enduring time-consuming and subjective credit approval processes. The diffi-

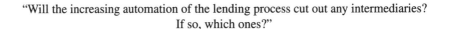

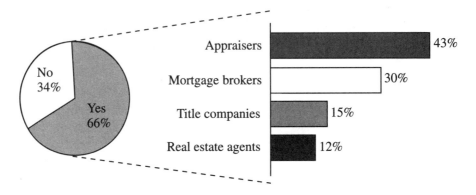

"Will the increasing automation of the lending process cut out any intermediaries? If so, which ones?"

Unprompted responses from 50 firms interviewed
(multiple responses accepted)

Source: Forrester Research, Inc.

FIGURE 12-4

Removing lending intermediaries.

culty of making ready comparisons of credit alternatives limited the consumer's ability to make well-informed choices.

The new model turns the equation around. Sites such as Financenter.com provide consumers with one-stop shopping for finding and closing credit instruments. In addition, the site provides a forum for consumer feedback on lender performance. Both kudos and criticisms are readily available for anyone to view. Savvy lenders will respond by learning from, and rapidly addressing, reasonable borrower criticisms and praise to structure their service to align with the features that consumers deem to be most important.

In addition, auction sites such as LendingTree in the consumer market, or Primestreet in the small-business space, have established a new model for applying for credit products. On these sites, the potential borrower provides information on what he or she is seeking, and multiple potential lenders respond with offers as long as the prospective borrower fits a preestablished profile. The resulting shift in knowledge and power from the lender to the borrower, combined with increased competition, has accelerated the compression of margins and commoditization of products.

FACILITATING NEW BUSINESS MODELS

The third major challenge presented by the Internet is for finance providers to understand and service new business models that have emerged in the virtual world that were not feasible in the physical one. The rise of electronic business-to-business and consumer-to-consumer communities presents new opportunities to use existing financing/credit instruments in new ways and to develop new instruments that support the new models.

Paypal provides an interesting example of the use of an existing credit instrument to support the financing needs of an electronic community. eBay is well known for its success in providing a retail auction service for consumers. However, establishing an effective, trusted means of payment between counterparties that are likely to be geographically dispersed, and usually have no prior knowledge of each other, has been difficult. The Paypal solution utilizes the existing infrastructure of the credit card payments system, along with e-mail, to provide a secure payment solution on which both the buyer and the seller can rely. (See Figure 12-5.)

Other players are moving to address similar issues in the business-to-business (B2B) market. In the B2B electronic communities that exist today, transactions are typically broken into two distinct groups of activity: procuring the good or service and financing the purchase. Companies such as eCredit.com and eFinance.com are moving toward establishing an integrated process that enables real-time decision making and activation for credit products that occur as the business transaction is being conducted. This type of integrated approach to Internet commerce is required in order to realize the full potential of electronic communities.

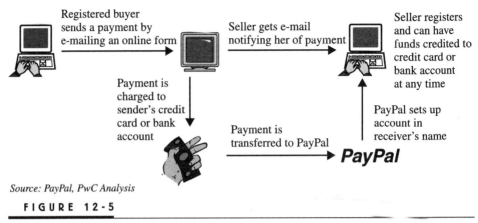

Source: PayPal, PwC Analysis

FIGURE 12-5

Diagram of PayPal flow.

POSITIONING TO WIN

Finding direction in this rapidly changing market requires that players realistically assess their competencies and how they are best positioned to compete. Through our work, we have identified five key competencies required to be an effective competitor in today's lending market:

1. *Virtual customer intimacy*. Competitors must leverage the data-capture capabilities of the Internet and other channels to establish a comprehensive picture of the customer. The knowledge gathered must be used to forecast and address customer needs by providing a seamless customer experience that is targeted to specific customer groups.

2. *Innovation and experimentation*. As credit providers use customer knowledge and new technologies to develop targeted offers customized to specific needs, they must develop the ability to rapidly take the new concepts to market, test them in the market, and continuously improve the offers based on market reaction.

3. *Alliances*. Building a successful Internet strategy requires adept development of strategic alliances to leverage the competencies of other market players. Alliances can take the form of teaming with companies that provide conduits for customer acquisition (distribution of your company's products and services) or that provide best-in-class products and services for delivery to your company's customer base.

4. *Service excellence*. The rapid growth of the Internet marketplace has left customer service as a casualty as competitors scramble for market share. Now, as market leaders move to consolidate their positions, they are turning to exceptional service as a potential differentiator. However, providing exceptional lev-

els of service requires an organizationwide commitment to ensure that consistent service is delivered across channels.

5. *Operational efficiency.* Successful competitors must be operationally efficient in order to be able to compete on a cost basis so that they can excel in a market exemplified by aggressive pricing models.

Developing these competencies requires building three foundation capabilities. First, winning organizations must become customer-centric. Only by truly understanding and thinking like your customer can your organization take the necessary steps to raise loyalty. Delivering customized solutions and creating unique customer experiences will increase the amount of pressure that competitors must apply to dislodge your customer relationships.

Second, the market winners must have the organizational agility to enable rapid reinvention and innovation. High-performing organizations are typically following one of two models. Some organizations have developed a "cocooned" Internet team that pulls together the best and brightest from across lines of business. Others have formed Internet teams that are truly separate from traditional business units. Regardless of the direction taken, management must inspire the ABCDs of an innovative culture:

- Aggressive time to market goals
- Bias toward action
- Competition and cooperation between units
- Dissension tolerance to foster innovative thinking

Lastly, winning requires alliance citizenship. An effective Internet strategy is not necessarily focused on building your own Internet presence; rather, it is built on understanding the direction of the Internet, and your company's strengths, and seeking the partners that can position your company to win. By establishing the capability to effectively partner with others, including current and potential competitors, market leaders will gain a better understanding of, and ability to influence, the direction of the market.

CHAPTER 13

Financial Information

Jeremy Pink, VP, News and Programming
CNBC Europe

In the late 1990s as online financial information exploded in the marketplace, banks, brokerages, mutual fund companies, Websites, and just about everyone connected to the financial services industry adhered to the mantra: Grow traffic at all costs and deliver as many eyeballs as quickly as possible. It was like a huge political campaign—only in this case, the candidates (banks, brokerages, etc.) didn't spend money to acquire voters; they spent untold millions to acquire consumers.

Like many campaigns, however, it's easy to spend money, but it's much harder to generate results. Remember the early success of Steve Forbes in the first 1996 Republican presidential primaries? He spent a fortune to acquire voters, dramatically outspending his opponents along the way. Eventually, that strategy proved costly not only to Forbes's pocketbook but to the retention of the voters themselves—they forged only a short-term attachment to their candidate, but lacked a meaningful long-term relationship with him.

That's essentially what happened to many firms that participated in the great financial services campaigns of the late 1990s. Consumers flocked to sites, but few of these sites had enough to offer viewers to keep them there for the long term. Many sites, in fact, offered one-time promotions to attract viewers. However, unlike the costs of switching between traditional financial services information companies, switching costs on the Internet are essentially nil, and those one-time promotional strategies proved costly.

Still, for a time, eyeballs ruled. It didn't matter how much money sites spent to get viewers until the spring of 2000, when Internet stocks and financial information providers literally crashed. That's because the game changed literally overnight, moving from eyeballs to profitability. It wasn't unusual for a fledgling financial information Internet site to command a lofty valuation based on traffic alone. But then a dirty word, "monetize," emerged, and suddenly eyeballs just didn't do it. Sites had to figure out a way to monetize those eyeballs, and that's where things went awry for many companies.

Many firms, which literally had to change business plans in midstream, watched as their valuations plummeted, investors reneged on their financing commitments, or they simply went out of business altogether. The spring 2000 bloodbath spared few and claimed many.

As we now sort through the rubble, some solid ideas and business concepts that took severe body blows remain standing. While Internet financial information companies no longer are the darlings of Wall Street, many do offer tremendous potential, and the survivors will reap huge rewards in the next 3 to 5 years. The winners will be those companies that focus on the message, not the medium. In other words, it no longer means much to be simply an Internet or an online financial information company. Rather, the winners will be those companies that deliver what consumers want and need. It just so happens that the best way for those companies to meet those needs will be via the Internet.

In the mid-1990s before Wall Street's huge gains, before online trading, and before the proliferation of Internet chat rooms and financial information sites, the retail investor really couldn't play on a level playing field with the professionals. Sure, some had access to 24-hour business television news or radio, but in order to execute the simplest trade, it cost the retail investor an average of $150 at a discount broker to several hundred dollars at a full-service broker. It was pretty pricey to execute a simple trade, and most consumers couldn't afford to trade that often and therefore didn't demand timely financial information the way they do today.

If you consider investing to be a linear process where the beginning point of the line is an investing idea and the end point is executing a trade, investing in the early 1990s really was difficult. Until trading became inexpensive, most retail investors only had a series of discrete data points along that line with which they could make their investing decisions. We call that, simply, the *investing continuum* (Figure 13-1).

Let's say you wanted to invest in AT&T, for example. As recently as 1993 or 1994, retail investors really had very little access to information. Perhaps they could obtain an annual report, get a dated analyst recommendation from a full-service broker, or hear a mention of the company on CNBC or CNN, or perhaps they might stumble across an article in an investing magazine. That was really about it—those choices represented a series of discrete data points—and investors were lucky if they had access to all those points before they executed a very pricey trade. What retail investors demanded and what the Internet's financial informa-

Investing idea   Trade execution

FIGURE 13-1

Investing continuum.

tion companies ultimately offered was a fluid way, or a continuum, to go from investing idea to trade execution.

Consider today's investor. Let's say she has the idea to invest in AT&T. She can do a number of things pretty easily and seamlessly. Maybe she starts out on a major financial information aggregator like Yahoo! Finance or AOL and types in AT&T's ticker symbol. That will lead her to a stock quote, a company profile, detailed charts and graphs, message boards, analyst recommendations, and more.

If that's not enough (and it isn't for many retail investors these days), she can get access to real-time quotes, real-time streaming quotes, company conference calls, and more. Now, that line (or continuum), which starts with an investing idea and ends with an execution of a trade, contains an infinite number of points along it, thanks in large part to the emergence of Internet financial information sites.

Online financial information companies come in all different shapes and forms and occupy virtually all those different points along that continuum. This creates a competitive environment that is both cutthroat and confusing. When business development executives from two different Internet financial services companies meet together, there's a familiar question at the end of just about every meeting. Both sides generally feel that there is business to do together, but just as the meeting concludes, you'll hear one executive ask the other, "Do I pay you or do you pay me?"

That shows just how much in their infancy Internet financial services companies are today. It's reminiscent of cable television in the late 1970s and early 1980s. Back then, most cable networks paid the cable providers to carry their programming. But as cable television programming matured, the tables turned and eventually the networks began getting fees (generally a few cents per subscriber) directly from those same cable providers. It was a classic push-pull strategy. Cable networks pushed their programming on viewers by paying the cable companies at first to reach potential consumers. Once those consumers showed that they wanted specific programming—the cable networks pulled in the viewers by offering compelling products—the cable networks began demanding fees from the cable providers.

The key to the successful cable network's strategy was to create programming (or in today's parlance, content) that met the specific needs and wants of consumers and that consumers would actually pay for, albeit indirectly via the cable providers. That's the same daunting challenge facing online financial information companies—to create content that simultaneously meets the needs of the consumer and generates meaningful revenue. Again, in today's Internet geekspeak, that's simply what "monetizing eyeballs" means.

So just who are the players in this race to monetize eyeballs? It's a pretty diverse group of businesses that cuts across your traditional "brick-and-mortar" companies to your pure, much ballyhooed Internet companies. Each type of company faces virtually the exact same challenges.

- *The brokers.* Firms in this segment run the gamut from Merrill Lynch, a full-service broker turned discount broker turned online broker; to Charles Schwab, a discount broker cum online broker; to Ameritrade, a pure online broker. Much as Merrill Lynch offered its research and other goodies to top clients in the early 1990s, Merrill, Schwab, and Ameritrade now must offer a host of tools and information in order to retain customers today. The brokers, unlike many in the online financial services space, have generated significant revenues through trading fees. But as trading becomes more and more of a commodity, those fees will undoubtedly decline, and all these brokers will need to figure out ways to monetize eyeballs in different ways.

- *The aggregators.* Consider Yahoo! Finance, AOL, and others as if they were the cable television providers of the late 1970s and early 1980s. Many consumers begin their search for financial information at these locations; and Websites, brokers, and others clamor to get good placement. As a result, AOL, for example, can charge brokers a stiff fee just to appear on its site. And, AOL can charge pure financial information providers like CBS Marketwatch for placement—much in the same way that cable providers charged programmers for placement two decades earlier. As we know, the tides ultimately turned against the cable providers, and the AOLs of the world certainly are aware of that. For the foreseeable future, though, the aggregators attract huge amounts of traffic, and they are the places where just about anyone who wants to be anywhere online must go to reach a critical mass of consumers.

- *Information providers.* Many pure Internet brand names have popped up in the past few years and have dramatically changed the way investors consume financial information. Players like CBS Marketwatch, Motley Fool, and TheStreet.com now command huge audiences both via the aggregators and directly from their own Websites. Still, even these companies are struggling to find a compelling way to turn a profit. TheStreet.com generates subscription fees, but recently decided to focus on collecting ad revenues and now allows free access to a major chunk of the site. CBS Marketwatch works on a pure advertising model with limited revenue from subscription products—it's far from turning a profit. Sites from major media products like the *Wall Street Journal* boast a huge subscription base, but the bulk of the information that it provides comes from services that generate revenue by traditional means. The *Wall Street Journal* is dancing a delicate line of creating a new revenue stream with its Web product without cannibalizing its existing, moneymaking operations.

- *Other major players.* There are a host of other Internet financial services that don't fall neatly into the above three categories. For example, Multex.com earns money by selling research on a pay-per-view basis to the retail investor as well as offering a suite of tools and applications that it sells directly to other Websites. Sites like Stockpoint.com and European Investor offer a suite of news feeds, stock quotes, research recommendations, and more to other Websites and compete with Multex. Go2Net collects subscription fees from to its message board, Silicon Investor, from the retail consumer while it also licenses proprietary technology to other Websites. GlobalNet Financial collects ad revenue from its many Websites by providing retail investors financial information, collects licensing fees with a suite of data products, and earns money via a brokerage unit.

- *Niche players.* As the Internet exploded in the past few years, a number of niche sites popped up. Those include sites focused on relatively small retail markets like foreign exchange trading, options trading, emerging markets information and more. Other sites are staking their claims as watchdogs for the retail investor and they appear to offer valuable services, but they aren't yet catching on with the retail investor. Those sites include Bulldog Research, which tracks Wall Street analysts, and Validea.com, which tracks the recommendations from some of the financial media.

Let's go back to that line that begins with the investing idea and ends with the execution of the trade. Most brokers occupy the far right of that line, while companies like TheStreet.com reside at the far left of the line. The real winners in the online financial services area will be those that can capture as much of the line as possible and somehow collect revenues along the way (Figure 13-2).

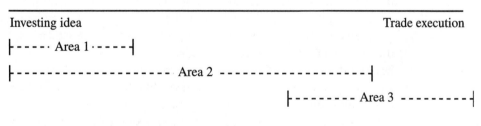

Area 1 = The Street.com, CBS Marketwatch
Area 2 = AOL Personal Finance, Yahoo! Personal Finance, Multex
Area 3 = E*Trade, Charles Schwab

FIGURE 13-2

Investing Continuum.

Here's a look at several of the companies among these various sectors that appear to be in the best position to thrive in the next 3 to 5 years. However, each top company faces a number of challenges, and each must execute its strategy flawlessly and with ruthless efficiency in order to survive.

Perhaps the company best poised to dominate this continuum is E*Trade, thanks to the sheer number of services that it offers and to an overlooked but powerful deal that the company made in May 2000. Today, E*Trade offers consumers stock trading, mutual fund trading, an Internet bank, news and information from outside vendors (including *Business Week*, Standard and Poor's, TheStreet.com, and others), a suite of data screening tools, analyst recommendations, and more. In other words, if you're a customer of E*Trade, you could do nearly all your trading, banking, and research directly from your computer. There's even talk that E*Trade plans to develop its own news division in order to take ownership of just about everything along that investing continuum.

Still, that's not enough for many consumers. Most have been reluctant to turn over their banking activities to an online firm for one simple reason—online firms usually don't have a physical presence. That's crucial if you're looking to make deposits or simply withdraw cash. Now, enter perhaps the most significant but overlooked deal that hit the financial services industry in 2000. E*Trade acquired the nation's largest network of independent ATMs. Literally overnight, E*Trade emerged with a physical presence that consumers demanded, the ATM. And remember the ATM essentially is an online service that consumers just happen to access from kiosks. It's now possible for E*Trade to infiltrate virtually every area of a retail investor's activity.

The big question is how will the company make money along the way. It's far from profitable, and its stock price performance shows that most aren't entirely convinced that the company will emerge as a winner in the long run. It faces competitive threats from brokers like Schwab, to banks like Citigroup, to even aggregators like AOL. Despite those competitive threats, E*Trade's management knew that it had to solidify and diversify its revenue stream, which was dominated by trading fees, in order to survive and flourish. It essentially implied that although it occupied that far right of that investing continuum, that wasn't enough. It needed to offer tools and services like news feeds in order to keep customers on its site so that they could make more transactions and the company could earn more trading fees. It also needed to offer additional services, like banking, in order to generate a host of new fees. Interestingly, E*Trade for all intents and purposes appears to show it doesn't expect to earn money from the left side of that investing continuum—it appears that other online players can earn money in that part of the line.

One stock in the Internet financial services space that Wall Street seems to hold in high regard is Multex.com. As of August 18, 2000, the market cap of Multex was roughly the equivalent of the combined market caps of TheStreet.com, CBS Marketwatch, and GlobalNet Financial. (E*Trade's market cap, by contrast, is seven times that of Multex.) Multex stands positioned to thrive for a number of reasons. First, it occupies a host of different points along that investing continuum and reaches the consumer directly and via relationships with other companies.

For example, Multex distributes an e-mail newsletter called the *Internet Analyst* designed specifically for the consumer market. It also has revenue-sharing relationships with the research arms of the Salomon Smith Barneys and Lehmans of the world. Finally, it offers a suite of tools and applications like company capsules, stock quotes, and analyst recommendations, which it sells in various packages to other Websites. The CEO of Multex views the mission of his company a bit differently. Isaak Karaev views his company as a financial information database company, which he feels just happens to package and present information to both the consumer and business markets in the most efficient way possible. Karaev's mission is consistent with hitting as many points along the investing continuum as possible. While revenues at Multex have grown dramatically from quarter to quarter, they have grown from a tiny base and as of the second quarter of 2000 stood at $19 million. Multex appears positioned to thrive in the future of online services, but the company's revenue for all of 2000 totaled less than $90 million, a tiny fraction of its offline competitors like Thomson Financial.

The most dominant players among information aggregators undoubtedly are Yahoo! Finance and AOL Personal Finance. Both offer tremendous amounts of information, attract huge viewerships, and rely heavily on advertising or sponsorship for the bulk of their revenues. However, in the second quarter of 2000, brokers, many of whom had paid huge sponsorship fees to appear in both Yahoo and AOL, began to question whether those fees were worth it. Since brokers measure their efficiency by the acquisition cost of a new consumer, the deals with these aggregators began to look expensive. Many analysts also question whether AOL and Yahoo can continue to demand top dollar for ads on their sites.

Interestingly, both AOL and Yahoo also derive additional revenue in the same manner as the cable providers derived it in the late 1970s and early 1980s. Yahoo and AOL are both paid by some of their content partners for carriage on their respective sites. In the short term, that has created a reliable, predictable flow of revenue for these two aggregators. But remember that there is a push-pull effect. When consumers begin to demand that AOL and Yahoo carry various content, the leverage shifts to the content providers and revenues once again would be under threat.

For the next few years, though, few sites if any will be able to create such a huge audience, and Yahoo! Finance and AOL Personal Finance will hold on to their market leading positions. Both boast impressive brand names and both are technologically superior to most of their competitors. AOL Personal Finance has gained an added advantage following its merger with Time Warner. AOL now has homegrown content via CNNfn, *Fortune*, *Money*, and other Time Warner financial news products. That gives it the edge over Yahoo, which has to rely on outside vendors for virtually all of its content. Look, however, for Yahoo's name to come up frequently in merger speculation with media companies. The bottom line: AOL and Yahoo each reach retail investors directly via the entire investing continuum, with the exception of the trade execution.

CBS Marketwatch, like AOL, benefits from its relationship with a huge media partner. In Marketwatch's case, that partner is CBS television, which promotes the Marketwatch site aggressively to its huge U.S. audience. Marketwatch also is developing television products and services, which many local CBS affiliates run on their stations. That partnership has helped Marketwatch generate the biggest online audience among all pure online content providers. That said, the bulk of its revenues come from advertising, and the amount that content providers can charge for advertising drops virtually every quarter. Marketwatch needs a critical amount of advertising revenue to support itself, and if it can come up with licensing deals or other revenue sources, it will emerge as a long-term survivor. It, like AOL and Yahoo, offers many points across the investing continuum, with the exception of the trade execution.

There are a number of wildcards that could threaten the dominance of any or all of these companies. Those wildcards include the emergence of broadband technology, widespread adoption of an alternative handheld medium (either the handphone set or the Palm Pilot), and the globalization of markets. While all these firms are making strides in each of these areas, as the future unfolds, a player might emerge that capitalizes on all three of these areas in a much more efficient way than the major players of today. In the meantime, the challenge for all online financial information providers remains to create meaningful revenue along the investing continuum. That means each successful company must deliver the message that the consumer (business or retail) wants and needs, and no longer can rely just on the medium itself, the Internet, to dominate a market or grow market capitalization.

CHAPTER 14

Financial Services Portals: The Winners in a New Era

Amy Butte, Financial Services Analyst and Managing Director
Bear Stearns
in collaboration with
Christine Haggerty, Managing Director
Bear Stearns

Contrary to the dire predictions made earlier this year, "old economy" retail securities and asset-management companies (and asset-gathering business models in general) are holding up well against the onslaught of online rivals. Rather than fighting change, many of these firms have embraced it, harnessing new technologies to broaden their services, improve efficiencies, and strengthen their competitiveness. And though technological transformation of the U.S. equity market could trigger a major shake-up of the industry, we also believe that a number of well-positioned players can continue to flourish in this new environment.

We expect the securities industry to gradually evolve into a barbell-shaped competitive hierarchy, with the scale providers (i.e., low-cost, volume-based business models) at one end and the full-service providers (i.e., value-added fee structure, margin-based business models) at the other (see Figure 14-1). Firms in the middle will be forced to choose between earning diminishing returns and being acquired. Many of them are seriously scale disadvantaged, meaning that they lack the critical mass to attain adequate economies of scale, generate long-term profits, and grow their businesses.

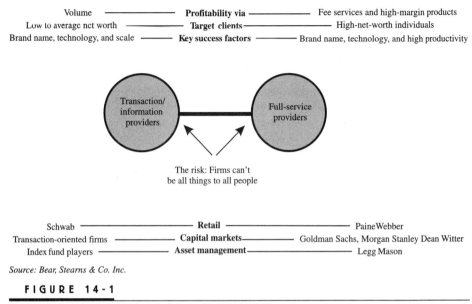

Volume ——————— **Profitability via** ——————— Fee services and high-margin products
Low to average net worth ——————— **Target clients** ——————— High-net-worth individuals
Brand name, technology, and scale ——— **Key success factors** ——————— Brand name, technology, and high productivity

The risk: Firms can't
be all things to all people

Schwab ————————————— **Retail** ————————————— PaineWebber
Transaction-oriented firms ——————— **Capital markets** ————— Goldman Sachs, Morgan Stanley Dean Witter
Index fund players ——————— **Asset management** ——————— Legg Mason

Source: Bear, Stearns & Co. Inc.

FIGURE 14-1

Choosing sides: A barbell-shaped competitive spectrum.

As we envision it, long-term success will hinge on how well each firm establishes itself as a financial services aggregator or as the primary source ("portal") for all its clients' financial services needs—whether it be through traditional broker-client relationships or newer online information-advisory-trading services, or a combination of both. Many of today's market leaders have already begun to capitalize on their scale advantages and strong brand images, and enjoy a good head start in the race to aggregate assets. They are also making the extensive investments needed to build the necessary infrastructure to compete in a more technology-driven business and to win new accounts.

ASSET GATHERING REMAINS A VIABLE GROWTH BUSINESS

There is a common perception (or misperception as the case may be) that the asset-gathering business is on its last legs. Proponents of this thesis argue that the firms in this business are doomed to watch their profits wither away as a result of increasingly fierce price competition, especially from new online entrants. We couldn't disagree more. Though the industry is likely to undergo great change over the next decade, we see plenty of growth opportunities, particularly as the baby-boomer generation starts to hit retirement age. Hence, we think the retail securities business (and asset-gathering strategies in general) remains a viable growth area capable of generating strong long-term returns for investors.

ADDRESSABLE MARKET CONTINUES TO GROW BRISKLY

We're projecting that compound annual organic asset growth could average 10 to 12 percent over the next 5 to 10 years. We define the addressable market as total household liquid financial assets—or assets accessible to financial companies offering products and services to U.S. investors. As of year-end 1999, these assets totaled an estimated $17.4 trillion, divided among banks, brokers, mutual fund companies, insurance companies, and other financial institutions (see Table 14-1). We estimate that the retail securities and mutual fund companies maintain market share positions of 40 percent and 25 percent, respectively. Total household liquid financial assets have expanded at a compound annual rate of nearly 15 percent over the past 3 years, up from an 11 percent rate in the 1990s and the 9.5 percent seen in the 1980s (see Figure 14-2). Obviously, these figures have been buoyed by strong equity returns in recent years. However, to be conservative, our estimates exclude options and warrants from our liquid asset totals.

RETIRING BABY BOOMERS COULD GENERATE AN ASSET BONANZA

The pace of organic asset growth could pick up again later in the decade as retiring baby boomers begin to seek alternative places to park their retirement funds and enter the consumption phase of their lives. To determine the size of this opportunity to the securities industry, we examined several data points:

- *The starting point: $2.5 trillion in liquid retirement assets.* Out of the $17.4 trillion (as the first half of 2000) in total U.S. liquid household financial assets, we know that at least $2.5 trillion is earmarked for retirement through vehicles such as IRAs (note the overlap in Figure 14-3). In addition to this

TABLE 14-1

Defining Household Liquid Financial Assets

Liquid Financial Assets from the Federal Reserve Flow of Funds	
	$, in Trillions
Total U.S. deposits*	4.3
Credit instruments*	2.0
Corporate equities	8.0
Mutual fund shares	3.1
Total household liquid financial assets	17.4

*As classified by the Federal Reserve, deposits include checkable deposits and currency, time and savings deposits, and money market fund shares; and credit instruments include open-market paper, U.S. government securities, municipal securities, corporate and foreign bonds, and mortgages.
Source: Fed Flow of Funds, Bear Stearns & Co.

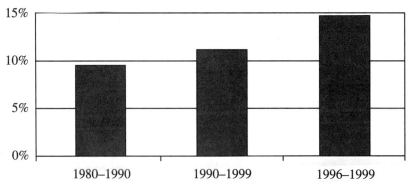

Source: Fed Flow Funds, SIA, Bear Stearns & Co.

FIGURE 14-2

Household liquid financial asset growth continues to accelerate historical CAGR of household liquid financial assets.

$2.5 trillion, two other sources could increase the available pool of retirement assets: (1) other liquid assets that have been earmarked for retirement but are not necessarily defined as such at this time (e.g., some portion of the $3.1 trillion in mutual fund assets could fit this description) and (2) some portion of illiquid retirement assets (e.g., "defined contribution" or "defined benefit" assets), which total an estimated $11.5 trillion.

- *Demographic trends.* According to industry data, on average, people over 60 years of age hold total assets of an estimated $210,000, with 27 percent invested in retirement vehicles. As shown in Figure 14-4, baby boomers begin

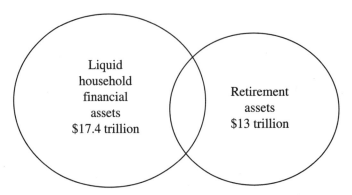

Source: Federal Reserve Flow of Funds, ICI, Bear Stearns & Co. estimates

FIGURE 14-3

IRA assets overlap liquid household financial assets.

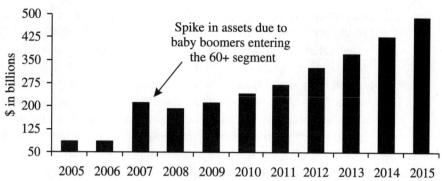

Source: Bear Stearns & Co. estimates; SRI MacroMonitor; U.S. Census

FIGURE 14-4

Assets up for grabs between 2005 and 2015. Estimated incremental assets available upon population reaching age 60.

to enter the 60-year-old age bracket in 2007, and the growth of this age group accelerates through 2020. Taking these two factors into account, we estimate that retirement assets of between $80 billion and $500 billion per year will be up for grabs between 2005 and 2015.

■ *The retirement rollover trend.* The key to understanding our view about the enormous opportunity opening up for the securities industry is the trend in retirement rollovers. Our research indicates that most retirement-related assets are "unsticky," or transitory, meaning that a significant percentage of people tend to change the domicile of their household financial assets (i.e., the financial institution that maintains the primary relationship with the owner of the

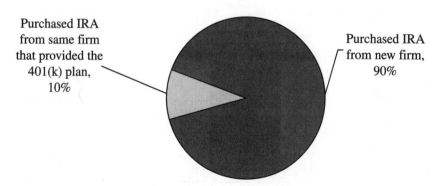

Source: VIP Forum; data from 1996–1997

FIGURE 14-5

Transitory retirement assets open up huge growth opportunities. Job changers and retirees' choice for IRA rollover destination.

assets) when they reach retirement age. According to data gleaned from VIP Forum, only 10 percent of assets owned by both job changers and retirees being rolled over into an IRA stay with the original plan sponsors (see Figure 14-5). Retirees withdraw less than 12 percent of available cash and roll the rest over into other IRA vehicles, thus further delaying tax consequences (see Figure 14-6). As important, there does not appear to be any definitive pattern or destination choice to their reallocated (or rolled-over) funds. As shown in Figure 14-7, the 401(k) lump sums rolled over by retirees into IRAs during the 1996–1997 period were spread across multiple investment firms.

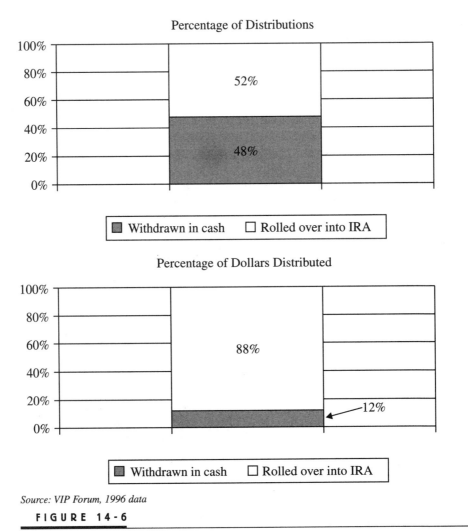

Source: VIP Forum, 1996 data

FIGURE 14-6

Retirees are rolling retirement plans into IRAs. Retiree 401(k) lump-sum distributions—Number of distributions versus the dollar volume of distributions.

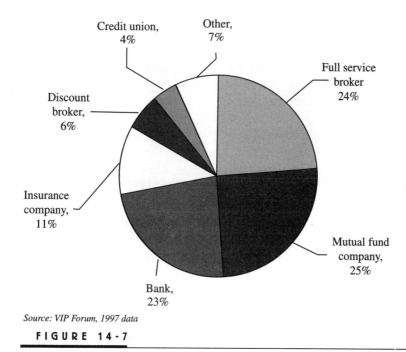

Source: VIP Forum, 1997 data

F I G U R E   1 4 - 7

Lump-sum rollovers Into IRAs are spread across the spectrum. 401(k) Lump-sum distribution destination of choice for rollover IRAs.

Assuming that current asset-allocation trends remain unchanged, we estimate that the industry could see net annual asset inflows climb from $7 billion in 2000 to roughly $190 billion by 2015. In aggregate, this implies an organic growth rate of 18 percent off the current base of assets. We expect that retail brokers could capture 50 to 80 percent of the available (or transitory) retirement-related assets per year, as a number of these firms have successfully positioned themselves as true financial aggregators and have effectively incorporated technology into their businesses. Accordingly, we estimate that incremental assets at the retail brokers can grow at a compound annual rate of 25 percent between 2000 and 2015. Assuming the upper end of the retirement asset take-away (or 80 percent), that sector's share could climb to 46 percent of the total asset pool by 2015, up from 40 percent today.

MUTUAL FUND COMPANIES: DEVISING NEW PLANS OF ATTACK

In our view, asset-management companies are at the most risk of losing assets, as a large percentage (roughly 49 percent) of the liquid IRA assets are domiciled with these companies. But despite the obvious challenges ahead for the mutual fund industry, a number of players have developed business strategies that we think could help them retain, if not increase, their share of the available business.

The Vertically Integrated Business Model

Fidelity Investments best exemplifies the vertically integrated asset-management company. Fidelity's three distribution channels—retail, institutional, and employer-sponsored retirement—have attracted best-in-class asset and account levels. Its broad offering of retirement products, mutual funds, and brokerage services and its use of active trader technologies provide retirees with plenty of places in which to roll over or reallocate their funds. In this way, if assets move out of a Fidelity fund, they at least stay within the complex. For this reason, we believe that Fidelity can maintain, if not increase, its market share over the coming years.

The Income-Focused Business Model

T. Rowe Price's recently launched Retirement Income Manager (RIM) program provides a good example of how new technology is changing the rules of the game for retirement relationships. Specifically, T. Rowe is moving the issue from asset accumulation to postretirement income management—hoping to reduce, if not eliminate, the rollover concern. The RIM product uses proprietary complex financial models to deliver a comprehensive solution that is tailored to individual goals and preferences. Once the client completes the detailed profile, RIM executes a Monte Carlo analysis—testing hundreds of retirement income strategies against 500 hypothetical scenarios of future market conditions. Furthermore, RIM uses multiattribute utility theory to consider the best fit based on the client's objectives. The personalized income and investment strategy—which recommends asset allocation and, more importantly, suggests an appropriate monthly income—is reviewed annually with a counselor. This personalized solution also considers minimum required distributions, tax-smart drawdown strategies, and annuities. According to management, the unique service differs from many of the Web-delivered retirement plans because of its combination of patent-pending technology and human interaction to provide a recommended retirement income strategy for clients receiving lump-sum retirement payments. We believe that this advanced "move-to-action" technology bodes well for the firm's strategic positioning. Early indications suggest RIM is attracting new accounts with average assets 10 to 15 times higher than the typical account.

New Technologies

There are also a slew of new technologies that currently exist on a stand-alone basis and that have been incorporated into the asset-gathering strategies of the traditional players. Financial Engines is a good example of the new technology popping up in workplaces across America. Founded by William Sharpe (1990 Nobel Prize winner), Joe Grundfest (a former SEC commissioner), and Craig Johnson (Venture Law Group), Financial Engines' mission is to provide impartial, personalized financial advice to individuals and Fortune 500 companies over the Internet.

The service forecasts how much the individual's portfolio might be worth in the future and offers personalized recommendations on how to invest retirement assets to meet those future goals. In many respects, these tools allow clients to take more responsibility for their retirement investment choices while also providing them greater access to information via the Internet. We believe that the growing acceptance of these tools indicates that traditional asset managers are starting to understand the power of these newer technologies and how they can be used to attract future rollovers into their complexes. For example, as part of its emerging affluent market strategy, PaineWebber uses mPower Technology (a competitor of Financial Engines) to help clients determine asset allocations in their 401(k) plans. As just one of the many programs featured on PaineWebber's corporate employee services' Web portal, we think it suggests how firms are seeking to incorporate multiple technologies into their asset-gathering strategies.

RETAIL SECURITIES–CONTINUING THE QUEST FOR AGGREGATOR STATUS

We believe that, similar to what has taken place in the Internet portal space, the retail securities firms that are able to secure a role as the primary source, or "portal," for all their customers' financial services needs—whether it be through traditional broker-client relationships or, newer online operations, or a combination of both—will dominate the business and enjoy the strongest long-term growth. In examining the potential of the various strategies currently being pursued within the retail securities industry, we focused on three key defining factors:

- *The cost of acquiring a new account.* This is an important criteron, since we believe that the lower a company's cost of acquiring a new account (Table 14-2), the greater its chance of becoming a financial services portal. Our research indicates that the more extensive the product offering, the less a firm will need to spend to attract a new client. As shown in Figure 14-8, TDWaterhouse and Schwab spend the least amount of money to win new business, while

TABLE 14-2

Client Acquisition Costs*

Marketing Spending as a Percentage of Net New Assets Acquired	
	Last 6 Months Annualized
PaineWebber Group	0.15%
Merrill Lynch	0.18%
Morgan Stanley Dean Witter	0.19%
Charles Schwab	0.23%

Source: Company reports; Competitrack; Bear, Stearns & Co. Inc. estimates.
*MWD acquisition costs were calculated based on changes in asset balances, net of the appreciation in the S&P.

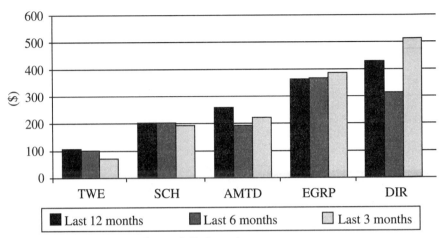

Source: Company reports; Bear, Stearns & Co. Inc. estimates

FIGURE 14-8

Client Acquisition Costs, marketing spending per new account. Note: For SCH, AMTD, and TWE, we use new accounts disclosed by the firms; for DIR and EGRP, we use change in active accounts. For EGRP, we assume 10 percent of its accounts are option accounts and exclude them from our analysis.

E*Trade, Ameritrade, and DLJdirect are currently being forced to spend $250 to $450 to lure clients to their sites, which leads us to believe that their value proposition to clients is below that of the first group.

- *Strategic focus.* A company with a horizontal focus competes on the basis of scale and generates profits as a result of inherent economies. A firm with a vertical focus tends to emphasize its broad product line and/or wide selection or high quality of services. A second-tier firm's primary focus is to acquire accounts and assets, which typically means that a large percentage of investment spending is plowed into advertising or marketing. In comparison, top-tier players (i.e., those we believe have the best chance of becoming financial services portals) do not need to spend as aggressively on advertising because they already possess adequate scale and strong brand equity and, hence, can afford to channel their investment dollars into incremental services or tools that will help them capture new clients and assets (see Figure 14-9).
- *Earnings power.* We also believe that a firm's earnings power is an important indicator of its potential to become one of the ultimate winners in this fiercely competitive business (see Figure 14-10). Aside from its obvious role in creating shareholder value, earnings power can help to determine a company's ability to "buy" market share (i.e., offer incremental products and services and invest in the brand) and to reinvest in the franchise (i.e., to stimulate future growth).

Under this analysis, E*Trade, Ameritrade, and DLJdirect appear to be the most susceptible to incremental competitive pressures and earnings shortfalls in

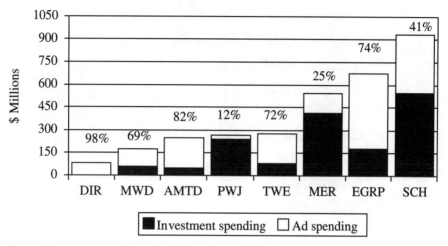

Source: Company reports; Competitrack; Bear, Stearns & Co. Inc. estimates

FIGURE 14-9

Horizontal versus integration focus. Advertising as a percent of total investment spending at retail competitors. Total investment is defined as estimated advertising costs plus purchases of furniture, equipment, and leasehold improvements.

the event of a sharp market downturn, while Charles Schwab, PaineWebber, and TDWaterhouse could experience the least amount of damage.

The Cutting Edge

We expect many of the following technologies to be incorporated into the broad product offerings of the retail securities companies. Thus, the lists below are not intended to promote specific companies, or to suggest that acquisitions are imminent, but rather to provide examples of how new technology can extend and is extending the reach of aggregator players.

Aggregation Vehicles

Aggregation vehicles facilitate the asset-gathering process through the use of technology and the Internet. In our view, the leading players include myCFO, Intuit's Quicken, IMWorth's Private Label system, X.com, and Vertical One's Account Keeper. For our part, we prefer myCFO, which is pioneering a new comprehensive service model that brings unprecedented round-the-clock financial management services to high-net-worth clients. The advanced technology of myCFO alleviates much of the administrative detail, thereby allowing advisers and CFOs to focus on delivering advice to clients. Finally, myCFO provides high-net-worth individuals with a single source for all their financial needs.

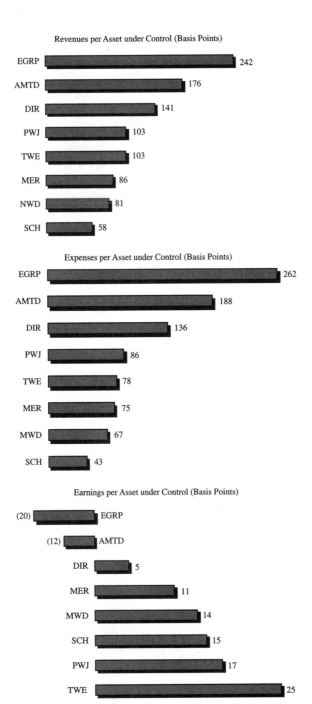

Source: Bear, Stearns & Co. Inc.; company reports

FIGURE 14-10

Differentiating retail securities model. Revenues and earnings per asset under control.

Insurance

Online insurance companies provide consumers ways to obtain the full range of insurance products—albeit in a less paper-intensive environment than that of the traditional insurance companies. In our view, Channelpoint, Quotesmith, Insweb, ebix, and Insurance Holding Company of America represent the most visible players in this niche today. Our favorite is Channelpoint. This company's business-to-business (B2B) technology enables financial services firms to expand their product offering, a competitive necessity in the fight among distributors to secure the role as the primary source of a client's total financial services needs. Channelpoint's advanced technology platform also eliminates the administrative functions of selling insurance and facilitates the incorporation of insurance products into total financial plans. Through Channelpoint, brokers will be able to offer insurance products as an option within an investment portfolio. It also creates incremental distribution channels for multiple insurance products.

Credit Providers

Credit providers make loans—ranging from home to auto—available to consumers via the Internet, thereby eliminating the time-consuming application process at many traditional providers. In our view, the players with the greatest market profiles include Lending Tree Inc., GetSmart.com, KeyStroke.com., E-LOAN, iOwn.com, LoansDirect, Loanworks.com, LoanCity.com, Mortgage.com, and IMX Exchange. Our favorite, however, is LoansDirect, mainly because of its direct-lender versus referral model. By incorporating this firm's direct-lender online platform into a brokerage business, a retail broker can save time without increasing its risk. For example, by adding a LoansDirect "button" to a client's home page, a retail securities firm would be able to (1) enhance its product offering, thereby reducing the risk that the client will go elsewhere; (2) enhance the client's portfolio view, by integrating the liability side of the balance sheet into the financial portfolio; (3) eliminate the need for advisers to learn an additional product, which thereby frees their time for providing incremental value-added; and (4) eliminate the need for the firm to take on incremental credit risk—a noncore competency at many retail securities firms.

Other Tools

We would count X.com, iexchange, escrow.com, Virtual Financial Services, and iescrow.com among the most well-known online asset-aggregation tools. Of these, we think escrow.com is a good company on which to focus. Through its advanced technology and user-friendly, secure Internet platform, escrow.com is positioning itself as the leading online transaction services provider. The firm's B2B, B2C, and C2C infrastructure provides an open, scalable, and 100 percent reliable business application for managing postsale transactions over the Internet. Furthermore, escrow.com's comprehensive e-commerce solution protects both buyers and sellers against fraud. While not completely analogous to the secure feeling that arises when entering the safe deposit department of the local bank, escrow.com creates a relatively "safe" financial environment for online clients. In our view, this will be important to users, whether or not they are transferring funds or buying and selling financial products via financial services aggregators.

Role Models

Retail securities firms are currently using technology in one of two ways: (1) to spur clients into action such that the firms attract a greater share of available investment dollars and (2) to increase the "stickiness" of the assets once they find a home. While all companies are incorporating some form of technology into their product offerings (e.g., Merrill Lynch uses online content and consumer goods sales), we believe that Charles Schwab and PaineWebber represent the most proactive approaches.

Charles Schwab: The Scale-Based Model

Schwab's scale-oriented model is based on the firm's ability to use technology and automation to keep expenses down and maintain its status as a low-cost provider of financial services. A chief part of the scale strategy rests in using technology to both (1) attract and aggregate assets and (2) continuously expand the service offering, giving the client little reason to want to switch to another firm. Beyond recent announcements relating to online bond trading (via eSpeed), direct-access trading technologies (via the acquisition of CyberCorp), and online loans (via E*Loan), Schwab incorporates many customizable (thus stickier) services into its arsenal. For example, MySchwab is an offering made available in connection with Excite that lets individuals create a personalized home page. With MyResearchReport, clients can generate customizable reports, by choosing data points (e.g., estimates and news) they find the most useful. Online bill paying, electronic funds transfers, Schwab Alerts, and eConfirms add to the Schwab experience. Finally, products such as the Portfolio Check Up provide tools for clients to analyze their portfolios—and, the hope is, create incremental incentives for bringing new assets to the Schwab complex.

PaineWebber: A Full-Service Model

PaineWebber's goal is to use technology to deepen the relationships between the client and the financial adviser, and PaineWebber and the adviser, such that both relationships are made stronger. As an example of its commitment to new technologies, the firm has recently invested in numerous e-related companies, including BondDesk.com, MuniDesk.com, and Charitableway.com (see Table 14-3). Furthermore, we expect PaineWebber to roll out incremental aggregation offerings, online credit and loan offerings, and portfolio allocation tools in the next few quarters. In our view, however, what makes PaineWebber's approach different from that of Schwab or other online firms is how it empowers the brokers, giving them responsi-

TABLE 14-3

PWJ E-Related Investments

Investment	Description/Function
BondDesk.com	Online retail fixed-income trading
Charitableway.com	Online charitable contributions
ClickThings	Website developer for small and medium-size businesses
Enba	European online bank
Investor Broadcast Network	Online broadcasting of corporate events
mPower	Online advice for 401(k) participants
MiniDesk.com	Online retail municipal bond trading
OneCore	Online financial services for small and medium-size businesses
W-Trade	Wireless trading and banking
Source: Bear Stearns.	

bility for disseminating information and for maintaining the client relationship. While the client receives easy access to information, PaineWebber's brokers receive tools with which to enhance their client relationships. For example, these brokers can customize their clients' home pages, receive information about their clients' online experiences, and generate on-the-fly analyses of their clients' portfolios.

CHAPTER 15

Online Asset Management

Kevin D. Freeman, Co-Founder and Chairman
Separate Account Solutions, Inc.

Erik H. Davidson, Co-Founder and President
Separate Account Solutions, Inc.

INTRODUCTION

Online financial services represent a revolution already under way. With the point and click of a mouse, individuals can easily pay bills, swap collectibles, trade stocks, bank, obtain loans, and perform a host of tasks that once required a much more formal setting. The common denominator for all these functions, however, is that they all can be performed without the delivery of external, professional advice.

Naturally, an advice component can augment any of the described tasks. Investors may seek guidance when buying or selling or even paying bills. Until recently, however, the advice component was delivered offline. This chapter will address the next generation of online financial services—the delivery of professional money management.

While the first generation of online financial services has already achieved substantial success (with more than 50 percent of all retail stock trades now performed online), it has also become commoditized. The price per stock trade has dropped below $10 and in some cases trades are free. Arguably, the second generation of service is far more complex, given its advice component. The question remains, however, whether or not it will also suffer commoditization over time.

This chapter will address the evolution and delivery of professional money management online. The changes already under way are radical. The landscape will never be the same again.

THE EVOLUTION OF PROFESSIONAL MANAGEMENT

For nearly as long as there has been a stock market, there has been a demand for advice relating to stock ownership. Pools of wealth were accumulated and then used by robber barons, bankers, and businessmen such as Vanderbilt, Fisk, Rothschild, Morgan, Drew, Astor, Gould, Keene, Sage, Gates, Rockefeller, and others. These men made and lost (and sometimes made again) fortunes for themselves and their backers. It was largely an unregulated (and often unscrupulous) enterprise.

Near the turn of the last century, the process of providing advice began to slowly shift to brokerage firms. Improved communications made it possible for the Wall Street brokers to maintain clientele across the country. In 1885, Burrill and Housman was formed in New York. It was later to become E. A. Pierce and Company. In 1915, Merrill Lynch and Company was formed. By 1940, the two had merged into what we know as Merrill Lynch today. Under the leadership of Charlie Merrill, stockbrokers became more than sellers of securities. Brokerage firms built research departments and provided market education and advice.[1]

With the bull market of the 1920s, the desire for professional management was so strong that blind pools were formed, offering individuals the chance to participate in market speculation. Never mind that the investors had no idea how the money was to be invested. That didn't matter nearly as much as who the blind pool operators were. In the best of cases such investments were risky. Some represented outright frauds. With the tremendous bubble building in the roaring twenties, however, demand for pooled vehicles continued to increase.

The truly wealthy have always been able to afford professional assistance when investing. Pooled vehicles made it possible for those of more average means to access such assistance. Sadly, however, these pools were largely unregulated. Stockbrokers also provided advice to the middle class although their advice was sometimes tainted by the sales commission they received. It wasn't until the Investment Company Act of 1940 that professional management truly became accessible in the form of the modern mutual fund.

Funds didn't become popular, however, until even later. As an example, noted mutual fund pioneer John Templeton began investing for clients in the 1930s, first with a brokerage firm and later with his own investment counsel firm for wealthy clients. He didn't get in to the mutual fund business until 1954 when he started the Templeton Growth Fund. Even then, available mutual funds were numbered in the dozens.

---

[1] Robert M. Sharp, *The Lore and Legends of Wall Street*, Dow Jones–Irwin, Homewood, IL, 1989.

Initially, funds were sold by brokers. These brokers were paid a "sales load" amounting to as much as 8.5 percent of the initial investment. Over the past 60 years, the fund industry has grown and evolved substantially. Now, investors buy no-load funds directly, without the services of brokers. The success of funds has been so spectacular that there are now more funds available than stocks listed on the New York Stock Exchange. Funds are available in every style and type. Index funds, foreign funds, convertible funds, sector funds, hedge funds, funds of funds, and others offer an extremely wide variety of alternatives. In addition, an entire industry has been built around providing advice and information regarding the professional managers of funds.

WHY FUNDS HAVE PROVED SO POPULAR

Mutual funds control in excess of $7 trillion today, from less than $100 billion just two decades ago, making them the most successful investment product in history.[2] The reasons for their tremendous success are simple. Mutual funds provide professional management, diversification, and simplicity, with low minimums and an affordable price. Most importantly, until recently, mutual funds were the only game in town available to most investors.

By pooling resources into funds, individuals can afford to hire the best managers and properly diversify investments. Until recently, most professional managers have had minimums of $10 million and some even $25 million. As late as 1989, I approached John Templeton on behalf of clients, asking that he consider personally managing their investments in the form of separate accounts. I was surprised to learn that his minimum outside of mutual funds was still $10 million. The Templeton funds were wildly popular, and John Templeton was named Mutual Fund Manager of the Year in 1990 by *USA Today*. Yet the only way for an individual to receive professional management from the Templeton organization at the time was to either buy a fund or invest more than $10 million.

Two reasons explained the high minimums. First, professional managers earned their fee as a percentage of assets under management. The cost of handling small accounts often exceeded the fee being charged, especially when accounting was done by hand instead of computer. Second, smaller client accounts couldn't afford the commission fees required by a diversified portfolio. If a manager held 50 stocks in a portfolio with annual turnover, the associated brokerage charges would have totaled several thousand dollars per year in the days of fixed commission rates. As a result, neither manager nor client could afford professional management for smaller accounts.

---

[2] Patrick McGeehan, "Online Funds, Built to Order," *The Wall Street Journal*, Aug. 13, 2000.

THE BIRTH OF AFFORDABLE SEPARATE ACCOUNTS

Two key factors made it possible for separate account minimums to decline. The first was a regulatory change. In 1971, the Securities and Exchange Commission ruled that commissions were negotiable for any trade involving $500,000 or more. Four years later, fixed rates were abolished for trades of any size. This now famous ruling was put in effect on May 1, 1975, and is known as "May Day" in the financial markets. Discount brokerage was allowed for the first time, giving rise to powerhouse Schwab and eventually the deep discounters such as E*Trade, Ameritrade, and other online brokers.

The ruling had another important effect. It allowed brokers to price their services in a variety of ways. Innovative E. F. Hutton seized the opportunity by pricing commissions as a percentage of assets for select clients rather than as a per-trade charge. Because all commissions are "wrapped up" in an annual percentage of assets charge (typically 2 percent), they became known as "wrap fees." Hutton offered this new approach to clients who utilized professional managers to pick their stocks in separate accounts rather than funds. This made it more affordable for individuals to access separate account management. There was no longer a fear that brokerage commissions would consume a portfolio. The account minimums dropped sharply, as low as $250,000 in some cases.

A separate account is a portfolio of securities owned by an individual (or institution) and managed directly for the benefit of that individual. Unlike a mutual fund, it is not a pooled vehicle with many owners. *The Wall Street Journal* made the following characterization:

> Essentially, separate accounts are custom made suits in a world of off-the-rack department store brands.[3]

While clients became able to afford separate accounts in 1975, it wasn't until much later that most managers could afford to provide them. The cost of tracking investment portfolios remained high well into the 1980s due to its labor-intensive nature. In addition, the best-performing managers were growing their business very nicely with mutual funds. With the bull market's start in August 1982 (when the Dow Jones Industrial Average was still well below 1000), professional money management through mutual funds became a booming business.

When I approached John Templeton in 1989, he did not believe it economical to manage separate accounts of less than $10 million. In fact, he was considering raising his minimum to $25 million. Yet ever the astute businessman, Mr. Templeton wrote to me a few months later asking for a business plan on how he might be able to lower his minimums and still make a profit. He sensed that the appeal of separate accounts was increasing and the demand would rise sharply. I

---

[3] "Dreyfus Joins Push to Pamper Its Clients," *The Wall Street Journal*, Feb. 23, 2000, p. C-27.

spent much of 1990 researching separate accounts and looking for the best way to affordably provide them. At the time, only a handful of brokerage firms offered separate accounts, with a total of only about $10 billion under management. Most of what the management firms offered (through the brokerage programs) were lesser known firms without a mutual fund alternative.

COMPUTERS WERE THE ANSWER

My research indicated that the money-management industry was slow in adopting the benefits of computerization. Certainly computers were used to provide stock quotes. Also, computers were used to keep track of mutual fund client rosters. For the most part, however, computers were not used in the areas of portfolio accounting, trading, and reporting. Yet these were the precise areas that made it uneconomical to manage smaller separate accounts. Fortunately, that was about to change—and change dramatically.

According to James Waller, senior vice president at CheckFree Investment Services[4]:

> In technology, Moore's Law indicates that processing price performance increases with the doubling of processing speed every 18–24 months. The productivity gains of wrap processing have mirrored that rate.
>
> In the 1980's, it was assumed institutional quality money management reporting would cost about $1,000 per year per portfolio—and that was just for the systems overhead allocation (never mind paying the portfolio manager or the broker consultant and their back office staff). Today, systems allow for sophisticated money management and reporting and trading solutions for under $100 per portfolio per year (and yes, the portfolio managers, brokers, and back office people still need to be paid).
>
> Technology has paved the way for these cost reductions. A decade ago, an institutional manager would typically have one reconciler for each account. Today, the "Kings of Wrap" have leveraged their operations so that one person can reconcile between five and eight thousand accounts.

Thus, the advent of the computer age combined with the deregulation of commissions has allowed both clients and managers the ability to afford lower separate account minimums. John Templeton caught the vision and asked me to come on board and help implement the business plan I had written. Less than a decade later, we profitably managed nearly $2.5 billion of separate accounts with a $100,000 minimum as a division of Franklin Resources.

---

[4] *Investment Consulting News and Wrap Fee Advisor*, Vol. 6, No. 2, 1999.

WHY CLIENTS FAVOR SEPARATE ACCOUNTS

Separate accounts offer a number of distinctive advantages over mutual funds. First and foremost, they allow clients to have customized portfolios unavailable through funds. Clients may choose not to hold a particular company or industry in their portfolio for any number of personal or economic reasons. For example, executives at Microsoft might prefer not to have any Microsoft or other technology shares in their managed separate account due to high levels of ownership in their option or profit-sharing plan. In a mutual fund, it would be virtually impossible to have the fund avoid ownership in these companies. In fact, fund shareholders have to wait as much as 6 months just to learn what the fund owns.

Similarly, many clients seek to apply social or personal screens on their portfolios. At Templeton, we managed a number of Catholic charities, which had a strict "no abortion" screen. As a result, we avoided ownership of certain health care providers for these clients. We also had clients who were concerned about the impact of deforestation on the environment. We avoided ownership in certain forest products companies in their portfolios. It would be impossible to enforce or even track these mandates in a mutual fund.

Another benefit of separate accounts involves tax control. Each year, mutual funds are required to distribute the vast majority of any gains or income enjoyed by the funds. These distributions then become taxable at the shareholder level. This system was implemented due to its relative simplicity. Unfortunately, it can also create some serious inequities. For example, more than 125 funds distributed more than 25 percent of their NAV in 2000,[5] and "More than 9% of the average fund's NAV was subject to capital gains taxes in 2000, according to a report by Wiesenberger."[6] These gains will be distributed to shareholders in the year they are realized. Yet it's possible that the shareholder wasn't in the fund when the gains were made, only when they were distributed. As a result, shareholders have absolutely no control over their tax liability and in some cases are taxed on gains they didn't even enjoy.

With a separate account, clients have much better control over their tax situation. In a given year, a client can request that shares not be sold at a gain or even that losses be taken if that would prove beneficial. At Templeton, we held a "tax loss derby" every year to see how many clients would take advantage of this benefit. We were always surprised by the number of clients that used the service and were pleased that we were able to help. One year, the very last request that came through was from the head coach of an NFL team. This individual had enjoyed a very good season and was receiving some bonuses that year. As a result, he asked us to sell every position that was below cost basis to provide some capital losses

---

[5] Michael Gaul, "Capital Gains in 2000: It's Payback Time!" *MorningStar*, Dec. 26, 2000.

[6] Collin Dodds, "2000 Was the Worst Tax Year Ever for Mutual Funds," *Ignites.com*, Feb. 14, 2001.

to offset the gains he was receiving. We were happy to oblige. By the way, his team went on to the Super Bowl that season!

Many other advantages could be listed. Perhaps one of the most important is that unlike mutual funds, separate accounts are not subject to the inflows and out-flows of other investors. One of the hardest things in managing a mutual fund has to do with managing the shareholders. Human nature is such that most investors will panic when markets fall and get greedy when markets are rising. As a result, fund managers are inundated with net redemptions as markets bottom and excess inflows when markets peak. Unfortunately, this is the exact opposite of the adage to "buy low and sell high." Even more unfortunately, it impacts every fund owner, even those who stayed the course and didn't buy or sell.

The best comparison here is between a private car and a public bus. Separate accounts are similar to a private car where the manager drives the client directly to his or her destination. While a public bus can also take passengers to destinations, it must stop at various points along the way to let people on and off. All other things being equal, a private car typically offers a superior experience to the public bus.

THE GROWTH OF THE SEPARATE ACCOUNT INDUSTRY

In 1990, approximately $10 billion was managed in broker-directed separate accounts. By 1993, the industry had grown to nearly $70 billion, according to Cerulli Associates. The Money Management Institute now estimates that total assets in separate accounts are in excess of $400 billion (see Figure 15-1).

One reason for this rapid growth is that the public is becoming more educated on the subject. For example, *The Wall Street Journal* has recently been touting the benefits:

> Clearly, separate accounts have strong selling points. Unlike investing in a mutual fund and immediately being exposed to the fund's imbedded capital gains, an investor has some say over stock purchases and sales in a separate account, giving him better control over his tax bills. Another advantage is that investors can say no to a stock they don't want to own—a tobacco company or defense contractor, perhaps—or one they already own in such quantity that they don't want any more.[7]

In addition, fund managers are rapidly entering the separate account market for fear of losing customers. In the early 1990s, Franklin-Templeton was alone among the very large mutual fund companies offering separate accounts. Recently, many other larger players have announced or are exploring plans to enter the separate account business:

---

[7] "Managed Accounts Win More Fans; Product Moves beyond the Rich," *The Wall Street Journal*, June 23, 2000, p. C-20.

SEPARATE BUT EQUAL?

Gaining fast in popularity are stock
portfolios managed on an individual
basis by professional stock pickers,
including mutual-fund managers. Total
assets in managed accounts, in billions.

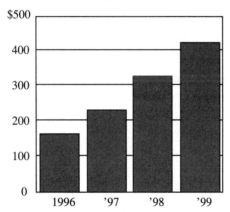

Source: The Money Management Institute

FIGURE 15-1

This graph from an article in The Wall Street Journal demonstrates the growth in the separate account market.
("Managed Accounts Win More Fans; Product Moves beyond the Rich," The Wall Street Journal, June 23,
2000, p. C-20.)

MFS and Oppenheimer Funds have just begun to target separate accounts for
sales. They join Janus, T. Rowe Price, Eaton Vance, Alliance and John Nuveen.[8]

As more investors bypass mutual funds, large fund-company Dreyfus Corp. is
following the money. Now it plans to roll out such a "separate account" alternative for investors interested in the services of managers who head the red-
hot Dreyfus Premier Technology Growth Fund as well as the socially
responsible Dreyfus Premier Third Century Fund. With the moves, Dreyfus
becomes the latest fund company to offer customized accounts to individual
investors.

In setting up separate-account businesses, fund firms are catering to
wealthy investors who want personalized attention and an upscale alternative
to mutual funds with their tax-inefficient, one-size fits all structure.[9]

Ultimately, we agree with Len Reinhart, chairman of the Lockwood
Financial Group and one of the pioneers of the separate account industry at E. F.
Hutton in the 1970s:

---

[8] "Fund Firms Step Up Separate Account Efforts," *Ignites.com*, Feb. 11, 2000.
[9] "Dreyfus Joins Push to Pamper Its Clients."

Five years from now, every major mutual fund company will have separate account products.[10]

The reason is very simple. As account minimums have dropped sharply due to computerization, account balances have simultaneously increased sharply due to wealth accumulation. This has dramatically increased the number of prospective clients.

It used to be that only a privileged few could afford their own money managers, but in the last few years assets in privately managed accounts have swelled. Credit, in part, a bull market that has more than doubled the number of millionaire households . . . to 5 million.[11]

THE DEATH OF MUTUAL FUNDS?

The modern mutual fund was "invented" in 1940 in order to provide professional management and diversification for investors at affordable minimums and fees. Clearly, with the deregulation of brokerage commissions and computerization of the industry, separate accounts can now carry on that mission in a superior fashion. The handwriting is already on the wall, and fund companies recognize it.

The challenge is for professional managers to recognize that they are in the money-management industry and not the mutual fund industry. In essence, they face the same challenge as the railroads did years ago when they should have realized they were in the transportation business. Those managers that adapt will continue to prosper. The mutual fund structure, however, will not be so lucky. Even the venerable *Barron's* asked, "Buggy Whip Funds?"[12]

And in the *San Jose Mercury News* was this quote about the imminent fate of mutual funds:

Coupled with a few other trends . . . mutual funds are in big trouble," said Jamie Punishill, senior analyst of online financial services for Forrester Research Inc. of Cambridge, Mass. "The standardized, commodity mutual fund we know today is dying."[13]

As minimums continue to fall (due in part to increasing computerization) and wealth levels continue to rise, separate accounts will ultimately displace the $7 trillion mutual fund structure. As summed up in *The Wall Street Journal*:

"Two years from now, with technology evolving so quickly, the question will be why be in a pooled product at all," says Leonard Reinhardt, CEO of Lockwood Financial."[14]

---

[10] "Fund Companies Told to Gear Up for Managed Account Competition," *Ignites.com*, June 21, 2000.

[11] "In Managed Personal Accounts, A Challenge to Traditional Funds," *The New York Times*, Sunday, July 9, 2000 p. BU 20.

[12] Mutual Funds Section, *Barron's*, June 26, 2000, p. F-3.

[13] "The Front Page," *San Jose Mercury News*, Aug. 12, 2000.

[14] "Managed Accounts Win More Fans; Product Moves beyond the Rich."

Another serious problem facing mutual funds is that they don't translate well in the Internet era. The technology of funds is so archaic that you can do little more with funds on the Web other than check daily prices, buy, and sell. Basically, that's the same thing as eBay does with Beanie Babies and other collectibles. You can't, however, do meaningful things such as take tax control, screen individual holdings, or even find out what stocks are in the fund on a real-time basis. In fact, you can't determine the price of the fund shares until after the market has closed for the day.

THE CHALLENGE FOR SEPARATE ACCOUNTS

Before separate accounts are able to displace funds, however, they will have to overcome a few limiting factors. First, distribution of separate accounts is tightly controlled by the five largest brokerage firms. Combined, these five firms control nearly 80 percent of the market, according to Cerulli Associates (see Figure 15-2).

These firms hold a tight grip on distribution and view separate accounts as their high-margin business to be protected at all costs. This group has already deeded traditional retail stock trading to the deep discounters and online brokers such as Ameritrade and E*Trade, with more than half of all trades now completed online. The major firms recognize the advice component inherent in separate accounts, however, and recognize that the e-brokers will struggle to compete. Unfortunately for clients and prospective clients, this factor has kept minimums

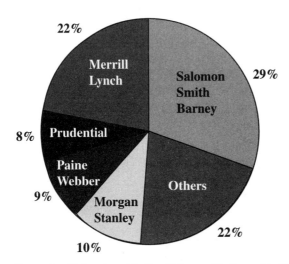

Source: Cerulli Associates, The Cerulli Report: The State of the Wrap and Managed Accounts Industry, 1999.

FIGURE 15-2

Asset share of top five consultant wrap providers—1Q 99.

high as the major firms have sought to serve wealthier investors, where the margins are higher. Stockbrokers continue to promote funds for smaller accounts because the cost of service is lower.

This creates a stranglehold of distribution for separate accounts somewhat similar to limited shelf space in a grocery store. Only the existing brand names have space, and new entrants find it difficult to offer their products. In addition, the cost of distribution can be almost prohibitive due to the high demands placed by the broker channel. Gavin Daly of Ignites.com notes:

> Getting into the separate account industry isn't easy, however. Industry officials estimate that it takes more than half a year to build the obligatory wholesaling staffs and back-office systems to support separate accounts. And that doesn't guarantee shelf space on the separate account platforms at brokerages and banks.[15]

We estimated the cost of a full-scale wholesaling effort for separate accounts to be more than $2 million per year for Templeton. This can be prohibitive for many managers. Others, however, such as Phoenix Investment Partners, see the potential as so large that they are making even greater commitments.

> Phoenix Investment Partners is increasing its wholesaling ranks by nearly half, to 40. The move is intended to accommodate the rapid growth of its separate account business.[16]

The second limiting factor is tied directly to the first. While the cost of nearly every other financial services product has declined sharply in recent years, the cost of managed products such as funds and separate accounts has remained stubbornly high. Fund expense ratios remain around 1.5 to 2.0 percent (not including the trading costs of the fund itself), and the average separate account fee was still 2.11 percent in 1999.

Interestingly, however, the cost of the professional management in separate accounts has actually declined sharply. For example, one of our first clients at Templeton paid 3 percent per year, and we retained 2 percent of that, with 1 percent paid to the broker. Less than a decade later, the average fee for clients industrywide was 2.11 percent, with 1.11 percent attributed to brokerage commission costs and distribution. That's pretty amazing in the Internet era, since the actual cost of trading has fallen sharply and distribution has also been sharply devalued.

The reason, of course, is the tight control of shelf space by the major firms. Having lost retail stock trades to e-brokers, these firms have kept separate accounts as their high-margin business. Individual brokers who sell these accounts average nearly $400,000 per year in income and receive 0.84 percent of each account for their services. What do they provide to warrant such an income? Many

---

[15] "Fund Firms Step Up Separate Account Efforts."

[16] "Phoenix Boosts Wholesaler Staff as Separate Accounts Business Booms," *Ignites.com*, May 16, 2000.

offer good asset allocation advice as well as monitoring the managers for clients. Too many, however, do little more than sit behind a mahogany desk, drink coffee with clients, and help them fill out forms.

Another serious problem with such limited distribution is that clients are forced to use the brokerage services of the program provider. Without competition, it's difficult to be certain that trade executions are as efficient as they should be. This was among our serious concerns at Templeton, and we regularly tracked the quality of these trades. Unfortunately, because we were beholden to the firm that brought us the account, we were limited in our ability to do anything regarding the quality of the trade. This can be devastating to long-term performance.

> The commission and impact costs are the tip of the iceberg, they are readily visible to all, but they only represent 32 bps in total. About three-quarters of the total (trading) cost is invisible to anyone who is simply looking at the transaction tape. The hidden costs of the iceberg are the costs of delay and of missed trades. We have performed several studies on the effect of using directed trades . . . and have always come to the same approximate conclusion . . . the place where it leaks out primarily is in delay and missed trades.[17]

Unfortunately, because the only access to managers is through brokerage firms, directed brokerage is automatically assumed without any potential for trade competition. While it's relatively simple to fire your manager in the current separate account system, it's very difficult to fire your broker or even to hold your broker accountable for the trading activity. Actually, it's even difficult to monitor the quality of the trades due to reporting delays. Sadly, even managers find it difficult to do anything about trade quality. The major firms have too strong of a lock on distribution.

These possible conflicts of interest can raise serious questions about the advice provided by brokers regarding managers. Most broker due diligence departments we encountered at Templeton did a fine job in evaluating our offerings. However, we did encounter several situations where the brokerage firm acted politically in the evaluation process and threatened to remove us from the program for what we deemed to be noninvestment reasons. We were even excluded from one major program based solely on a personality conflict between one of our employees and one of theirs. In addition, we noticed numerous examples where the firms acted in a parental fashion, preventing clients from engaging the manager of their choice. Finally, the simple limitation of due diligence resources for "on-site" visits limited the available choices offered to clients.

Until the distribution stranglehold is broken and fees come down, separate accounts will be unable to take their rightful place in fully displacing mutual funds. As a result, other products have cropped up as "competitors" to traditional

---

[17] Wayne H. Wagner, Chairman, Plexus Group, "Measuring, Controlling, and Allocating Trading Costs," *Ethical Issues for Today's Firm*, AIMR Conference Proceedings, July 2000.

funds. These include the customized baskets (such as FOLIOfn, Netfolio, Netstock's ShareBuilder, and E*Trade's Electronic Investing) as well as exchange-traded funds (ETFs).

While the customized baskets offer some value, such as individual tax control and screening of unwanted securities, they ignore one of the true benefits of mutual funds and separate accounts—active professional management.

> "FOLIOfn's product is caught between an index fund and someone who manages a stock portfolio themselves . . . . It's caught in no-man's land a little bit," said Dan Burke, senior analyst of online investing for Gomez Advisors Inc. of Concord, Mass. "The question is: Will mainstream investors bite on this? Those are the people who are coming online now. With FOLIOfn, you own the stock. That means you, not a portfolio manager, determine when or if to sell shares."[18]

Without the appeal of professional management, these customized baskets actually appear to be a greater threat to e-brokers (due to their very low trading costs) than to active mutual funds.

Similarly, ETFs are offered as an alternative to traditional funds. They boast lower fees, tax advantages, and flexibility. But as with the customized baskets, they do not provide an active advice component. This will prevent them from competing with the 90 percent of mutual funds that are actively managed.

> One reason for ETFs' limited competitiveness versus mutual funds is that they are passively managed. The study notes that index funds, even at their peak, never comprised more than 12% of the overall fund market. It also notes that index funds have lost ground to actively managed funds as of late. There is speculation that a number of companies are working on actively managed ETFs. But such a product is more than a year away, according to the report. Despite offering lower fees, tax advantages and more flexibility, other factors will make it hard for ETFs to steal market share from mutual funds. They are not advisor-friendly. They have no built-in way to retain investors. And they have short or no track records. The public knows very little about them.[19]

In addition to having greater appeal to investors, separate accounts also have greater appeal to brokers and managers. Brokers would find their commissions and margins squeezed even further if baskets or ETFs replaced mutual funds. Managers would lose their asset-based fees altogether. By supporting separate accounts, brokers can still enjoy trading commissions or wrap fees and managers are still paid for assets.

Clearly then, separate accounts are the logical successor to the mutual fund throne from every perspective. Institutional money managers have recognized this

---

[18] "The Front Page."

[19] "Report: ETFs Growing Fast, But Don't Threaten Mutual Funds," *Ignites.com*, July 25, 2000.

and are entering the separate account market as a result. The media have also taken notice and produced dozens of articles on this very subject this year alone. For example,

Jeffery M. Laderman, and Amy Barrett, "What's Wrong with Funds," *Business Week*, Jan. 24, 2000.

John Waggoner, "New Investments Challenge Mutual Funds," *USA Today*, May 26, 2000.

Ken Brown, "Fund Firms Go After Custom Accounts," *The Wall Street Journal*, Nov. 1, 2000.

Tony Chapelle, "Managed Accounts Growing Faster Than Funds," *On Wall Street*, Jan. 1, 2001.

"Forrester Research Predicts the Demise of the Mutual Fund Reign, Resulting in a Loss of More Than $1 Trillion in Invested Assets," *Business Wire*, Dec. 18, 2000.

Paul J. Lim, "Investments That Take the 'Mutual' out of Mutual Funds," *U.S. News & World Report*, Oct. 23, 2000.

Collin Dodds, "Dark Days Seen for Fund Industry," *Ignites.com*, Dec. 7, 2000.

THE FUTURE OF SEPARATE ACCOUNTS

In the past 25 years, two factors allowed the separate account industry to grow dramatically. One was a regulatory change, and the other was technological innovation. Over the next few years, two related changes likewise will allow separate accounts to displace mutual funds.

The first change actually took place in 1997 and is known as the SEC's safe-harbor ruling 3(a)4. This ruling essentially exempted separate accounts from registration as mutual funds even if they were managed similarly as long as a few key criteria were met. These include allowing individual clients to opt out of any specific security or class of securities, segregating all holdings in the client name, and providing the ability to contact the manager.

If the SEC had not provided this ruling, the separate account business would have been limited to very high minimums. With the ruling and the use of computers, however, the criteria could be met with minimums as low as $100,000. Unfortunately, the human element of a stockbroker interface has kept minimums higher than otherwise necessary. The reason is that brokers have a limited amount of time to spend with clients. They naturally want to have the highest average client size possible to maximize their earnings potential.

Fortunately, the second key factor solves the problem of the first. With the 3(a)4 safe harbor in place, clients can virtually meet the requirement without the involvement of a broker via the Internet. In fact, in most ways the Internet offers a superior interface for clients to list their specific criteria (such as no tobacco stocks), keep track of their individual holdings, and directly communicate with the manager. As a result, the Internet holds the promise of allowing a substantial lowering of account minimums and fees while bypassing the distribution stranglehold of the broker. After all, in the Internet age, distribution and brokerage commissions (the two primary costs charged by separate account brokers) have been greatly reduced.

Already, we've seen a few traditional brokers begin to offer their separate account services via a retail Website. Rob Jorgensen offers the First Union/Lockwood program at a discounted fee through RunMoney.Com. Wrapmanager.com is an offering from a broker with the Investment Center, which clears through Wexford Clearing and offers an Internet version of the Prudential program. E*Trade's recent purchase of PrivateAccounts.com in the fall of 2000 offers a data point on the cost of buying a program.[20] Finally, myMoneyPro.com is offering a limited number of smaller managers with custody and trading at Fidelity. While these offerings show promise in lowering minimums and fees somewhat, they remain controlled by the major brokerage firms.

As previously stated, e-brokers have yet to offer separate accounts due to the sticky issues related to providing advice. Most states and the SEC have ruled that the distribution of separate accounts requires registration as an investment adviser. The e-brokers have strategically avoided such registration due to the implications therein. If they were advisers, they could be held responsible for the various trades placed unsolicited by clients which might be viewed as inappropriate. Every time such an inappropriate stock declined in price, the e-broker could be considered liable for the loss.

Ultimately, the Internet solution will put control of separate accounts where it belongs—with the client. Clients should be free to choose any separate account manager, not just the select few afforded shelf space at the major brokers. In addition, the Internet can provide clients with very sophisticated tools to allow customized asset allocation, manager search, and portfolio monitoring. In addition, clients should have the ability to evaluate and choose any broker, including the very low-cost e-brokers. The Internet can also allow the careful monitoring of execution quality.

Every step of the separate account process can and will be Web-enabled. The account opening process can be done more conveniently through a Web-based application. Clients could also determine which type of manager will best suit their particular investment goals. Then, they could search for the manager who would best meet those goals over the prescribed time horizon. They could review

---

[20] According to E*Trade's 10-K filed November 9, 2000, the value of the deal at the time of the purchase was approximately $40 million. It should be noted that PrivateAccounts.com had never launched its services when it was bought by E*Trade.

the qualitative factors, and even view a brief presentation, all online. In addition, they could do very complex statistical comparisons with no more effort than a point and click.

Similarly, clients would enjoy the convenience of using their existing e-broker relationship or have the opportunity to search and evaluate from a variety of alternatives. Once the relationship is established with both the e-broker and money manager, the client would then establish his or her personal profile. This would allow an exclusion of any security or class of securities as required by the 3(a)4 safe harbor. After that, clients are free to settle back and let the money manager work on their behalf. Monitoring is simple to do but powerful in results. Performance can be viewed "live," and a number of reports can be produced with simple keystrokes. This allows the ultimate benefits of customization without the unnecessary hassles or cost.

The connectivity between e-brokers and institutional managers combined with creative and sophisticated Web-based applications is the future of separate accounts. E-brokers are desperately in need of products to attract wealthy clients. Fortunately, separate accounts would provide steady trading activity and higher wallet share, not to mention the prestige of conducting institutional-level trades. Overall, this will lower client acquisition costs on an asset basis as well.

> Internet brokerages will be challenged to show they can attain or maintain profitability. To do so, analysts say, they'll have to broaden their range of products and services . . . the desired audience is wealthy investors . . . .[21]

Institutional managers will be able to break the distribution stranglehold and access the rich client base already captured by e-brokers. In addition, they will be able to enter the separate accounts business without fielding a multimillion-dollar wholesale effort. This will make their business more profitable than traditional brokerage channels.

Ultimately, clients will be the biggest winners. We project that fees could reach as low as 1 percent plus minimal e-brokerage charges, with a measurable increase in program quality. In addition, account minimums should first fall to $50,000 and could ultimately get below $20,000. This would make separate accounts both affordable and accessible for most investors. We believe that separate accounts will even be offered in 401(k) plans within a few years.

Earlier, we quoted *The Wall Street Journal* in stating that separate accounts are like custom-made suits. The benefits are obvious. Unfortunately, the downside has been cost and accessibility. Most Americans still buy their suits off the rack for these reasons. Similarly, most Americans still own mutual funds. However, having recently traveled to Hong Kong, I learned that custom-made suits can be both affordable and convenient. I had a suit delivered to my hotel in 24 hours at a

---

[21] "Online Brokerages Regroup as Market Sink," *Investors Business Daily*, June 7, 2000.

price well below any suit I could buy off the rack. The best part is that this suit was the best quality I've ever worn. As a result, Hong Kong residents never buy suits off the rack in department stores. In the next few years, the Internet will become to separate accounts what Hong Kong is to suits. In fact, the Internet is even better. Clients will get customization with convenience and affordability without ever leaving home!

CHAPTER 16

How to Build and Monitor E-Commerce Insurance

Burke A. Christensen, Vice President, Operations and General Counsel
Quotesmith.com, Inc.

The Quotesmith.com slogan, "A New and Better Way to Buy Insurance," emphasizes the difference between the way that insurance has been sold traditionally and the way that it is being marketed in e-commerce. The traditional marketing practices in the insurance business are firmly based upon the historical view (especially as applied to life insurance) that insurance is sold, not bought. This opinion is not shared by the Internet aggregators, Internet insurance agencies, and insurance companies operating Websites.

The marketing philosophy of the traditional insurance company relies upon an army of agents and brokers who are trained to find prospects, persuade those prospects that they need insurance, help them find the money to pay the premium, make a presentation, and close the sale. The training and compensation structure created for traditional agents and brokers encourages them to sell higher levels of coverage and the more expensive types of products. In addition, these agents and brokers are trained and encouraged to sell only the products of a limited number of companies.

The e-commerce philosophy is to give consumers complete knowledge about the products available in the market. Putting consumers in charge of the flow of information gives them the widest possible choice and permits them to buy if they want, what they want, and when they want it. The Internet provides consumers with choice, convenience, accuracy, and speed. Self-directed consumers who are armed with more complete market knowledge will then be able to make their own better-informed buying decisions. In this consumer-driven insurance market, no "selling" in the traditional sense is required.

The capacity of the Internet to aggregate information and permit consumers to independently compare and contrast that information is particularly suited to the marketing of insurance. There are several reasons for this: First, an insurance policy is nothing more nor less than an insurance company's unilateral promise to pay a death benefit under certain circumstances at some time in the future. Unlike books, computers, and toys, all of which are sold successfully on the Internet, an insurance policy does not require the warehousing of goods or the physical delivery of a tangible product. A policy is merely the current legal convention and need not be required for the product to be sold and the promise to be binding.

Second, comparing the qualities of insurance products in cyberspace is a real, not a virtual, experience. When you shop for vacations, computers, flowers, or toys on the Internet, you are comparing the "almost-real" virtual representations of the product you wish to buy. The arrival of the actual product will be similar, but cannot be identical, to the virtual representation of the product on your monitor. This is not the case with insurance. The cyberspace representation of the contract will be exactly the same as the real-time printed version of the contract upon its arrival at your home. In fact, there is no reason, other than current legal convention, that the contract needs to arrive at your home at all. The printed version of a contract is merely the written manifestation of mutual assent that represents the agreement entered into by the parties.

Third, the high level of regulation imposed upon insurance contracts means that there is substantial uniformity in the contractual language of the policies from different insurers and in the minimum kinds of benefits provided by contracts of similar types. Thus, the Internet's ability to sort and compare similar things is perfectly designed to permit consumers to compare insurance products.

Fourth, the traditional face-to-face sales method of marketing insurance is expensive. Most of those who begin training to become an insurance agent fail to survive after 5 years. This training process is very expensive to the carriers. The cost of compensating those who survive the training period is also high. Cochran, Caronia Securities, LLC estimates agent costs average 10 to 15 percent of the insurance premium dollar, depending upon the product. The mass marketing techniques of the aggregators may enable them to produce insurance sales in such volume that the commission structure can be revised to make the Internet insurance product more competitive yet still profitable for the carrier to produce and the aggregator to sell.

The traditional method using local agents and brokers restricts the consumer's ability to compare. From the traditional agent or broker, the consumer will learn about only those few carriers about which the agent is knowledgeable. The consumer's power to choose will be further restricted to those few carriers with whom the agent has an agent or broker relationship. This screening power possessed by the agent restricts the consumer, because the agent controls the information about the products available to the consumer. If the agent is not aware of a particular product or is aware and elects not to tell the customer about it, for all practical purposes, that product does not exist.

An experienced and diligent insurance agent or broker may have adequate up-to-date knowledge about the products of 10 or 15 carriers. It is likely that the great majority of his or her clients are given product information from only a few of those. It is even more likely that the traditional agent places most of his or her business with two or three of those carriers. Thus, the traditional agent screens the flow of information and the freedom of choice made available to the consumer.

Many consumers desire and appreciate the agents who provide this counseling and advisory service. Those experienced agents who provide high-touch service and competent advice, and who select the carriers they represent and the products they sell based upon the factors that are in the best interests of their clients, will not likely feel much competitive pressure from the Website aggregators.

In contrast, the Internet insurance aggregator provides market knowledge about hundreds of insurance companies and their products. Unless the aggregator has established a special relationship with a limited number of carriers or restricts its database to a limited number of carriers, the aggregator is generally indifferent with respect to which policy a consumer may elect to purchase. Like the Internet sellers of books, toys, or computers, the Internet marketer of insurance cares that the consumer will find the policy he or she wants to buy.

The producer who represents a limited number of carriers based upon the commission paid to the producer and who does not adequately address the needs of the client faces extinction. This will happen because, whether a consumer elects to purchase an insurance product using an Internet aggregator or not, the information about the products is available to any consumer who takes the time to look. Any consumer can take the limited information provided to him or her by the traditional agent and compare it with the information available on the Internet. The traditional agent or broker is no longer the only method through which the client can gain market knowledge. The single company site and the agent site or aggregator site with a database that is limited to only a select few carriers have the same deficiencies.

For the self-directed insurance consumer there is a very wide range of choice. For an Illinois resident who is a nonsmoking male age 35 seeking $250,000 of term insurance coverage with the premium guaranteed for 20 years, the Quotesmith.com database provides detailed product information on 124 insurance carriers offering 209 policies with premiums ranging from $325 per year to more than $2000. Other Website insurance information aggregators such as InsWeb (with about 45 carriers) and SelectQuote (with about 25 carriers) can also provide market research of this type. The scope and depth of this information is limited only by the size of the database maintained by the aggregator.

For the prospective insurance applicant who is in good health, a nonsmoker with no adverse family medical history and no high-risk hobbies, the size of the Website aggregator's database is important only to the extent that it provides a wide range of premium choices from a diverse group of quality carriers. However, for the applicant who is not a preferred risk, the size of the database is extremely important. There are, for example, term insurance carriers whose products are not intended to compete on price with the most aggressive term carriers. These companies compete by offering more favorable underwriting for selected health hazards, such as adverse family medical history, smoking, weight, or hazardous activities. An aggregator with a limited database may not include the carriers that have a product specifically designed for a prospective customer's particular problem.

The history of Quotesmith.com and the Internet insurance information aggregators shows how rapidly this market segment has grown in a very short period of time. In 1984, Quotesmith and SelectQuote were founded. In 1995, InsWeb was founded. It is estimated by Cochran, Caronia Securities, LLC that less than 1 percent of insurance transactions are currently conducted via the Internet. According to Forrester Research, Internet-influenced sales of auto, home, and term insurance in 1998 equaled $1.5 billion.

Nevertheless, Cochran, Caronia also estimates that the Internet's share of the consumer insurance market could increase to between 2 and 10 percent by 2003. A 2 percent share would total approximately $7 billion in annual premiums. Forrester Research estimates Internet insurance sales for 2003 to be $11.1 billion in annual premiums.

The Internet insurance aggregators operate under a limited number of business models. Some, in fact, are not aggregators at all. For example, some insurance companies operate their own Websites. These "one-company site" Internet marketing models generally offer fast underwriting and, in some cases, lower premiums than are available elsewhere from that carrier. The one-company sites generally do not offer the same level of consumer choice and comparison capacity that is available from the aggregators.

All the aggregators provide free consumer information at their Websites about the insurance policies and products of a greater or lesser number of insurance companies. Some of the aggregators, such as InsWeb and SelectQuote, operate on the referral model, and some, such as Quotesmith.com, provide full quote to policy delivery service and do not refer leads to insurance agents and brokers.

Under the referral model, if a Website visitor wishes to purchase an insurance policy from a company whose products are displayed on the aggregator's Website, the visitor's request is referred to an insurance agent of that company. Under the full-service model, the aggregator provides the application, processes the applicant's request for insurance, and monitors the insurance company's underwriting progress until the policy is delivered. This latter model requires that the aggregator be appointed as an agent or broker for the insurance companies and be a licensed insurance agent in all jurisdictions.

One of the consequences of the full-service model is that the Website aggregator is regulated by every state (plus Washington, D.C.) where it does business. This requires that the aggregator meet the licensure and continuing education requirements of all 51 jurisdictions. It also means that the aggregator, as an insurance producer, must comply with all laws regarding advertising materials, illustrations, and replacements that govern the activities of an insurance agent or broker. With respect to these laws, the full-service model also requires that the aggregator must satisfy any additional requirements imposed by the insurance carriers. A failure to abide by these laws or the requirements of the carriers may result in the suspension or revocation of licensure by a state or the cancellation of an agency contract by the carrier.

Ensuring compliance with the differing laws of 51 jurisdictions can be a daunting task when an Internet insurance aggregator is conducting radio, television, and print advertising campaigns nationwide. Although the aggregator's Website and home office have a fixed location, the information on the Website is available in each of those jurisdictions and subject to regulation in each one.

The marketing of insurance on the Internet is in its infancy, but every indication suggests that this e-commerce segment is poised for rapid growth. When legal conventions are altered to permit electronic signatures and when insurance carriers develop products designed to take advantage of the economies of scale inherent in the e-commerce market, even today's most aggressive projections of market growth may turn out to be too conservative.

Burke A. Christensen is a graduate of Utah State University and the University of Utah College of Law. He began his career in 1975 as an attorney with the Northwestern Mutual Life Insurance Company at its home office in Milwaukee, Wisconsin. For 10 years he served as Vice President and General Counsel for the American Society of CLU & ChFC in Bryn Mawr, Pennsylvania. He has been engaged in the private practice of law with Bell, Boyd & Lloyd in Chicago and is currently employed as Vice President, Operations and General Counsel, for Quotesmith.com, Inc., in Darien, Illinois.

Mr. Christensen is the coeditor of *McGill's Life Insurance* and *McGill's Legal Aspects of Life Insurance*, both published by the American College. From 1985 to 1998, he was the author of "Strictly Speaking," a column on business and professional ethics for the insurance industry, published in the *Journal of the American Society of CLU & ChFC*. For 18 years, he was the author of "Law & Life Insurance," a monthly column on the law, regulation, and taxation of life insurance, published in *Trusts & Estates Magazine*.

CHAPTER 17

The Insurance Industry E-Volves

Thomas Holzheu, Ph.D., Senior Economist
Thomas Trauth, Ph.D., Senior Economist
Ulrike Birkmaier, Senior Economist
Swiss Re Economic Research and Consulting

INTRODUCTION

The Internet has developed from a purely information and communication medium into an important distribution channel. It allows companies to deliver high-quality, personalized information to a large audience in a way that was previously inconceivable. This effectively removes the information economy's conflict between the scope and depth of information.

While the focus in the early days of the Internet was on selling products to consumers (business to consumer, or B2C), the emphasis is now shifting toward commercial clients (business to business, or B2B), and this segment is likely to be the most important focus of Internet distribution in the future. Internet technologies not only have consequences for distribution, but influence a company's overall business processes as well. The more the production process depends on the processing of information, the greater the potential for change. As a result, e-business as dealt with in this article is understood to mean the use of information and communication technologies—and specifically the Internet—to continuously optimize an organization's business processes.

E-BUSINESS TRENDS IN THE INSURANCE INDUSTRY

Where does the insurance industry stand today? To date, insurers have regarded the Internet mainly as a further channel of distribution for their products. Compared with online brokerage and online banking, development of the Internet in the insurance industry has been somewhat cautious. Websites mainly serve to provide information about the company and its products. The opportunities created by e-business for making all business processes more efficient, beginning with the online conclusion of policies, have not been seized by established insurers. What are the reasons for this reluctance? A host of special factors make the online selling of insurance products difficult:

- The complexity of some products—for example, tax-efficient life insurance policies—increases the consumer's need for specific advice. It has not yet been possible to automate the provision of information, although it can be assumed that advances in technology will create new opportunities for automated solutions. The complexity of many insurance products can also be reduced by design modifications.

- In many cases, it is difficult to standardize claims settlement, as this process consists of rather complex investigations and decision making. Furthermore, often people and institutions are involved that are not bound by a contract with the insurer (e.g., liability insurance).

- The Internet is particularly suitable for products where contacts with the company occur frequently. Insurance is usually taken out infrequently, perhaps every couple of years or even once in a lifetime. Once a policy has been concluded, with some types of insurance the insurer and the customer have no more contact—unless an insured event occurs.

- Many consumers still view the Internet as an insecure medium. This prevents large transactions from being concluded via the Internet, and it deters the transmission of confidential information, both of which are essential aspects of insurance policies.

- In personal lines especially, regulatory hurdles make Internet distribution difficult. In the United States, for example, an insurer who wants to sell policies nationwide must obtain a license in all 50 states, and some lines of business require the involvement of a licensed broker (e.g., workers' compensation).

Which Insurance Products Are Suitable for E-Business?

Not all insurance products are equally suited to Internet distribution. Their suitability depends chiefly on how much advice is required. The more complex the product and the bigger its financial scale (transaction volume), the greater the client's willingness to pay for advice. This relationship is illustrated in Figure 17-1.

Products that are particularly suitable for marketing on the Internet are those that can be described and rated using a small number of parameters, such as motor, private liability, buildings, household contents, and term life insurance. Those

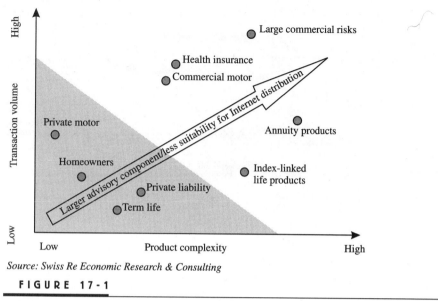

Source: Swiss Re Economic Research & Consulting

FIGURE 17-1

Internet suitability–transaction volume versus complexity.

lines account for about $ 250 billion, or one-third of total market volume in the United States. These types of cover are also suitable for online price comparisons, which makes the Internet even more attractive for potential clients.

Online Insurers Stand to Gain Substantial Market Share

Despite the obstacles mentioned, *sigma* expects Internet insurers to gain substantial market shares, especially in personal lines. By 2005, this market segment will represent a 5 to 10 percent share of the U.S. market and around 5 percent in Europe. Figure 17-2 shows how online purchasing of personal lines is set to grow in Europe and the United States. In 1999, only 15 percent of clients in Europe had an Internet connection, while the figure was as high as 44 percent in the United States. Only 1.5 percent of customers used the Internet to purchase financial services in Europe, compared with around 20 percent in the United States. In 1999, however, only 0.02% of premiums in Europe and roughly 0.2 percent of premiums in the United States were generated via the Internet. *Sigma* estimates show that by 2005 the percentage of clients using the Internet to purchase insurance and financial services could rise to 20 percent in Europe and just under 30 percent in the United States. Premiums generated via the Internet would therefore equal to $6.7 billion in Europe and $17 billion in the United States, equivalent to online market shares of 5 percent and 7.5 percent, respectively.

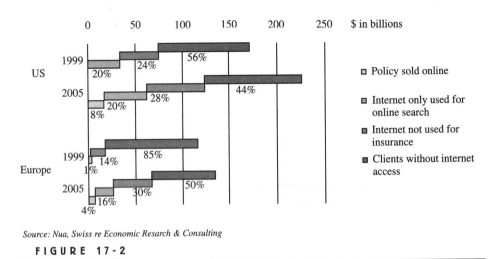

Source: Nua, Swiss re Economic Resarch & Consulting

FIGURE 17-2

Online market potential in personal lines.

The Internet—Much More Than Just an Extra Distribution Channel

Products that are not necessarily suitable for online marketing include most life and pension products, health insurance, and many commercial lines. But even these products can benefit from the excellent opportunities for quality and service improvements presented by e-business:

- If clients already have extensive product and risk expertise, the Internet can still be used as a marketing tool, despite the high complexity and transaction volume. Internet team rooms, for example, could support the consulting and negotiation process.

- Even if the conclusion of the policy and the associated advisory services occur with little or no online support, policy administration or claims settlement can still benefit from such support. For example, when choosing a private health insurer, a client who seeks independent advice may well be prepared to use online facilities to process and settle doctors' bills.

- Brokers can use e-business solutions to bundle together the needs of a large number of clients, handle the administration themselves, and then forward the data to the insurer. In the United States, for example, this type of Internet broker has become established in health insurance products for medium-sized companies.

- Modern communication technologies allow more personalized products, faster response times, greater flexibility in covers, and better support for risk management.

As stated earlier, the use of Internet technologies in the insurance industry is not just limited to distribution, but also has a fundamental impact on almost all other production areas. The integration of all business processes in a unified information flow significantly reduces the cost of gathering and analyzing information. Since the efficient processing of information is a key factor for insurers in the creation of added value, the use of new information and communication technologies enables them to revamp and rationalize key links in the value chain.

Newly established insurers are not burdened by legacy business systems and are able to exploit modern information and communication technologies in order to set "best-practice" benchmarks for the entire industry. This will exert significant pressure on established insurers to adapt their business model to the changing requirements for greater efficiency, speed, and quality of service.

In the past, the added value created by insurers has centered on the aspects of distribution, administration, and claims settlement. In these areas there are many routine tasks that could be automated through the efficient use of information and communication technologies. The tasks would therefore embody less added value. In the future, insurers will have to create a greater proportion of their added value through a higher standard of service.

HOW DOES E-BUSINESS AFFECT COMPETITION?

E-Business Lowers Market Entry Barriers

In the past, many insurance products have been distributed mainly through brokers tied to insurance companies or operating on a freelance basis. Since enormous investments are needed to build up such a distribution network, established insurers were generally well protected against new competitors. Now the Internet provides new companies with instant access to the insurance market at an affordable cost. In addition, market transparency is improving, since product and price information is more readily available through the Internet. Lower market entry barriers and higher market transparency are combining to intensify competition and force prices down. This also makes it increasingly difficult for an insurer to pass the comparatively high costs of traditional distribution on to the prices it charges for its products.

In life insurance especially, online distribution may change the nature of the competition. Acquisition costs traditionally play a key role. They often amount to more than 100 percent of the new premiums, and are amortized over the course of a long policy term. For new entrants to the market, such a big cost burden at the start of the insurance contract is a major barrier to entry, as they are unable to draw on a constant premium flow to finance the client acquisition costs. If Internet insurers manage to reduce these acquisition costs significantly, it would become far easier for them to break into the market. On the other hand, even Internet insurers need to attract clients through advertising, and this entails substantial costs as well. Furthermore, a certain amount of advice is normally required for many life insurance products, because of their transaction volume and complexity.

Even if e-business lowers market entry barriers, newly founded companies in particular need to become fairly well known if they want to win significant market share (branding). Another important factor—particularly in the insurance industry—is that the client must have confidence in the insurance company. Online sales still carry an element of uncertainty for many clients, particularly in Europe. This is mainly due to unresolved legal aspects of online policy sales and premium payment, as well as concerns about data protection. Insurers with an established brand name therefore have a competitive advantage, as they naturally command a greater degree of confidence.

New companies need to build up this goodwill from scratch, and this usually involves high advertising and marketing expenses. Here an analogy can be made to online stockbrokers. The newly founded companies E*Trade and Ameritrade, with online market shares of 11 percent and 7 percent, respectively, spent 54 percent and 40 percent, respectively, of their revenues on advertising in 1999. By contrast, the market leader Charles Schwab, whose telephone brokerage operations had already given the company a strong brand name and an online market share of 24 percent, only spent 6 percent of its revenues on advertising.[1]

The current disadvantages experienced by new Internet insurers should gradually become less important over time. First, confidence in the Internet as a distribution channel will improve as its penetration increases. Second, newcomers will be able to build up their weak reputations through solid credit ratings or alliances with well-known Internet brand names. Successful alliances for Internet insurers are feasible with online banks or online brokers, as well as with quality portals such as AOL, Yahoo, or Microsoft.

"Lateral entrants" from other sectors can break into the insurance business with the help of the Internet. The most likely candidates are companies that already have a well-known brand name and strong customer loyalty. These companies, such as banks, asset managers (e.g., Fidelity), or Internet providers, could set up new, efficient e-business systems, without the burden of legacy systems or conflicts with other distribution channels. They could also transfer their brand name to the insurance industry and utilize their financial resources.

The importance of a brand name on the Internet is illustrated by the examples of Charles Schwab (online brokerage), Dell (online computer sales), and Amazon (online books, CDs, etc.). All three companies have managed to acquire substantial market share, despite charging higher prices than their competitors in some cases. Even well-established companies that attempted to break into the online market at a later stage, such as Compaq in computers or Barnes&Noble in books, have to fight an uphill battle.

---

[1] Sources: Various annual reports.

E-Business Helps Cut Costs Significantly

The new e-business capabilities bring significant efficiency improvements in distribution, administration, and claims settlement. The biggest cost block for non-life insurers is claims payments, which typically consume almost two-thirds of total premium volumes. About a third of premiums covers the cost of distribution, administration, and claims settlement. Distribution costs account for 12 to 26 percent of premiums, administration costs for around 9 to 15 percent of premiums, and claims settlement costs for about 4 to 12 percent of premiums.

Modern information technologies also bring cost savings for claims payments. For example, better data analysis may improve risk selection,[2] and better detection of insurance fraud as well as tighter cost control of, for example, repair companies or medical service providers can help to further reduce claims costs.

In life insurance, claims costs account for 15 to 20 percent of premium income, much less than in non-life insurance, because of the high savings component. Distribution costs represent the biggest cost block, accounting for between 50 and 75 percent of total costs, which means the bulk of the cost savings can be achieved in distribution. However, many life insurance products require a lot of advice, and are therefore only partly suited to pure Internet distribution.

What are the potential savings for the U.S. insurance industry? We attempt to answer this question with the aid of a scenario that assumes that over time all insurers come to exploit the entire range of business opportunities. Online distribution will gain a market share of 10 to 20 percent in personal lines and 5 to 10 percent in commercial lines. Table 17-1 shows the implications of these assumptions: *sigma* expects e-business to produce cost savings of around 10 percent in claims settlement, 30 percent in policy administration, 30 percent in distribution, and 5 percent in claims payment. Claims settlements can be reduced through improved control of partner companies and the avoidance of insurance fraud. This results in total potential savings of $15 billion, or around 12 percent of premiums.

In commercial lines, the greater complexity of the processes involved means that most of the efficiency improvements will be in the areas of administration and claims settlement. *Sigma* therefore assumes a greater potential for efficiency improvements—in other words, 15 percent lower claims settlement costs and a 35 percent reduction in administration costs. The savings potential for distribution costs will be considerably less (10 percent) because of the substantial advisory and service content. Claims payment expenses also hold less cost-cutting potential in commercial lines because of the very intensive exchange of information. *Sigma* assumes a maximum savings of 2.5 percent. The total cost-saving potential therefore totals $11 billion, or 9 percent.

---

[2] This is only possible for insurers that achieve a better risk selection than the sector average. For the industry as a whole, this is a zero-sum game.

TABLE 17-1

Savings Potential in U.S. Property and Casualty Insurance

Savings in % of Expenses	Distribution	Administration	Claims Settlement	Claims Payments	Total
Personal lines	30%	30%	10%	5%	12%
Commercial lines	10%	35%	15%	2.5%	9%

Considerable Margin Pressure on Traditional Insurers

Morgan Stanley expects new e-business insurers to enter the market with roughly 10 percent lower premiums.[3] The aggressive premium level is necessary if insurers are to win market share in the fiercely competitive market. Hence, claims and expense ratios are higher because of the lower premium income. Efficiency improvements, additional marketing costs, and lower premium income more or less balance each other out.

This puts pressure on traditional providers to react with lower premiums as well. Without any adjustments to the cost structure, premium rate reductions have the immediate effect of pushing up combined ratios. However, the average profit earned by insurers in U.S. personal lines during the period 1994–1998 was equivalent to just 7.1 percent of net premiums.[4] A reduction in the underwriting results of only a couple of percentage points would therefore lead to a significant and unacceptable decline in profits.

The margin pressure described above will force traditional insurers to implement sweeping cost-cutting measures. This is not always possible without shedding jobs. Three-quarters of the costs run up by German and U.S. non-life insurers are attributable to personnel costs (commissions included). Efficiency improvements therefore entail the automation of work processes through new information technologies. Assuming that nonpersonnel expenses are likely to rise in the future because of the investments required, *sigma* estimates that personnel costs will have to be cut by around 10 to 15 percent. Cost savings will be necessary in other lines of business as well, notably commercial business and life and health insurance.

Even though the employment rate will fall in the insurance industry, this does not necessarily imply mass layoffs. There is a good chance that falling insurance prices will stimulate demand for insurance. This will in turn generate higher growth and compensate for some of the job losses. Since the overall structural

---

[3] Morgan Stanley Dean Witter, "Internet and Financial Services Teach-In," conference in New York, Mar. 9, 2000.

[4] Source: A. M. Best.

change is likely to take several years, much of the adjustment can be achieved through natural fluctuation. In addition, advances in information and communication technologies will themselves create new employment opportunities. As with every structural change, employees must try to adapt their qualifications to meet new requirements. Some of the cost savings in the insurance industry will also be achieved through savings in supplier companies. For example, better cost control means that car repair workshops could be forced to improve their efficiency.

For traditional insurers, the need to adapt to new e-business opportunities not only entails direct costs in the form of substantial investments in the new information and communication technologies, but also frictional costs resulting from the change of existing business models. Companies will have to revamp their business processes and corporate structures, resulting in internal conflicts. Internet marketing threatens traditional distribution channels and therefore tends to meet with strong resistance within a company (channel conflict). Many insurers solve this problem in the short term by not passing on the efficiency gains created by electronic distribution to the customer. Some insurers pursue a dual strategy and try to establish a foothold in countries where they have no significant market share by offering e-business solutions while maintaining traditional distribution channels in their home market. This is not a strategy for long-term success, however, because the potential efficiency gains in the home market are abandoned.

Traditional Insurance Brokers Will Have to Redefine Their Roles

The impact of e-business on insurance brokers depends a lot on the insurance products in question. If these can be standardized and readily compared with each other, and do not require extensive consultation, then the competitive pressure on traditional insurance brokers is considerable. A number of providers already act as "aggregators," providing comparisons of quotes from different insurance companies. However, in cases where products require extensive advice and benefits and prices are difficult to compare, brokers will continue to play a key role. This will be particularly true of the more complex benefits packages available in life insurance, in the rapidly growing markets of integrated risk management, and in commercial lines. As advisory and risk management services become increasingly important, demand for independent insurance brokers is likely to rise. This will be reflected in a different payment structure, with advisory fees increasingly replacing premium-based commissions.

SUMMARY

E-business is expected to have a strong impact on the insurance industry's way of conducting business. The opportunity presented by the Internet to transact online business more quickly and efficiently is compelling. However, the Internet is much more than just a new distribution channel: The ability to process transactions online enables companies to overhaul and rationalize many of their traditional business processes.

Using the Internet saves new market entrants the considerable cost and time usually required to set up their own distribution networks. Newcomers can realize substantial efficiency gains by exploiting the Internet's advanced communication capabilities to optimize their business processes.

Newly established Internet insurers have tended to pursue a consistent outsourcing strategy. The ability to exchange large volumes of information very quickly allows companies to deconstruct the value chain and outsource some of the links to specialized providers.

As well as start-up companies specializing in selling insurance via the Internet, there will also be "lateral" entrants to the insurance market, including providers crossing over from the financial sector (banks or brokers, for example) and established Internet companies. These companies will try to use a strong brand name or an established Internet presence to extend their current range of products to insurance.

The influx of new competitors and the opportunities for enhancing efficiency present a major challenge to the insurance industry. Overhauling and adapting existing business processes will meet with considerable opposition within the established insurers but will be a prerequisite for future success.

BIBLIOGRAPHY

Booz-Allen Hamilton, "Insurance: Setting a Course in Unchartered Waters," *insights*, 1997.

Conning, "Internet Insurance Distribution," *Strategic Study Series*, Hartford, CT, 2000.

"Continuing the E-volution," *Best Review*, September 1999.

Donaldson, Lufkin & Jenrette, "Insurance: The Impact of the Internet on the European Insurance Industry," March 2000.

Ernst & Young, "FS Internet Value Creation Study," January 1999.

Evans, P., and Wurster, T. S., "Blown to Bits," Harvard Business School Press, November 1999.

Evason, M., "E-Commerce Strategies," *Reuters Business Insights*, 1998.

Fox-Pitt, Kelton, "Dreams and Realities: European Insurers and the Internet," May 2000.

Garven, J. R., "On the Implications of the Internet for Insurance Markets and Institutions," *Working Paper*, September 1998.

Goldman Sachs, "United States: E-insurance: If You Build It, Will They Come?" September 1999.

Gora, J. C., "European Insurance Multinationals Expand Internet Activities," *Resource*, July 2000, pp. 34–36.

Gough, K., "Insurance Distribution: Navigating the Web of Strategies," *Society of Insurance Research: Research Review*, 3, 1999, pp. 17–21.

Hollman, K. W., Hayes, R. D. and Zietz, E. N., "Impact of Advances in Information Technology in the Insurance Industry," *Society of Insurance Research: Research Review*, 3, 1999, pp. 1–11.

"Insurance: The State of Allstate," *The Economist*, July 22, 2000, pp. 72ff.

"Managing eMarketplace Risks," *Forrester Report*, 1999.

Meyer, S., and Krohm, G., "An Overview of the Regulation on Insurance Transactions on the Internet," *Journal of Insurance Regulation*, Vol. 17, No. 4, 1999, pp. 550–570.

Morgan Stanley Dean Witter, "The Internet and Financial Services," Jan. 31, 2000.

Salomon Smith Barney, "Net Winners & Losers: The Impact of the Internet on European Business," Boston, 1999.

Stephens Inc., "Online Sales of Insurance—Which Business Models Make Sense and Which Don't," February 2000.

Shapiro, C., and Varian, H. R., "Information Rules: A Strategic Guide to the Network Economy," Harvard Business School Press, 1999.

Swiss Re, "The Impact of E-Business on the Insurance Industry: Pressure to Adapt—Chance to Reinvent," *sigma*, 5,2000.

Trencher, M. L., "Life Insurance Execs Give Industry a 'C' on Distribution Effectiveness," *Society of Insurance Research: Research Review*, 3, 1999, pp. 13–15.

Ibid., "Direct/Tech: The New Frontier of Insurance Distribution," *Society of Insurance Research: Research Review*, 3, 1999, pp. 23–26.

"The Web They Weave," *Best Review*, May 2000, pp. 28–52.

Thomas Holzheu, Thomas Trauth, and Ulrike Birkmaier are senior economists of Swiss Re's Economic Research & Consulting unit in New York and Zurich and also recently authored *sigma* 5/2000, "The impact of e-business on the insurance industry: Pressure to adapt—chance to reinvent."

Leading Financial Services Websites

Company	Website	Type	Description
American Express Co.	www.americanexpress.com	Bank/broker	Financial portal, planning, and brokerage services
Atlantic Financial	www.atlanticfinancial.com	Bank/broker	Online bank broker
BA Investment Services Inc.	www.bankamerica.com	Bank/broker	Online bank broker
Bank of Montreal Investor Services Ltd.	www.investorline.com	Bank/broker	Online bank broker
Citicorp Investment Services	www.citibank.com/us/investments	Bank/broker	Online bank broker
Comerica Securities Inc.	www.comerica.com	Bank/broker	Online bank broker
Crestar Investment Group	www.maxxinvest.com/crestar	Bank/broker	Online bank broker
First Chicago NBD Investment Services Inc.	www.fcnis.com	Bank/broker	Online bank broker
First Citizens Investor Services	www.firstcitizens.com	Bank/broker	Online bank broker
First Tennessee Brokerage Services	www.ftb.com	Bank/broker	Online bank broker
First Union Brokerage Services Inc.	www.firstunion.com	Bank/broker	Online bank broker
Huntington Investment Co.	www.huntington.com	Bank/broker	Online bank broker
Los Alamos National Bank	www.lanb.com	Bank/broker	Online bank broker
NationsBanc Investment Inc.	www.nationsbank/investments.com	Bank/broker	Online bank broker
Peoples Securities Inc.	www.peoples.com/invest	Bank/broker	Online bank broker
PNC Brokerage	www.pncbank.com	Bank/broker	Online bank broker
Royal Bank Action Direct Inc.	www.royalbank.com	Bank/broker	Online bank broker
Scotia Discount Brokerage Inc.	www.scotiabank.com	Bank/broker	Online bank broker
Security First Network Bank	www.sfnb.com	Bank/broker	Online bank broker
The State National Bank	www.statenb.com	Bank/broker	Online bank broker
U.S. Bancorp Investments	www.usbank.com/invest	Bank/broker	Online bank broker
United National Bank & Trust Co.	www.united-bank.com	Bank/broker	Online bank broker
Wachovia Investments Direct	www.wachovia.com/pcinvest	Bank/broker	Online bank broker
Wells Fargo Securities Online Brokerage	www.wellsfargo.com/wellstrade	Bank/broker	Online bank broker
Bond Connect	www.bondconnect.com	Bond trading	State Street and Bridge affiliated site provides information on bond markets.
Bond Net	www.bondnet.com	Bond trading	The Bank of New York's BondNet Division delivers a live, screen-based marketplace for U.S. fixed-income securities.
Bond Page	www.bondpage.com	Bond trading	Online bond broker provides information and analysis of all bonds.

Company	Website	Type	Description
Bond Resources	www.bondresources.com	Bond trading	Information on all types of bonds, bond funds, and fixed-income market.
Bonds Online	www.bondsonline.com	Bond trading	Information on all bond markets.
BradyNet	www.bradynet.com	Bond trading	Emerging market debt.
Broker Tec	www.brokertec.com	Bond trading	A consortium of 12 of the world's leading securities dealers that was formed to develop a global, interdealer brokerage of fixed-income securities and derivatives.
MuniAuction	www.muniauction.com	Bond trading	MuniAuction provides auction hosting services for primary-market offerings, or new issues, of fixed-income securities. Early developer of secondary market for municipal bonds.
Municipal Trade	www.municipaltrade.com	Bond trading	Municipal bond trading site.
MuniDirect	www.munidirect.com	Bond trading	Municipal bond trading site.
Trade Web Inc.	www.tradeweb.com	Bond trading	Business-to-business e-commerce in U.S. fixed-income markets.
Trading Edge Inc.	www.tradingedge.com	Bond trading	Comprehensive bond trading site dealing in most fixed-income markets.
Treasury Direct/U.S. Bureau of the Public Debt	www.publicdebt.treas.gov	Bond trading	Purchase U.S. government debt directly online.
A. B. Watley Inc.	www.abwatley.com	Broker	A NASD member, SIPC-protected, broker-dealer, founded in 1958, provides high-quality trading technology and service and low cost.
Accutrade Inc.	www.accutrade.com	Broker	Online broker.
America First Associates	www.aftrader.com	Broker	Online broker.
American Century Investments	www.americancentury.com	Broker	Online broker.
Ameritrade Inc.	www.ameritrade.com	Broker	Low commission, 24-hour customer service, convenient account access, and a secure online trading experience.
AmeriVest Inc.	www.amerivestinc.com	Broker	Online broker.
Andrew Peck Associates	www.andrepeck.com	Broker	Online broker.
Bidwell & Co.	www.bidwell.com	Broker	Discount brokerage services.
Bluestone Capital Partners	www.trade.com	Broker	Access to investment options and information 24 hours a day, 7 days a week, from a virtual trading station.

Company	Website	Type	Description
Brown & Co. Securities Corp.	www.brown.com	Broker	Deep discounts and service.
Burke Christensen & Lewis Securities Inc.	www.bclnet.com	Broker	
Bush Burns Securities Inc.	www.bushburns.com	Broker	
Charles Schwab & Co. Inc.	www.schwab.com	Broker	Largest online broker with high-end products and fees, including real-time quotes, bill paying, First Boston research, and options.
Christopher Street Financial Inc.	www.csfin.com	Broker	
CIBC Investor Services Inc.	www.investoredge.cibc.com	Broker	
CompassWeb Brokerage Inc.	www.broker.compassweb.com	Broker	
CompuTel Securities	www.rapidtrade.com	Broker	
CT Securities International Inc.	www.ctmarketpartner.com	Broker	
Datek Online	www.datek.com	Broker	A pioneer in online trading with link to affiliate Island ECN.
DeLong, Friedman & Suknick Inc.	www.dfs-futures.com	Broker	
Delta Equity Services Corp.	www.deltaequity.com	Broker	
Discover Brokerage Direct		Broker	
DLJ Direct Inc.	www.dljdirect.com	Broker	Discount brokerage as well as special services for high-deposit users, including IPOs and private equity deals, DLJ research, and with $1 million and more, a personal adviser.
Downstate Discount Brokerage Inc.	www.trade4.less.com	Broker	
Dreyfus Brokerage Services Inc.		Broker	
E*TRADE Group Inc.	www.etrade.com	Broker	At $14.95 a trade, the site provides news, research, online banking, mortgages, bill paying, etc.
E-Commodities	www.e-contracts.com	Broker	
Empire Financial Group Inc.	www.lowfees.com	Broker	
FarSight Financial Services LP	www.farsight.com	Broker	
Fidelity Brokerage Services Inc.	www.powerstreet.com	Broker	Highly rated online and wireless trading with link to Fidelity fund, 401(k) accounts, Lehman Brothers research.
First Flushing Securities Inc.	www.firstflushing.com	Broker	
First Trade Securities, Inc.	www.firsttrade.com	Broker	Rated one of the best brokers online. Real-time streaming quotes, lowest margin lending rates, and free S&P research. Over 6000 mutual funds online.

Company	Website	Type	Description
Freedom Investments Inc.	www.freedominvestments.com	Broker	
Freeman Welwood	www.freemanwelwood.com	Broker	One of the first online brokerages in the country to discount commissions.
Green Line Investor Services Inc.	www.greenline.com	Broker	
Harris Investor Direct Inc.	www.harrisinsight.com	Broker	
Howe Barnes Investments Inc.	www.netinvestor.com	Broker	Secure 24-hour online and telephone trading of stocks and options. Over 4000 mutual funds available, including over 900 no-load funds.
Interactive Brokers	www.interactivebrokers.com	Broker	At the forefront of the electronic brokerage industry since 1993.
internetTRADING.com	www.internetrading.com	Broker	
Investex Securities Group Inc.	www.investexpress.com	Broker	
Investrade Discount Securities	www.investrade.com	Broker	
Ira Epstein & Co.	www.iepstein.com	Broker	
Jack White & Co.	www.jackwhiteco.com	Broker	
JB Oxford & Co.	www.jboxford.com	Broker	Stock quotes and advanced charting, the latest news and commentary, and stock screening and company profiles.
Lind-Waldock & Co.	www.lind-waldock.com	Broker	
Main Street Market	www.mainstmarket.com	Broker	
Marquette de Bary Co. Inc.	www.debary.com	Broker	
Max Ule & Co. Inc.	www.maxule.com	Broker	
Merrill Lynch & Co.	www.mldirect.com	Broker	Access to extensive research, news, and tools, and for bigger accounts, access to brokers.
Momentum Securities LLC	www.tradescape.com	Broker	High-technology brokerage, execution, and trading technology firm.
Money Garden Corp.	www.forx.mg.com	Broker	
Montgomery Asset Management	www.montgomeryfunds.com	Broker	
Morgan Stanley Dean Witter	www.msdw.com	Broker	Research, asset allocation, and planning tools, with more services at $100,000 deposits.
Mr. Stock Inc.	www.mrstock.com	Broker	Provides one-stop shopping for option traders.
Muriel Siebert & Co.	www.msiebert.com	Broker	
National Discount Brokers Group	www.ndb.com	Broker	Servicing active traders with analytical and market information tools.
Newport Discount Brokerage Inc.	www.newport-discount.com	Broker	

Company	Website	Type	Description
Pacific Century Investment Services Inc.	www.boh.com/invest	Broker	
Patagon.com	www.patagon.com	Broker	The premier financial destination in Latin America and Spain.
Peremel & Co. Inc.	www.peremel.com	Broker	
Preferred Capital Markets, Inc.	www.tradeoptions.com	Broker	The Preferred Trade System is a custom, low-cost, electronic securities execution and real-time account access software for self-directed investors and active traders.
Priority Brokerage	www.prioritybrokerage.com	Broker	
Professional Discount Securities	www.prodiscount.com	Broker	
ProTrade Securities	www.protrade.com	Broker	
Prudential Securities Inc.	www.prusec.com	Broker	
PT Discount Brokerage	www.ptdiscount.com	Broker	
Putnam Investments	www.putnaminv.com	Broker	
Quick & Reilly Inc.	www.quick-reilly.com	Broker	
Recom Securities Inc.	www.trutrade.com	Broker	
Regal Discount Securities	www.eregal.com	Broker	The deep-discount electronic stock brokerage division of Regal Discount Securities.
Ryback Management Corp.	www.ryback.com	Broker	
Scottsdale Securities Inc.	www.scotttrade.com	Broker	Low commissions, local service, fast execution, low margin interest, real-time accounting, electronic confirmation, $5 million account protection.
SII Investments Inc.	www.siionline.com	Broker	
Southwest Securities Group, Inc.	www.mydiscountbroker.com	Broker	Substantial savings trading through personal brokers or via the Internet.
Soverign Securities Inc.	www.mydiscountbroker.com	Broker	
Stanford Federal Credit Union	www.sfcu.org	Broker	
Stein Roe Mutual Funds	www.steinroe.com	Broker	
Stocks4Less	www.stocks4less.com	Broker	
Summit Financial Services Group	www.sfsg.com	Broker	
Sunlogic Securities Inc.	www.sunlogic.com	Broker	A discount brokerage firm.
SureTrade	www.suretrade.com	Broker	Low-cost, high-quality research and easy, efficient trading for serious investors.

Company	Website	Type	Description
Swift Trade Securities Inc.	www.swifttrade.com	Broker	An Ontario-based securities dealer established in 1997. The firm's primary business is to provide electronic day trading and training facilities.
T. Rowe Price Discount Brokerage	www.trowprice.com/brokerage	Broker	
TD Waterhouse	www.tdwaterhouse.com	Broker	Low-cost broker with national branch office network provides reports from S&P and First Call and an IPO center.
The Net Broker	www.netaxis.qc.ca	Broker	
The Net Investor	www.netinvestor.com	Broker	
The R.J. Forbes Group Inc.	www.rjforbes.com	Broker	
Tradecast Securities Ltd.	www.tradecast.com	Broker	Front-end system with Web link.
TradeStar Investments Inc.	www.4tradestar.com	Broker	
Tradewell Discount Investing LLC	www.trade-well.com	Broker	
Trading Direct	www.tradingdirect.com	Broker	
UBOC Investment Services Inc./ Pacific Alliance Capital Management	www.uboc.com	Broker	
Vision Securities Inc.	www.visiontrade.com	Broker	Provides superior execution at a reasonable fee.
Wall Street Access	www.wsaccess.com	Broker	
Wall Street Discount Corp.	www.wsdc.com	Broker	
WallStreete Electronica Inc.	www.wallstreetelectronics.com	Broker	Highly rated online brokerage with highly automated capabilities and strong options information and execution services.
Wang Investment Associates Inc.	www.wangvest.com	Broker	
Waterhouse Securities	www.waterhouse.com	Broker	TDWaterhouse offers a full range of brokerage, banking, and mutual fund products and services.
Web Street Securities Inc.	www.webstreetsecurities.com	Broker	Complete, user-friendly online trading and investing service.
Westminster Securities Corp.	www.livebroker.com	Broker	
White Discount Securities	www.wdsonline.com	Broker	
WIT Capital	www.witcapital.com	Broker	
XPressTrade LLC	www.xpresstrade.com	Broker	
Your Discount Broker Inc.	www.udb.com	Broker	
Ziegler Thrift Trading Inc.	www.ziegler-thrift.com	Broker	
Zions Investment Securities Inc.	www.zionsbank.com	Broker	

Company	Website	Type	Description
All-Tech Direct, Inc.	www.attain.com	Electronic communication network	A pioneer in direct-access electronic stock trading.
archipelago	www.archipelago.com	Electronic communication network	
Brass Utility	www.brassutility.com	Electronic communication network	
Btrade	www.btrade.com	Electronic communication network	
Instinet	www.instinet.com	Electronic communication network	The world's largest agency brokerage firm and a wholly owned subsidiary of Reuters Group PLC. Trading daily in over 40 global markets and a member of 19 exchanges in North America, Europe, and Asia.
Island	www.island.com	Electronic communication network	Computerized trading system that gives brokerages the power to electronically display and match stock orders for retail and institutional investors.
ITG	www.itg.com	Electronic communication network	
MaketX	www.maketx.com	Electronic communication network	
NextTrade	www.nextrade.com	Electronic communication network	
OptiMark	www.optimark.com	Electronic communication network	Leading provider of exchange solutions to electronic marketplaces and communities.
Primex	www.primex.com	Electronic communication network	
Redibook	www.redibook.com	Electronic communication network	Competes with market makers in NASDAQ's over-the-counter market with the ease of execution previously found only in the listed market.

Company	Website	Type	Description
StrikeTechnology	www.striketechnology.com	Electronic communication network	
SuttonOnline	www.suttononline.com	Electronic communication network	Sutton provides real-time trading software for domestic and international markets and a gateway to these markets for its subscribers.
TransPoint	www.transpoint.com	Electronic communication network	
ADR.com	www.adr.com	Financial information	Information on American depository receipts.
Barrons	www.barrons.com	Financial information	
Bloomberg	www.bloomberg.com	Financial information	Comprehensive financial, economic, and market analysis with news, data and tools.
Bond Market Association	www.investinginbonds.com	Financial information	
Bridge	www.bridge.com	Financial information	Provides stock information.
Briefing	www.briefing.com	Financial information	Commentary and analysis on important news affecting the markets.
BusinessWire	www.businesswire.com	Financial information	Market commentary, quotes, charts, portfolio tracking and company reports.
CBS MarketWatch	www.marketwatch.com	Financial information	Financial and investment information; portfolio tracking and charting.
CNBC	CNBC.com	Financial information	Information, data, tools, and analysis of stocks and funds.
CNET	www.cnet.com	Financial information	Information on an array of topics. Cnet offers links to news, hardware, downloads, builder, games, jobs, auctions, prices, and tech help.
CNN Financial News	www.cnnfn.com	Financial information	Information on deals and debuts, economy, industry watch, markets, stocks, bonds, mutual funds, and more.
Company Sleuth	www.companysleuth.com	Financial information	Aggregates Internet-based information on various companies.
CyberInvest	www.cyberinvest.com	Financial Information	Links to investment-related sites.
Dow Jones Inc.	www.dowjones.com	Financial information	Media site that reports on business news, markets, industry center, and more.
Emerging Markets Companies	www.emgmkts.com	Financial information	News, quotes, and financial data on emerging markets.
Equity Analytics	www.equityanalytics.com	Financial information	Financial and investment information along with IPO information.

Company	Website	Type	Description
Europe Online	www.europeonline.com	Financial information	Links to exchanges, companies, and news sources.
EuropeanInvestor.com	www.europeaninvestor.com	Financial Information	Links to and news and information on European markets.
Financial Times	www.ft.com	Financial information	Comprehensive information and analysis of global markets.
FreeRealTime.com	www.freerealtime.com	Financial information	Media site that provides real-time quotes, delayed quotes, market summary, and more.
GlobalNetFinancial.com	www.globalnetfinancial.com	Financial Information	An international provider of online financial news, investment tools, and transaction services. Provides iNvest Websites around the world and has developed transaction Websites in the U.S. stocks and Forex trading.
InsuranceNewsNetwork.com	www.insurancenewsnetwork.com	Financial information	Online resource for the insurance industry.
InvestmentHouse.com	www.investmenthouse.com	Financial Information	Provides insight on many aspects of stock market investing and financial planning.
Investorama.com	www.investorama.com	Financial information	Links and information on stock markets, online investing, mutual funds, taxes, real estate, and retirement investing.
InvestorBroadcastNetwork.com	www.investorbroadcastnetwork.com	Financial information	Links to Internet investment sites.
InvestorGuide	www.investorguide.com	Financial information	Links to Internet investment sites.
Investorville	www.investorville.com	Financial information	Message boards, IPO information, stock research, charting.
IPO Maven	www.ipomaven.com	Financial information	Information and company reports on IPO filings, performance, and pricing.
IPO.com	www.ipo.com	Financial information	Information, news, and data on IPOs.
IPOMonitor.com	www.ipomonitor.com	Financial information	Provides daily e-mail messages to alert members of all significant events in the life of an IPO. Website offers additional information for the IPO market in general.
MarketGuide.com	www.marketguide.com	Financial information	Specializes in compilation, integration, display and delivery of a superior-quality database of descriptive and analytic information on more than 12,000 publicly traded domestic and foreign corporations.
News.com	www.news.com	Financial information	Affiliated with cnet.
Newsalert.com	www.newsalert.com	Financial information	
Nikkei Net Interactive	www.nni.nikkei.co.jp	Financial information	News and analysis on Asia and Japan.

Company	Website	Type	Description
On24.com	www.on24.com	Financial information	Original and syndicated streaming broadcast news and opinion created for the online investor.
OptionSites.com	www.optionsites.com	Financial information	Links to options brokers and information.
PCQuote.com	www.pcquote.com	Financial information	Information on news, stocks, IPOs, earnings, trading, equities, finance, futures, and more.
Primark.com	www.primark.com	Financial Information	Comprehensive databases and a full range of information services to its customers, combining quality data with software tools, analyses, and forecasts for complete decision support.
PRNewswire.com	www.prnewswire.com	Financial information	Provides comprehensive public relations and investor relations services ranging from Internet.
Quote.com	www.quote.com	Financial information	Information on a variety of financial topics such as stocks, fixed income, markets, funds, IPOs, news, and more.
QuoteStream.com	www.quotestream.com	Financial information	Offers real-time financial information, updates, detailed stock quotes, customizable news and stock tickers, and technical analysis.
RadioWallStreet.com	www.radiowallstreet.com	Financial information	Multimedia financial information over the Internet.
Raging Bull	www.ragingbull.com	Financial information	Message boards, news, and stock data.
Reuters.com	www.reuters.com	Financial information	News, quotes, trading, investor information such as annual reports, financial reports, company information, and analyst presentations.
S&P Personal Wealth	www.personalwealth.com	Financial information	Comprehensive information, retirement and personal financial planning.
SecorBase.com	www.sectorbase.com	Financial information	Directed toward providing the most thorough and accurate picture of the market by industry, sector, product, or service within the shortest amount of time.
Silicon Investor	www.siliconinvestor.com	Financial information	
Stock House	www.stockhouse.com	Financial information	Media site that offers information on new releases, markets, IPOs, and quotes and provides a resource center for research.
Stock Point	www.stockpoint.com	Financial information	
StockScape.com	www.stockscape.com	Financial information	Investor information enhanced by a unique relationship with an ever-growing stable of leading financial newsletter writers.

Company	Website	Type	Description
Telewaquote.com	www.telewquote.com	Financial information	Securities information for intraday, end-of-the-day, and historical data; quotes, charts, news, statistics, and a securities search engine.
TheMarkets.com	www.themarkets.com	Financial information	Portal founded by seven securities houses to provide financial information and analysis.
TheStreet.com	www.thestreet.com	Financial information	Latest stories, market briefing, and news, stocks, personal finance, commentary, analysts' rankings and international.
Thomson Investors Network	www.thomsoninvest.com	Financial information	Comprehensive site offering portfolio management, stock and mutual fund data and analysis.
UK-iNvest	www.ukinvest.com	Financial information	Stock analysis and recommendations on U.K. markets.
Vcall.com	www.vcall.com	Financial information	
Wall Street Journal Interactive	www.wsj.com	Financial information	Offers online service of *The Wall Street Journal*.
Wall Street Research Net	www.wsrn.com	Financial information	Links to investment-related sites.
WallStreetForum.com	www.wallstreetforum.com	Financial information	
WorldlyInvestor.com	www.worldlyinvestor.com	Financial information	Comprehensive global investing portal that provides timely, proprietary, and investable stories about financial markets, stock, bonds, and mutual funds. Acquired by Advisor Software Inc.
401(k) Advocate	www.timyounkin.com	Financial planning	Advice and tools.
401Kafe	www.401kafe.com	Financial planning	Retirement planning site.
401kExchange.com	www.401kexchange.com	Financial planning	Exchange matching of 401(k) plans and plan providers.
Advisor Software Inc.	www.myinvestmentsonline.com	Financial planning	Financial planning tools for high-net-worth investors, 401(k) plans, and financial planning professionals.
American Academy of Estate Planning Attorneys	www.estateplanforyou.com	Financial planning	Estate planning strategies.
Deloitte & Touche Online	www.dtonline.com	Financial planning	Estate planning strategies.
DirectAdvice.com	www.directadvice.com	Financial planning	Retirement financial planning and asset allocation.
EfficientFrontier.com	www.efficientfrontier.com	Financial planning	Retirement planning and asset allocation.
Estate Planning Links.com	www.estateplanninglinks.com	Financial planning	Estate planning strategies.
FinancialEngines.com	www.financialengines.com	Financial planning	Technology that provides a view of how investments might perform.
LifeNET.com	www.lifenet.com	Financial planning	Estate planning strategies.

Company	Website	Type	Description
MoneyAdvisor	www.moneyadvisor.com	Financial planning	Financial calculators and planners.
mPower	www.mpower.com	Financial planning	Financial planning tool for 401(k) plans.
National Network of Estate Planning Attorneys	www.netplanning	Financial planning	Advice and Information on estate planning.
Reliastar Financial	www.ihatefinancialplanning.com	Financial planning	
TeamVest	www.teamvest.com	Financial planning	
AOL Personal Finance	www.aol.com	Financial portal	Offers highlights, breaking news, chat, and stock quote information.
CEOExpress Company	www.ceoexpress.com	Financial portal	Comprehensive source of data and information on finance, investments, and the economy.
Excite	www.excite.com	Financial portal	Links and information on stocks, bonds, and mutual funds.
Financenter.com	www.financenter.com	Financial portal	Financial topics explored are stocks, mutual funds, real estate, money managers, bonds, insurance, money markets, mortgage lenders, and more.
MSN Money Central Investor	http://moneycentral.msn.com	Financial portal	Offers comprehensive personal finance information including investing, banking and bills, retirement and wills, taxes, insurance, saving and spending, family and college, and real estate. Also provides stock and fund screening, information, and reports.
Netscape Corp.	www.netscape.com	Financial portal	Links and information on stocks, bonds, and mutual funds.
OnMoney	www.onmoney.com	Financial portal	Provides tools to make managing money less frustrating and the information to make more informed decisions about personal finances.
Prodigy Services Co.	www.prodigy.com	Financial portal	Links and information on stocks, bonds, and mutual funds.
Quicken.com	www.quicken.com	Financial portal	Offers highlights, breaking news, chat, and stock quote information. Data for stocks and funds and coverage of banking and mortgages.
Yahoo Finance	http://quote.yahoo.com	Financial portal	Stock and fund screening, market information and planning. Extensive links and financial planning information.
Yodlee, Inc.	www.yodlee.com	Financial portal	
1stQuote.com	www.1stquote.com	Insurance	Comparison shopping for term life insurance with quotes from a database of more than 400 companies.

Company	Website	Type	Description
Accu Trade	www.accuquote.com	Insurance	Compare the price, features, and financial strength of over 1100 life insurance products.
AmericaQuote	www.americaquote.com	Insurance	An interactive life insurance Website to help users determine which company and plan is right for them.
AnnuityNet	www.annuitynet.com	Insurance	Three-variable annuity products traded online.
AnnuityScout.com	www.annuityscout.com	Insurance	Screens for variable annuities based on fees and investment options.
AnswerFinancial	www.answerfinancial.com	Insurance	Family needs in insurance, health protection, and finances.
FinPortfolio.com	www.finportfolio.com	Insurance	Variable annuities.
InstantQuote.com	www.instantquote.com	Insurance	Helps the consumer choose a company and product based on all the factors that are considered by the insurance companies when they underwrite a case.
Insure.com	www.insure.com	Insurance	Online VA calculator.
InsureOne Financial Services	www.insureone.com	Insurance	InsureOne Financial Services tailors individual and group life, health, and disability insurance plans, including Medicare supplement and long-term care policies. It also offers annuities, money-market accounts, and mutual funds.
InsurePoint Community	www.insurepoint.com	Insurance	The InsurePoint Community is part of a very targeted campaign to support new and growing technology firms.
InsureRate	www.insurerate.com	Insurance	Information about insurance products and services.
InsureZone	www.insurezone.com	Insurance	
InsWeb	www.insweb.com	Insurance	InsWeb is a free service that compares insurance quotes from leading insurance companies to find the best rates available.
MasterQuote of America	www.masterquote.com	Insurance	Term life insurance comparison service.
Quicken Insurance	www.quickeninsuremarket.com	Insurance	Receive and compare real-time quotes, obtain information, connect with agents, and purchase policies from the nation's leading insurance carriers.
QuickQuote	www.quickquote.com	Insurance	Online information and full-service insurance brokerage.
TIAA-CREF	www.tiaa-cref.com	Insurance	Leader in variable annuities.
Variable Annuities Online	www.variableannuitiesonline.com	Insurance	Screens online VAs.

Company	Website	Type	Description
Friedman Billings Ramsey	www.fbr.com	Investment banking	Source, finance, and advise companies with respect to the capital markets through dynamic research, market-making capabilities, venture capital, investment banking services, and an online platform.
Garage.com	www.garage.com	Investment banking	Garage.com helps entrepreneurs and investors create, build, and fund promising early-stage technology companies.
M&A Online	www.maol.com	Investment banking	Connects sellers and buyers of companies.
mevc	www.mevc.com	Investment banking	Offers professionally managed, diversified venture capital funds to individuals.
OffRoad Capital	www.offroadcapital.com	Investment banking	Allows investors with as little as $25,000 to bid on private equity investments.
University Angels.com	www.universityangels.com	Investment banking	Information on university campus start-ups for angel investors.
Vcapital.com	www.vcapital.com	Investment banking	Geared to investors with $200,000 or more and professional venture capitalists with 65 deals concluded.
VentureHighway.com	www.venturehighway.com	Investment banking	Small venture capital firms backed by broker.
WIT Soundview Group Inc.	www.witcapital.com	Investment banking	Wit Capital was founded in 1996 with a mission: to empower investors and issuers alike by transforming the capital-raising process through the use of the Internet.
WR Hambrecht & Co.	www.wrhambrecht.com	Investment banking	WR Hambrecht takes stakes in ventures and sells some to investors.
Yahoo!NetRoadshow	www.netroadshow.com	Investment banking	Yahoo!NetRoadshow provides investment banks with the ability to produce road shows on the Internet.
Yazam	www.yazam.com	Investment banking	Yazam acts as lead investor and provides access to angels to Israeli investments.
Vanguard University	www.vanguard.com	Investment education	
Alliance for Investor Education	www.investoreducation.org	Investor education	
American Association of Individual Investors	www.aaii.com	Investor education	
Dow Jones University	dju.wsj.com	Investor education	
IBM	www.ibm.com/investor/financialguide	Investor education	
Investor Education Center	www.quote.com	Investor education	

Company	Website	Type	Description
The Armchair Millionaire	www.armchairmillionaire.com	Investor education	Internet investor conference call directory.
BestCalls.com	www.bestcalls.com	Market analysis	Provides access to professional-level research tools
Bigcharts	www.bigcharts.com	Market analysis	like interactive charts, quotes, industry analysis, and intraday stock screeners, as well as market news and commentary.
Bull & Bear Securities Inc.	www.bulldogresearch.com	Market analysis	Ranks and evaluates stock market analysts.
Chicago Board of Options Exchange	www.cboe.com	Market analysis	Options information, education, and tools.
Dailystocks	www.dailystocks.com	Market analysis	The Web's first and biggest stock research site.
Earnings.com	www.earnings.com	Market analysis	An application service provider that builds highly scalable and efficient multimedia broadcast solutions for the financial vertical.
Emergent Advisors.com	www.emergentadvisors.com	Market analysis	Affordable, objective, online advice.
FinancialWeb	www.financialweb.com	Market analysis	Websites on stock quotes, screening, research, fund data, and reports.
FreeEdgar.com	www.freeedgar.com	Market analysis	Since 1997, the FreeEDGAR Website has set the standard for delivering processed EDGAR filings to the financial community.
Gomez.com	www.gomez.com	Market analysis	High-quality community ratings and reviews of online businesses.
Hoovers	www.hoovers.com	Market analysis	Information on company profiles, financial data and screening tools.
Individual.com	www.individual.com	Market analysis	Business, trade, and financial news that is custom-built and delivered to your e-mail every business morning.
Individualinvestor.com	www.individualinvestor.com	Market analysis	Investment news for the online environment.
insiderSCORES	www.insiderscores.com	Market analysis	
Investools.com	www.investools.com	Market analysis	Advice for independent investors.
Money.com	www.money.com	Market analysis	Investment information including stocks, funds, tech investing, insurance, real estate, retirement, etc.
MotleyFool.com	www.motleyfool.com	Market analysis	Market commentary, quotes, charts, portfolio tracking, and company reports.
Multex Investor	www.multexinvestor.com	Market analysis	Searchable database of Wall Street and independent stock market research.
My Stock Options	www.mystockoptions.com	Market analysis	
NetStock.com	www.netstock.com	Market analysis	Customer-focused provider of low-cost, easy-to-use, online investment products and tools.

Company	Website	Type	Description
OneLineInvestor.com	www.olineinvestor.com	Market analysis	Investing search engine.
Optionetics	www.optionetics.com	Market analysis	Options research and analysis.
Riskgrades.com	www.riskgrades.com	Market analysis	Risk management for investors.
SchaeffersResearch.com	www.schaeffersresearch.com	Market analysis	Option strategies from author of "The Option Advisor" letter.
SiliconInvestor.com	www.siliconinvestor.com	Market analysis	One of the Internet's leading networks, providing consumer services, business services, and enabling services.
Smart Money Interactive	www.smartmoney.com	Market analysis	Stock and fund screening, market information and planning tools.
Stock Detective	www.stockdetective.com	Market analysis	A global business-to-business aggregator, developer, and distributor of e-financial content in multiple languages.
Validea	www.validea.com	Market analysis	Investment information, screening, and research.
WallStreetCity.com	www.wallstreetcity.com	Market analysis	
WallStreetOnline.com	www.wallstreetonline.com	Market analysis	
WallStreetSource.com	www.wallstreetsource.com	Market analysis	A system, developed by street professionals for street professionals, to deliver only pertinent, concise, decision-making data in a user-friendly format.
WealthHound.com	www.wealthhound.com	Market analysis	Online source for quotes, news, investing, mortgage, insurance, banking, etc.
Whispernumbers.com	www.whispernumbers.com	Market analysis	Unofficial earnings estimates.
Wright Investors' Service	www.wisi.com	Market analysis	Data on 18,000 companies around the world.
Zacks Investment Research	www.zacks.com	Market analysis	Provides the investment community with the most widely used stock earnings estimates and fundamental data.
BestRate	www.bestrate.com	Mortgage and credit	
CardWeb	www.cardweb.com	Mortgage and credit	
FiNet.com	www.finet.com	Mortgage and credit	Online mortgage service shops hundreds of mortgage products and rates.
GlobalMortgage	www.globalmortgage.com	Mortgage and credit	Custom-tailored mortgage online.
HomeLoanDirect.com	www.homeloandirect.com	Mortgage and credit	Home loans processing software and automated underwriting systems.
HomeOwners.com	www.homeowners.com	Mortgage and credit	Find a mortgage rate.
ImxExchange	www.imxexchange.com	Mortgage and credit	Mortgage brokers and lenders price and lock quotes in real time.

Company	Website	Type	Description
InstMortgage	www.instmortgage.com	Mortgage and credit	Offers mortgage rates online.
iOwn	www.iown.com	Mortgage and credit	Helps customers find a home and a mortgage.
Mortgagebot.com	www.mortgagebot.com	Mortgage and credit	Provides instant interest rate quote and review of applications for online approval of mortgage or home equity loans.
MortgageIT, Inc.	www.mortgageit.com	Mortgage and credit	Rate quotes, closing costs, online loan status, online applications, and lower-cost residential mortgages.
Pedestal	www.pedestal.com	Mortgage and credit	Resource for secondary-market mortgage professionals.
QuickenMortgage	www.quickenmortgage.com	Mortgage and credit	Information and links to home mortgages.
RealEstate.com, Inc.	www.realestate.com	Mortgage and credit	A business-to-business application service provider that delivers Web-based, real estate solutions to real estate agents, brokers, lenders, and appraisers.
UltraPrise.com	www.ultraprise.com	Mortgage and credit	Mortgage professionals come together in a secure Web environment to buy and sell funded whole loans.
AIM	www.aim.com	Mutual funds	Mutual fund family.
American Century	www.americancentury.com	Mutual funds	Mutual fund family.
Dreyfus Investor	www.dreyfus.com	Mutual funds	Mutual fund family.
Fabian	www.fabian.com	Mutual funds	Mutual fund "lemon list."
Fidelity.com	www.fidelity.com	Mutual funds	Mutual fund family.
Find-a-Fund	www.findafund.com	Mutual funds	Compares mutual funds by stocks they own. Includes portfolio selection tools.
Fund Alarm	www.fundalarm.com	Mutual funds	Tool for deciding when to sell a fund.
iDayo Investor	www.idayoinvestor.com	Mutual funds	
IndexFunds.com	www.indexfunds.com	Mutual funds	Education and information on index funds.
Invesco	www.invesco.com	Mutual funds	Mutual fund family.
Janus	www.janus.com	Mutual funds	Mutual fund family.
MAXfunds	www.maxfunds.com	Mutual funds	
MetaMarkets.com	www.metamarkets.com	Mutual funds	Fully transparent mutual fund.
Micropal	www.micropal.com	Mutual funds	Information on 38,000 funds worldwide.
Morningstar.com	www.morningstar.com	Mutual funds	Comprehensive mutual fund database searchable along every criterion. Asset allocation and screening of stocks and funds.
Mutual Fund Education Alliance	www.mfea.com	Mutual funds	

Company	Website	Type	Description
Mutual Fund Investor's Center	www.mfea.com	Mutual funds	Retirement center and search of mutual funds by cost.
Oppenheimer	www.oppenheimer.com	Mutual funds	Mutual fund family.
Personal Fund	www.personalfund.com	Mutual funds	Calculates breakeven costs and comparisons between funds.
Sage	www.sageonline.com	Mutual funds	Mutual funds portal.
Scudder	www.scudder.com	Mutual funds	Mutual fund family.
Strong	www.strong-funds.com	Mutual funds	Mutual fund family.
T. Rowe Price	www.troweprice.com	Mutual funds	Mutual fund family.
Van Kampen	www.vankampen.com	Mutual funds	Mutual fund family.
Vanguard	www.vanguard.com	Mutual funds	Mutual fund family.
Catex Inc.	www.Catex.com	Nonequity trading	Online exchange for trading weather and catastrophe options and other derivatives.
CFOWeb.com	www.cfoweb.com	Nonequity trading	Single-source destination for capital markets requirements.
Creditex	www.creditex.com	Nonequity trading	Allows traders to buy and sell credit derivatives.
GainCapital.com	www.gaincapital.com	Nonequity trading	Foreign exchange trading online.
American Express	www.americanexpress.com	Online banking	
Bank of America	www.bankamerica.com	Online banking	
Chase Manhattan	www.chase.com	Online banking	
Citibank	www.citibank.com	Online banking	
"Commerce Bancshares, Inc."	www.commercebank.com	Online banking	
CompuBank	www.compubank.com	Online banking	A broad range of banking services.
DoughNET	www.doughnet.com	Online banking	Online bank or credit account used to shop and donate.
First Internet Bank of Indiana	www.firstib.com	Online banking	
NetB@nk	www.netbank.com	Online banking	Opened in October 1996, NetBank, a member of the FDIC, is the nation's largest federal savings bank to operate exclusively through the Internet.
Ohio Savings Bank	www.ohiosavings.com	Online banking	
Telebank	www.telebank.com	Online banking	
Wells Fargo	www.wellsfargo.com	Online banking	
WingspanBank.com	www.wingspan.com	Online banking	WingspanBank.com, a division of First USA Bank, N.A., founded in mid-1999.

Company	Website	Type	Description
BuyandHold.com	www.buyandhold.com	Online investing	
FOLIOfn	www.foliofn.com	Online investing	
myMoneyPro.com	www.mymoneypro.com	Online investing	
Net Stock Direct	www.netstockdirect.com	Online investing	Extensive information and links to direct stock purchase programs.
NetStock Investor	www.sharebuilder.com	Online investing	
Universal Network Exchange	www.UNX.com	Online investing	
4Credit	www.4credit.com	Online lending	Search for loans, order credit reports, or browse through free consumer credit information.
Bankrate.com	www.bankrate.com	Online lending	Bank rates and personal finance news.
CyberLoan	www.cyberloan.com	Online lending	Formed in 1989, CyberLoan.com is a leader in online lending automation technologies.
ecredit	www.ecredit.com	Online lending	Links businesses that want to borrow with those that want to lend.
E-Loan Inc.	www.eloan.com	Online lending	Mortgages, loans, and credit cards.
GetSmart	www.getsmart.com	Online lending	Financial Marketplace with SmartMatch System to help shop for many online financial services.
InterLoan	www.interloan.com	Online lending	Interloan is a direct lender that also represents the most competitive investors in the nation.
Keystroke Financial Network Inc.	www.keystroke.com	Online lending	Partner with the largest, most diverse lenders in the industry. Offers low-rate home loans.
LendingTree Inc.	www.lendingtree.com	Online lending	Online loan marketplace where lenders compete for borrowers' business.
LiveCapital, Inc.	www.livecapital.com	Online lending	Provides loan information for small business.
LoanCity.com	www.loancity.com	Online lending	Underwrites loans efficiently and rapidly. Designed to help mortgage brokers close more loans.
LoanWeb.com	www.loanweb.com	Online lending	LoanWeb has established a network of lenders who are ready to compete for borrowers' business.
LoanWorks.com	www.loanworks.com	Online lending	Helps customers find a loan online.
NextCard.com	www.nextcard.com	Online lending	NextCard provided the first real-time, online approval system for a VISA card in 1977 and was the first company to offer a choice of customized credit card offers and personalized PictureCard designs.
PeopleFirst.com	www.peoplefirst.com	Online lending	The leading online vehicle lender, originating and servicing customer auto and motorcycle loans via the Internet.

Company	Website	Type	Description
Bills.com	www.bills.com	Online payments	e-mail payment services.
Ecount	www.ecount.com	Online payments	e-mail payment services
Gmoney	www.gmoney.com	Online payments	e-mail payment services.
MoneyZap	www.moneyzap.com	Online payments	e-mail payment services.
PayMe.com	www.payme.com	Online payments	e-mail payment services.
PayPal	www.x.com	Online payments	PayPal allows you to send money instantly and securely to anyone with an e-mail address.
USPS eBillPay	www.usps.com	Online payments	e-mail payment services.

Publicly Traded Internet Financial Services Companies

Symbol	Name	Stock Price 12/31/1998	Stock Price 12/31/1999	Stock Price 12/31/2000	Stock Price 6/4/2001	PE Ratio 6/4/2001	Market Capitalization 6/4/2001
SVNX	724 Solutions Inc.	N/A	N/A	25.94	9.5	N/A	550,000,000
ABWG	A.B. Watley Group Inc.	N/A	10.38	12.13	9.4	N/A	103,000,000
ACS	Affiliated Computer Services, Inc.	45.56	46	54.44	73.25	30.9	3,681,325,000
AT	ALLTEL Corporation	59.81	79.81	62.81	58	8.7	18,164,034,256
AOL	America Online, Inc.	38.78	76.5	52.81	52.3	117.2	230,951,826,682
AMTD	Ameritrade Holding Corporation	5.25	20.5	14.44	8.53	N/A	1,610,267,760
BLLS	billserv.com, Inc.		7.75	4.88	2.4	N/A	37,452,001
BVSN	BroadVision, Inc.	3.56	56.5	32.63	6.5	N/A	1,778,179,500
SCH	Charles Schwab Corporation	18.73	28	34.19	18.3	51.1	25,392,856,937
CKFR	CheckFree Corporation	23.38	103.84	58.75	37.0	N/A	3,210,712,000
DLX	Deluxe Corporation	36.56	27.44	22.56	27.76	9.6	1,961,521,616
DBD	Diebold, Incorporated	35.69	23.13	27	31.74	19.8	2,272,298,324
DGIN	Digital Insight Corporation		36.38	15	15.76	N/A	460,538,727
EELN	E-Loan, Inc.		17	2.56	1.31	N/A	70,512,057
ET	E*Trade Group, Inc.	11.7	28.5	13.5	7.72	129	2,486,658,252
FDC	First Data Corporation	31.88	47.44	48.5	67.25	28.6	26,346,263,500
FISV	Fiserv, Inc.	34.29	38.63	50.06	55.1	38.4	6,857,351,190
INSW	InsWeb Corporation		25.38	2.09	0.9	N/A	38,093,399
INTD	InteliData Technologies Corporation	1.31	4.25	4.5	5.5	N/A	250,921,000

Symbol	Name	Stock Price 12/31/1998	Stock Price 12/31/1999	Stock Price 12/31/2000	Stock Price 6/4/2001	PE Ratio 6/4/2001	Market Capitalization 6/4/2001
ICPT	InterCept Group, Inc.	7.25	29.25	27.5	30.0	N/A	424,530,000
INTU	Intuit Inc.	24.17	59.94	63.44	31.2	N/A	6,513,553,000
ITG	Investment Technology Group, Inc.	38.9	28.56	39.94	52.0	24.2	1,646,684,000
JKHY	Jack Henry & Associates, Inc.	24.88	26.25	57.31	29.6	50.3	2,618,593,634
JBOH	JB Oxford Holdings, Inc.	1.81	7.69	3.28	1.88	N/A	26,423,400
NITE	Knight Trading Group, Inc.	11.97	46	27.13	14.26	12.3	1,764,232,968
LAB	LaBranche & Co. Inc.		12.75	33.88	40.1	25.0	2,300,256,212
TREE	Lending Tree, Inc.	N/A	N/A	4.74	6.0	N/A	112,422,000
MSFT	Microsoft Corporation	69.34	116.75	70.75		40.8	377,123,885,498
NETZ	Netzee, Inc.		16.63	2	4.7	N/A	15,816,180
ORCC	Online Resources & Communications Corporation		16.63	3.81	2.05	N/A	23,943,999
QUOT	Quotesmith.com, Inc.		11.38	0.94	2.75	N/A	15,174,500
SONE	S1 Corporation	15.25	78.13	10.25	11.0	N/A	646,190,787
SCAI	Sanchez Computer Associates, Inc.	14.63	41.19	16.94	12.9	N/A	331,798,547
SIEB	Siebert Financial Corp.	10.69	14.75	5.88	5.1	20.9	115,224,298
SYBS	Sybase, Inc.	7.41	17	23.69	15.95	18.6	1,627,171,131
TWE	TD Waterhouse Group, Inc.		16.56	16.5	12.05	36.7	9,576,457,522
TSAI	Transaction Systems Architects, Inc.	50	27.5	14.75		213.4	6,189,000
ULTR	Ultradata Systems, Incorporated	2.25	1.13	1.72	0.8	N/A	2,780,800
VDSI	Vasco Data Security Intl	2.97	8	9.13	5.0	N/A	138,040,645
VRSN	VeriSign, Inc.	14.78	190.94	123	54.6	N/A	10,959,522,036
WEBS	Web Street, Inc.		12.38	1.38	1.35	N/A	34,927,201
WITC	Wit Soundview Group, Inc.		17	6.81	2.72	N/A	327,455,363

INDEX